Understanding
Greek Sculpture

709.
5

NIGEL SPIVEY

Understanding Greek Sculpture

Ancient Meanings, Modern Readings

With 142 illustrations

Thames and Hudson

To

J.H. BLEACH

Magister Artium

Frontispiece: Herakles supporting the world – a detail of a metope from the temple of Zeus at Olympia.

© 1996 Thames and Hudson Ltd, London

First published in the United States of America in 1996 by
Thames and Hudson Inc., 500 Fifth Avenue,
New York, New York 10110

First paperback edition 1997

Library of Congress Catalog Card Number 95-60560

ISBN 0-500-27876-8

Printed and bound in Slovenia

CONTENTS

Acknowledgments

This is an eclectic study. The chapter bibliographies, collected at the end of the book, indicate most of my scholarly debts, but of course some further acknowledgments are due. I must thank especially Paul Cartledge, Amanda Claridge, Joan Connelly, Robert Cook, Birthe Lundgreen and Frank Walbank for commenting on parts of the manuscript.

All ancient sources referred to are translated. For the benefit of those readers with philological curiosity, I have given indications of the original where it might be of interest. There is, I am afraid, no system to the transliteration of Greek throughout the book: hence 'Akropolis' rather than 'Acropolis', yet 'Daedalus' rather than 'Daidalos'. No glossary of terms has been provided, but efforts have been made to explain academic jargon as and when it is used.

I should record that the book was written because of my students, not despite them. But it would not have been written at all without the facilities and support of the Faculty of Classics at Cambridge, and Emmanuel College.

Nigel Spivey, Museum of Classical Archaeology, Cambridge, April 1995

Map showing principal sites mentioned in the text.

1

INTRODUCTION

Iconology must start with a study of institutions rather than with a study of symbols.

E.H. Gombrich, *Symbolic Images* (London 1972), 21

'Take care when you look at old statues'

'Take care when you look at old statues, especially Greek ones.' The author of this caveat is commenting on a rather distressing episode. He has been wandering around Constantinople with a local man of learning (*chartularius*), looking at the many statues (*eikones*) to be seen in that city in the early eighth century AD. As they gaze up at one of the statues, and the guide begins his speel, the statue ('small and squat, but very heavy') topples down from its pedestal. The guide is killed instantly. The sightseer panics: after unsuccessfully trying to drag the statue into a river, he seeks refuge in a church. Relatives of the felled guide gather round; a philosophical bystander blames divine providence. The emperor Philippicus (AD 711–13) then orders that the statue be buried, before it causes any more damage.

Take care when you look at old statues. It was a useful rule in Late Antiquity, when many Greek bronzes still survived in public places, and nowhere more abundantly than at Constantinople, whose founder (in the censorious phrase of St Jerome) 'had virtually the entire city filled with nudes'. Constantine's conversion to Christianity in 312 did not, evidently, entail an aversion to Greek statues, though it was not long before the adjective 'Greek' (*Hellenikos*) became, in Byzantine parlance, simply equivalent to 'pagan'.

We have some idea of what the collection of statuary in Constantinople looked like. It appears from drawings that part of a now-lost column, probably of Arcadius, showed a view of the Hippodrome, with statues conspicuously occupying the central spine of the race track (*ill. 1*). Constantine's clerical biographer, Bishop Eusebius of Caesarea, who

probably supplied St Jerome with Christian disgust for nude exhibits, specifically mentions that there were Delphic tripods in this area: and indeed one bronze fragment survives of the gigantic victory tripod originally dedicated at the sanctuary of Delphi after the battle of Plataea (479 BC, in which Greek forces defeated the Persians). It is a single serpent head, not much to look at now, but it belonged to a specially tortuous snaky column, made to elevate the golden tripod it once supported, and the monument stood intact until broken up by a drunken Turkish warlord. All that can be seen *in situ* today is the lower stump of the twisty bronze column, still rising to a height of over 5m (16ft).

Adjacent to the Hippodrome was the Gymnasium of Zeuxippos. No image of this baths complex survives, except a poetical series of 'word-pictures' (*ekphraseis*) attributed to an early fifth-century AD visitor from Upper Egypt called Christodorus. These hardly constitute great poetry – poor Christodorus rarely manages to do other than praise the lifelike qualities of the eighty bronzes he sees in the Gymnasium, though occasionally he will salute an appearance as 'divine' (*theoeikelos*) – but at least they give us an idea of the range of statuary displayed in the area. There were a few worthy Romans to be seen – Caesar, Pompey, Vergil – but otherwise it was a museum of the best representatives of Hellenic mythology, poetry, drama, philosophy and politics, perhaps laid out according to a sophisticated interest in pagan learning.

1 A sixteenth-century Italian drawing of part of the reliefs on the column, probably of Arcadius, erected at the beginning of the fifth century AD but now lost. This section seems to show a procession through the Hippodrome of Constantinople, with numerous statues in niches in the background.

Now Eusebius tells us that the emperor only displayed old statues in order to expose them to ridicule, to clear them of inherent superstitions and to release their viewers from 'the dotage of mythology'. And Constantine's troops, claims Eusebius, regularly received imperial orders to strip temple cult statues of their precious accoutrements. But if indeed Constantine was so motivated, it has to be said that his programme of demystification failed. Not only are there numerous attestations of popular belief in the animate qualities of Greek statues, but it is also clear – from our opening anecdote, among others – that some of Constantine's successors shared in that popular belief. (One ninth-century empress, rejoicing in the name Euphrosyne, or 'good sense', is recorded as having had a colossal statue of Herakles flogged: the reason for this punishment is not given, but presumably she was expecting weals to appear.)

The imputation of demonic powers to Greek statues must have cut two ways in the Byzantine world. On the one hand, figures like Eusebius tut-tutted at the dangerous ubiquity of pagan images; on the other, the emperors firmly buttressed the legitimacy of their own rule by exploiting what residual 'Classical' magic was contained by those same images. If Constantinople was eventually to be hailed as the 'New Rome' (*Nea Roma*), then the circumstances of Classical urban decoration associated with the old Rome had to be replicated.

Constantine certainly used statues of himself: enormous ones, of which only vast pieces remain (*ill*. 2). And some of his successors – Constantius, for example, and Julian the Apostate – deliberately tried, when making triumphal entrances into cities, to assume a 'statue-like' appearance. In the margins of the Empire it might be possible to declare that all idolatry had been damned on the morning of Christ's nativity: such was the message of the Syriac preacher Jacob of Saroug (AD 451–521), in his powerful homily *The Fall of the Idols*; but in the capital and elsewhere, the idols enjoyed prolonged reverence. Indeed, zealous Christians, especially monks, often had to be reprimanded by their own clerical superiors, the bishops, who were hurt by the sight of damaged pagan idols. A letter attributed to St Augustine tells of the trouble caused in the city of Sufes (now Tunisian Sbiba) when, probably following an edict in AD 399 from the emperor Honorius sanctioning iconoclasm, a statue of Herakles was broken. Sixty Christian citizens apparently died in the resultant tumult, and Augustine hastens to reassure the local councillors that the statue shall be restored (*saxa non desunt*: 'there's no shortage of stone'), complete with paintwork. It is almost as if the loss of a statue regarded as talismanic can only lead to disaster.

The Byzantine respect or tolerance towards conspicuous Classical images – not only nudes, but also reliefs showing scenes of animal sacrifice or other such *anathemata* – is an intriguing phenomenon. It was partly a reverence born of fear: if statues were removed, or even just moved, earthquakes and other disasters were threatened. It was partly a reverence born of proper aesthetic admiration: one emperor, Theodore II Lascaris (AD 1254–58), has left us a letter in which he notes how magnificent the old monuments of Pergamum are when compared with contemporary squalor. (This is a significant admission, given that in the second chapter of Revelations, Pergamum is described as 'the place where Satan has his throne'.) And it must partly have been a reverence born of sheer conservatism: what was good enough for Augustus, Hadrian and others was thereby good enough for Constantine and his successors.

It is tempting to claim that Classical art was conserved in Constantinople *as art*. However, as specialists in Byzantine art have pointed out, there is curiously little evidence to show that the intimidating presence of Greek statuary actually had much influence on the artists of the time. The theory that the Olympian Zeus (see *ill. 109*) once stood in the Palace of Lausus at Constantinople, and shaped the iconography of a bearded Christ Pantocrator, is (if true) exceptional. As one scholar puts it: 'What . . . preserved the city was not Jupiter but the benign presence of the True Cross, the Rod of Moses, or other holy relics'. The statues assembled in the Hippodrome and elsewhere may have been dynamic when they fell on top of sightseers, but otherwise they were remarkably inert, exercising no aesthetic claims on their circumstances (in fact, the production of any

Byzantine marble or bronze free-standing sculpture, let alone Greek-influenced, was negligible). It was not until the Turks arrived that a serious programme of iconoclasm occurred; before then, the Greek statues of Constantinople were more or less tolerated. Beyond whatever good intentions lay behind their original Constantinian assemblage they were, we might say, simply knocking around: components of an urban pastiche which was effectively meaningless, were it not for those certain occasions when the statues demonstrated a capacity for homicide.

Living among the wreckage

Late Antique; *Post* Modern. To draw a parallel between present circumstances and those of the Byzantine capital is probably appropriate. In the language of the Postmodernists, Constantinople was a 'collage city': packed with architectural and ornamental 'quotations', reassuringly 'heritagized'. In no sense was a Renaissance implied by Constantine's assemblage of Classical statuary, no invention of some great historical distance between Constantinople and the Athens of Perikles or the Rome of Augustus. Constantine had not 'discovered' exemplary works of art, nor had he brought them to his capital, like some proto-Lord Elgin, to encourage the improvement of aesthetic taste and artistic standards. Originally, some proper sense of affinity, as we have noted, may have been intended with Rome as the precedent capital: Rome was heavily adorned with Classical sculpture, for various reasons (ranging from military triumphalism to an intellectual inferiority complex), and so a 'New Rome' transplanted eastwards should in this respect resemble old Rome. Considering that Rome as a cultural capital was indebted to Pergamum (quite literally, Rome inherited the Anatolian city and all its treasures in 133 BC), and that Pergamum in turn styled itself as a new Athens (see Chapter 9), we might like to envisage this process as a torch of artistic enlightenment, passed from one 'capital' city to another, and always rekindled at the same essential source: Classical Athens.

But quite apart from the religious and political reasons why the foundation of Constantinople is historically considered as the terminus of Classicism in general, there are art-historical considerations which encourage one to locate the debasing of Greek sculpture in Late Antiquity. In Rome itself, the collapse of Classical form has been blamed on Constantine, most passionately by the art historian Bernard Berenson (1865–1959), who saw in the Arch of Constantine (AD 313–15) a clear testimony of decline. Berenson's was an absolute condemnation ('In my point of view', he wrote, 'decline is decline and not simplification, symbolization, sublimation or any other "-ation" that they may admire if they

3 Detail of the north front of the Arch of Constantine in Rome, commemorating Constantine's victory over Maxentius at the Battle of the Milvian Bridge in AD 312. The different parts were assembled from earlier monuments.

will'); and his aesthetic arrogance makes most modern readers of his essay antipathetic to its argument. But looking up at the Arch (*ill. 3*) we are bound at least to sympathize with Berenson's purism. This monument is a hotch-potch: cannibalized tondo-reliefs from earlier imperial arches are dumped on top of the hieratic registers of diminutive minions themselves compressed into obeisance to Constantine and his colleague Licinius, who in turn are wearily supported by two flabby river-gods in spandrels where airy Victory-nymphs would be better placed. 'Design' has been replaced by 'chance': and chance, or opportunism, is the keynote of Postmodernity.

There is some evidence that the eclecticism of the Arch of Constantine was dictated by a lack of skilled workmen. Scholars on Constantine's side argue that his choice of earlier monuments to incorporate was sensitive and selective (choosing only images pertaining to 'good' emperors: Trajan, Hadrian and Marcus Aurelius). But this cannot gloss over the obvious aesthetic disjunction we see on the Arch, nor account for the curiously redundant agglomeration of statuary collected in Constantinople. The truth is that for Constantine, Classical sculpture had lost its original significance. He used it more for play than purpose. In this respect, his situation may be judged very similar to our own.

Pausanias and the understanding of Greek sculpture

It may be true that museums now function as almost self-conscious parodies of temples, and that tourists, in the Postmodern world, have become the new pilgrims; but we shall never understand why Greek sculpture looks as it does so long as we refuse to recreate, imaginatively, its original circumstances of production and the responses to it.

St Paul, when he visited Athens in the first century AD, found it *kataeidolos*: 'a forest of idols'. The sheer quantity of statues standing around the Greek world would truly unnerve us if we could ever visualize them *en masse* in their sanctuaries, like a second population made of marble, wood and bronze. How shall we begin to recover the institutional contexts of this statuary?

Fortunately, we have a guide who takes us some way there. One of the first tasks for anyone wanting to understand Greek sculpture is to read Pausanias. Pausanias was a Greek, perhaps from Lydia, travelling in the Roman world during the mid-second century AD. He wrote a descriptive account of his travels around Greece (*Periegesis tes Hellados*) at a time when the sites of Greece were beginning to cater for virtual tourists such as himself, yet still functioning as sanctuaries. Like his near-contemporary Plutarch (who served for thirty years in the priesthood at Delphi), Pausanias had a serious interest in ritual behaviour. Though he is sometimes considered a gullible traveller, ready to swallow any tale the locals feed to him – one of his favourite verbal tags is *hos legetai*, 'as it is said' – Pausanias comes across as an honest and uncomplicated witness, whose religious reflexes are still lively. And so we have a valuable testimony of the ancient significance of Greek sculpture: while Pausanias is writing about statues that may have been made up to a millennium before he saw them, their function was more or less intact.

This makes for a discourse of appreciation that deserves our brief notice. Here, for example, is Pausanias approaching the Parthenon:

> Here there are statues of Zeus, one made by Leochares, and the other called Zeus of the City [*Polieus*], whose traditional sacrifice I shall now describe (though not its legendary origins). Upon the altar of Zeus Polieus they place barley mixed with wheat and leave this unguarded. The ox they have ready for sacrifice goes up to the altar and nuzzles the grain. A priest whom they nominate as ox-slayer despatches the beast, drops his axe and runs away. The other priests, pretending they do not know who did the act, then put the axe on trial. The ritual is as I describe it.
>
> (I. 24.4)

What we see here is an ambivalence of response on the part of Pausanias: both attributionist – informing us that one statue of Zeus was made by

Leochares; and functionalist – describing the ritual performances ordained in front of the statue of Zeus Polieus. Who made the statue of Zeus Polieus? Pausanias switches his interest, as he does whenever possible, to an alternative question: what was the statue of Zeus Polieus for? And he devotes more space to answering that second question. When it comes to talking us through the sculptural decoration of the Parthenon itself, he has remarkably little to say – perhaps precisely because it was not so much a temple as a great civic treasure-house, with no great surviving ritual traditions.

By the time Pausanias was writing, the attribution of sculptures to named sculptors was a well-established aspect of Roman connoisseurship. Pausanias could not help but be aware that some of the statues he examined were 'works of art'. He duly notes down details of authorship when he thinks them significant. Yet his encounters with Greek sculpture take place predominantly in sanctuaries, and his sense of art as visual theology is keener than his disposition for making attributions. With Pausanias at our side, we are closer to the original significance of Greek sculpture than we would be with most modern handbooks. It is the objective of this present study to take us even closer: to restore to Greek sculpture not only its sacred functions, but also to attempt to resurrect its proper historicity. This may involve a serious shift of emphasis: away from the actual makers of sculpture, and back to those who commissioned it, those who used it and those who once simply viewed it.

The death of the author?

'La mort de l'auteur' is an obituary phenomenon chiefly observed in modern literary theory, though some art historians have subsumed it under the phrase, 'the social production of art'. They seek (to adopt their own jargon) to 'desacrilize' the author (or the artist), and deny the power of individual originality. Originality, they say, is merely the construction of a society fascinated by personality. More powerful sociological forces shape works of art more effectively than individuals ever can. So it is, according to this dogma, that the very notion of the author be executed. (Curiously, the theorist who advocated most influentially the author's death, Roland Barthes, who died in 1980, shows no sign of falling victim to his own proposition: his posthumous popularity as an author, not to mention an intellectual authority, burgeons by the year.)

'Authors' – names, sculptors, individuals of genius or skill – are traditionally the principal means by which Greek sculpture has been approached. The reason for this is obvious: whenever art becomes capital, names have more than a simply taxonomic usefulness. They serve as economic guarantors, price labels, signatures of authenticity. Students of Greek sculpture are encouraged to look for sculptors even when their work no longer exists: so it is that most handbooks of Greek sculpture describe the career of a Classical Athenian sculptor called Myron, despite the fact that our only acquaintance with his work is through secondary references to it, or else what we take to be 'copies' of it.

Quick consultation of the index to this book will show how little dependence is here placed on a history of Greek sculpture by reference to named sculptors. And some readers will find that odd. After all, it is a tenet of the historical understanding of images – what we may broadly call 'iconology' – that a work of art means what its author intended it to mean. In the words of Michel Foucault (1926–84), who made valuable adjustments to the theory of Barthes, 'the author is the principle of thrift in the proliferation of meaning'. How, then, can the historical meanings of Greek sculpture be fathomed without primary reference to the sculptors themselves?

In an ideal state of iconological research, we should indeed consult the transcripts of meetings held between Greek sculptors and their patrons. None, needless to say, exist. Perhaps, then, we might search the treatises written on their work by the sculptors themselves? Alas, though we believe such treatises to have been written, again none survives – at least not beyond a few gnomic citations by later writers. So what course is left open to us?

The solution adopted here is not, in fact, the complete effacement of the author, nor a denial of individual ability, nor any dull Marxist insistence on some supposed collectivity of purpose in ancient Greece. As Nietzsche and others have commented, it is difficult to escape the impression that art flourished in Greece largely as a result of ambition, or competitiveness (the Greek *eris*), becoming a god. But even that competitiveness has its social basis. Following Foucault, we may allow 'author-functions'; but names are not the ultimate sanction of the works illustrated in the following pages. Names, as far as they mean anything, are woven into the overall contexture of art and its production. Foucault is fundamentally right: art belongs to a game of power. And in that game, institutions and customs are more powerful than individuals. That is why the understanding of ancient Greek sculpture rests, essentially, with the understanding of ancient Greek society.

2

'THE GREEK REVOLUTION'

Some years ago I was in the British Museum looking at the Parthenon sculptures when a young man came up to me and said with a worried air, 'I know it's an awful thing to confess, but this Greek stuff doesn't move me one bit'. I said that was very interesting: could he define at all the reasons for his lack of response? He reflected for a minute or two. Then he said, 'Well, it's all so terribly rational, *if you know what I mean.'*

E.R. Dodds, *The Greeks and the Irrational* (California 1951), 1

The making of an *Urpferd*

A horse is a horse is a horse. But in art, some horses are more horsey than others. So it is that one particular horse, from the East pediment of the Parthenon (*ill. 4*), has become the acme of all horsiness. Philip Hunt, the cleric who so eagerly assisted Lord Elgin in his removal of the Parthenon sculptures to London, was one of the first moderns to eulogize the beast, claiming that it 'surpasses anything of the kind . . . in the truth and spirit of the execution. The nostrils are distended, the ears erect, the veins swollen, I had almost said throbbing. His mouth is open and he seems to neigh with the conscious pride of belonging to the Ruler of the Waves.'

In fact this particular horse probably pertains to the chariot of a symbolic figure who is either Nyx (Night) or Selene (the Moon); and where Hunt saw throbbing eagerness in the features of the horse, others register (more appropriately) a degree of equine fatigue. But the response to this horse has been almost universally enthusiastic, to the extent that it is referred to as the *Urpferd* – the original horse, the Platonic idea of a horse, the horse-archetype – a horse by which all other horses must be measured.

This is a high accolade for a piece of Greek sculpture, and it can be traced directly to Goethe (1749–1832), who became mildly obsessed with finding *Ur*-forms in other fields: an *Urpflanze*, for example, 'the primal plant', from which all plant varieties must be descended ('auf alles übrige lebendige'). Referring simply to 'the Elgin horse-head' in one of his essays

4 *(opposite)* The *Urpferd*: a horse belonging to the chariot of Nyx (Night) or Selene (the Moon), from the east pediment of the Parthenon, Athens.

on morphology, Goethe argued that the statue was so overpowering and yet 'ghostly' in appearance, that if you compared it to actual horses in nature, you could only conclude that the sculptor had created 'the primal horse'.

Goethe's later compatriot Ernst Buschor would exclaim: 'Das Pferd ist durch den Parthenon geadelt, ja geheiligt' – 'On the Parthenon, the horse is ennobled, even sanctified'. Those who watch the behaviour of visitors to the British Museum will observe the great effort it takes for most viewers of the *Urpferd* not to reach forward and stroke it. But why is it such a compelling image?

Goethe's own reasons for enshrining this (and other works of Classical art) as exemplary and endowed with an almost divine validity, are partly explained by his contribution to a conversation in which some of the company opined that the Greeks had not been faithful in portraying animals, often creating very stiff, unshapely and 'imperfect' creatures. Here is Goethe's response:

> I will not argue about that. But above all else we must distinguish at what time and by what artist such works originated. For no doubt examples could be produced in large quantities to show that Greek artists, in their representations of animals, not only equalled Nature, but surpassed it. The English, who are the best judges of horses in the world, are forced to admit that their two antique horseheads [from the Parthenon] are more perfect in form than those of any breed extant today. These heads date from the best period of Greek art. But our wonder and admiration is not to be explained on the assumption that those artists were working from more perfect models than those which exist today. The reason is rather that they had, with the progress of time and art, themselves become such that they brought an inner greatness of spirit to their observation of Nature.

(Goethe, in conversation with Eckermann, 20 October 1828)

5 Detail of a horse on an Athenian Late Geometric vase; eighth century BC.

Goethe's final phrase ('so dass sie sich mit persönlicher Grossheit an die Natur wandten') requires further exegesis. Conceptual art is art produced not from the observation of nature, but a concept, a mental image – a typical representation, undifferentiated by such features as are individual or accidental. There is no need, as many art historians do, to trawl examples of conceptual art from Egypt: Greek art in the eighth century BC offers plenty of examples. Horses that appear on the neck of a Late Geometric Athenian pot, for example (*ill. 5*), are entirely conceptual. Their artist may or may not have had particular horses in mind when he drew these: what is important is that they came from the mind, and are not an attempt at direct representation. Apart from the lack of detail, there is no depth to the picture: even the background patterns bear no semblance to an actual context or landscape.

On an Athenian vase painted almost two hundred years later we can see the extent of artistic change (*ill. 6*). Landscape is still not a major concern,

6 A horse on an Athenian black-figure amphora by Exekias; sixth century BC.

but form, detail and a degree of naturalistic conviction have materialized in a way that invites the word 'progress'. The horse here has been drawn by an artist who has studied equine anatomy. This is not to say it constitutes a portrait of a 'real' horse: it belongs to a named mythical character, Kastor, and is being patted by Kastor's father in a scene of homecoming or departure; yet it too has a name, Kyllaros ('The Scuttler'), and, despite its mythical status, it is not a fantastical beast, but rather an enviable thoroughbred. Not only has myth been domesticated, it has been rendered credible, while at the same time retaining the enchantment of the rare and special. And that, perhaps, is what Goethe intended when he spoke of the Greeks grafting 'an inner greatness of spirit to their observation of Nature'.

In an age such as ours, when 'primitivism' has been saluted as an aesthetic virtue, the force of describing Greek art in its Geometric style – its conceptual stage – as 'primitive' is obviously diminished. Prior to movements such as Cubism, however, art historians were inclined to characterize conceptual representation as either primitive or childish, so that any movement in the direction of illusionistic art seemed like a step towards civilization or an achievement of maturity. In an influential book at the turn of the century, Emmanuel Loewy used the language of growing-up and 'emancipation' to denote what happened when Greek artists ceased using mental images as a source. Two examples mentioned by Loewy will suffice to summarize his case. He took a piece of early cult statuary from Olympia – the head commonly referred to as belonging to the cult image of Hera, though it may not be (*ill. 7*) – and pointed out that the ears of this head had not been carved according to their natural appearance, but attached on the principles of 'mental abstraction': inorganically, just as spikes on the neck of a Geometric horse imply a mane, without the cogency of naturalistic depiction. Later on, the Discobolus (*ill. 8*) is congratulated on the number of views it offers up, thanks to the desertion of mental images. 'Each part of it seeks to exhibit itself to the spectator in a full and exhaustive aspect': thus Greek art graduated, by about 600 BC, to what Loewy called 'the discovery of nature'.

The releasing effect of this new attentiveness to the ways in which things really appear, and the sophistication of devices developed for its transmission to the viewer – the development of planes, of rounding, of foreshortening – were, in Loewy's eyes, both new and unique to the Greeks. But he stopped short of the more dramatic appellations subsequently given to the same art-historical process. In his now canonical handbook, *The Story of Art* (first published 1950), Sir Ernst Gombrich hailed it as 'the Great Awakening'. In another of his books, *Art and Illusion* (first published 1960), he calls it 'the Greek Revolution'. We are also offered a further, and similarly momentous name for this phenomenon: 'the Greek Miracle', a phrase first coined by Waldemar Deonna in the 1930s, and which also served as the title of a recent exhibition of fifth-century BC sculpture at the New York Metropolitan Museum.

However we choose to describe this 'discovery of nature', we do seem justified in reaching for superlatives when faced with some of the results, such as the prize item of the New York exhibition, Kritian Boy (*ill. 9*). Created in Athens just before 480 BC, Kritian Boy stands at the end of a series of statues of nude male figures usually referred to as *kouroi*, or 'young men'; he also stands at the end of a voyage of technical exploration, which Gombrich describes as well as anyone ever has.

> The sculptors in their workshops tried out new ideas and new ways of repre-
> senting the human figure, and each innovation was eagerly taken up by others
> who added their own discoveries. One discovered how to chisel the trunk, another
> found that a statue may look much more alive if the feet are not both placed firmly
> on the ground. Yet another would discover that he could make a face come alive
> simply by bending the mouth upwards so that it appeared to smile.
>
> (*The Story of Art*, London 1995, 78)

But what prompted these 'discoveries'? Why were Greek sculptors compelled towards naturalism? Gombrich's own account partly revives a tenet of eighteenth-century Enlightenment scholarship, which is that the 'liberty' of Greek citizens fostered artistic licence (discussed below); but primarily he was inclined to argue that it was the impulse of narrative, the need to tell a story, which pushed artists towards involving viewers (or 'audience', perhaps) by making the story's figures more lifelike in appearance. That is to say, a story acquires dramatic verisimilitude through its enaction by 'real-looking' characters: emotions are given – if we can borrow a phrase from literary criticism – their 'objective correlative'.

This summary of Gombrich's argument does it scant justice: but it has been noted by others that Gombrich acts with the air of a conjuror in resolving the causes of 'the Greek Revolution'. The apparently mythological significances of early Greek figurative art enable him to produce 'narrative' like a rabbit from a hat; the particular social and historical forces operating upon Greek artists hardly concern him at all. Here, we shall try to compensate for that, and see how such forces may have contributed to this stylistic change (which for reasons of verbal economy we may continue to call 'the Greek Revolution').

To take the case of Kritian Boy. Though he was probably not the richest of early fifth-century BC dedications on the Athenian Akropolis (his scale is under lifesize, and a bronze statue would have been more conspicuous at this time), he has become the 'cover boy' of the Greek Revolution. That is, his delicate form has been loaded with huge stylistic significance. As Humfry Payne wrote: 'There is . . . no statue which looks forward more

9 'Kritian Boy'; *c.* 480 BC.

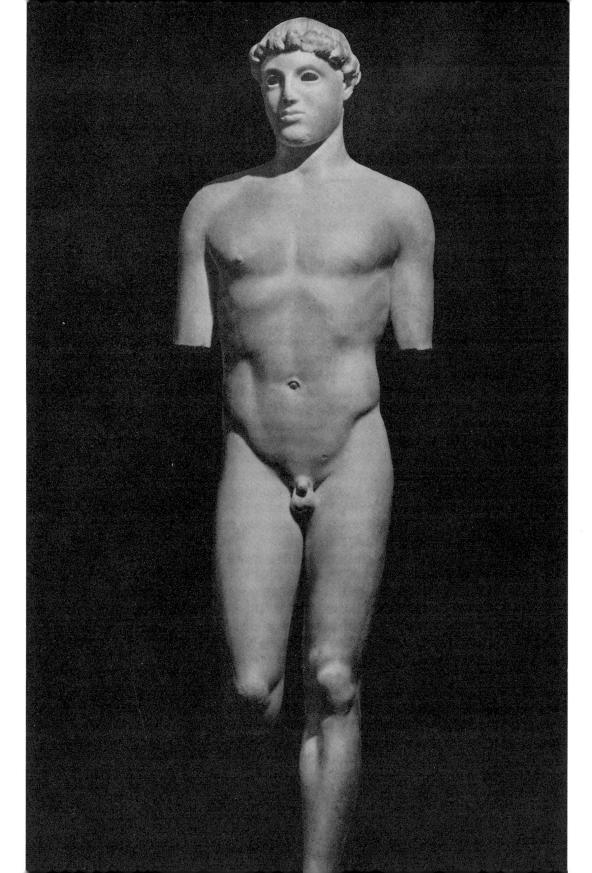

clearly to the full development of early Classical sculpture, none which is less reminiscent of the past.' More than that, Kritian Boy has been saluted as 'the first beautiful nude in art' (Kenneth Clark, *The Nude*, 1956, 29). So it is easy to forget that this statue once possessed a proper identity. One guess (and it is only a guess) is that the statue was a representation of the Athenian founding hero Theseus; another theory, more cogently, holds that the statue can be reinstated with a base recovered from the Akropolis – a simple Ionic column capital which is inscribed with a pair of hexameter verses. These verses draw attention not to the artist (who must remain unknown, since 'Kritian' only implies a resemblance to a copy of a work attributed to an artist of whose original *oeuvre* nothing survives), but to the Athenian who paid for and dedicated the statue:

> Victor in the boys' foot-race of the Panathenaia
> Kallias, son of Didymaios, dedicated this statue to Athena.

If the base indeed belongs to Kritian Boy, then it provides a simple legend to the statue which may, in aesthetic terms, explain why the figure of the boy is at once both restrained and assertive. He is an athletic victor, hence proud; he is dedicating his image to Athena, hence grateful. But what measure of piety was demonstrated by dedicating a statue at a sanctuary such as the Akropolis? How significant was it to win the foot-race at the Panathenaic Games? Why was it important to name the father as well as the victorious youth? And is this, in any meaningful sense, a portrait of young Kallias; or else a thing of beauty by itself, presented *ex voto* to a goddess who will enjoy its contemplation? As noted, the statue is under lifesize: would a larger image have been regarded as too much in the way of self-promotion, perhaps a real political risk in a community which had just invented the device of ostracizing potential grandees?

Such questions are rarely asked of the statues that are said to represent the Greek Revolution. Once ensconced in our museums, detached from their bases, such pieces are not easily returned, in the mind's eye, to their original situation. But here we shall try to recapture something of that context. To do this is not to repress the implied excitement of an artistic 'awakening'. If anything, it should make the process seem even more lively than it already is.

Style and democracy

The New York exhibition mentioned above, 'The Greek Miracle', was a timely event: part of a series of celebrations organized in Greece, America, Britain and elsewhere to mark the 2500th anniversary of the world's first democracy. Its subtitle was 'Classical Sculpture from the Dawn of

Democracy', and in his preface to the catalogue, the President of the United States (then George Bush: writing, as it happens, just prior to his own electoral rejection) urged visitors to the exhibition to be grateful for their 'democratic heritage' as they gazed on the art of fifth-century BC Athens. What precisely constitutes the miracle is not defined in the catalogue: but the viewer was supposed to see statues like the Kritian Boy as both symbols and products of the political system which the Greeks knew as *demokratia*, or 'rule of the people'.

The vagueness of the catalogue is not a surprise. For the truth is that no one has properly explained the connection which the organizers of the New York show sought to make between naturalism as a style and freedom of expression as a political ideal. Perhaps such ideological substructures are impossible to demonstrate so far in retrospect. But the fruits of continued excavation in the Agora, the hub of democratic Athens, at least encourage a reconsideration of the issue: for loose as it is, the association of naturalism and democracy has a distinguished academic pedigree.

It was J.J. Winckelmann (1718–68) who first asserted that the 'perfection' of Classical Greek art was indebted to the circumstances of individual liberty. Winckelmann himself was influenced by the philosophical assertions of the Third Earl of Shaftesbury (1671–1713), whose three-volume *Characteristicks of Men, Manners, Opinions, Times* contains 'profound reflections on the periods of government, and flourishing and decay of Liberty and Letters'. Shaftesbury's ideas must be taken into account in any discussion of Winckelmann, because (not surprisingly, coming from a member of the English aristocracy) Shaftesbury's definition of 'Liberty' hardly equates with 'democracy'. Benign princes may very well create excellent conditions for artistic self-expression: what is important is that they do not dictate an agenda – the sort of vainglorious autocracy Shaftesbury deplored, for example, at the court of Louis XIV at Versailles. So although Winckelmann was writing on the eve of the French Revolution, it would be wrong to translate his oft-invoked *Freiheit* as 'democracy', even though it carries direct connotations of *political* freedom. Nevertheless, Winckelmann was prepared to make artistic quality dependent on some sort of civic mentality of egalitarianism, and he sounds very much like a convinced democrat when he describes the overthrow of tyranny at Athens ('in which the whole people participated'), and the subsequent rules of ostracism whereby 'it was not the right of one person . . . to immortalize himself at the expense of others'.

The project of Winckelmann's 1764 *History of Ancient Art* (*Geschichte der Kunst des Alterthums*) was to make art 'systematically intelligible': to create an ordering of Egyptian, Greek, Etruscan and Roman art that would clarify the rise and decline of styles, and chart them chronologically. Based on the Papal collections in Rome (Winckelmann never went to

Greece, and saw very few Greek originals), and mostly concerned with sculpture, this system gained wide currency almost as soon as it was published. Winckelmann's approach provoked plenty of dissent in general (especially from fellow Germans J.G. Herder and G.E. Lessing), and disagreement in detail, but he succeeded in setting an almost canonical regard in the West for fifth-century BC Greek sculpture. Though Winckelmann never saw the Parthenon sculptures, they would have fitted perfectly into his scheme: exemplary fruits of Classical Greek *Freiheit*.

By hingeing great art on the circumstances of 'liberty', Winckelmann set some awkward traps for himself. The Vatican collections contained pieces of sculpture he considered sublime: the Laocoon Group, the Belvedere Torso, the Apollo Belvedere. None of these, unfortunately, can be matched with the *floruit* of Greek democracy in the fifth century BC. Indeed, Winckelmann could see as well as anyone else that the Belvedere Torso bears an inscription that rules out such a date: it must in fact be post-Alexander, and therefore produced in a less than perfectly 'free' environment. A similar difficulty arises with a colossal head of Antinous, now in the Louvre, which Winckelmann much esteemed: how could a portrait of the emperor Hadrian's boyfriend be attributed to an artist enjoying 'liberty'? Here Winckelmann falls back, implicitly, on the sort of liberty defined by Shaftesbury, allowing Hadrian to be a beneficent patron. But it is clear that Winckelmann wants more from his *Freiheit*, for he adds that when this portrait was done, Hadrian was 'planning to restore to the Greeks their original freedom, and had begun by declaring Greece to be free'.

Such casuistries did not go uncriticized. But, broadly speaking, the phenomenal posthumous reputation of Winckelmann has ensured a long life for the connection of 'perfect' Classical art to the circumstances of democratic Greece, and in particular Periklean Athens. Ernst Curtius and Alfred Zimmern were just two of a number of highly influential archaeologists and ancient historians who enthusiastically endorsed that connection.

Gombrich himself explicitly links his 'Great Awakening' to 'the Dawn of Democracy' when he tries to explain why the discovery of natural forms happened where and when it did. Athenian artists, he says, may not have been rich or distinguished, but, unlike their counterparts in Egypt or Assyria, they had a 'share in the life of the city' and took some part in the 'business of government' – because Athens was a democracy (*The Story of Art*, 82). To illustrate his case for a 'Great Awakening' Gombrich uses an Athenian vase-painting by Euthymides. The date of the painting may be fixed at some time between 510 and 500 BC: conveniently enough, because the date usually given for the initial establishment of democracy in Athens is 508/7 BC. Gombrich writes (and it is worth italicizing): '*It was a tremendous moment in the history of art when, perhaps a little before 500 BC, artists dared for the first time in all history to paint a foot as seen from the front.'* The vase in fact features a fairly routine scenario for Greek vase-painting: a warrior donning his armour and preparing to set off from home, with his wife and father standing on either side. But the warrior's pose makes the vase, in Gombrich's eyes, a revelation – a frontal foot. An entirely new trick of representation has apparently been 'discovered', and we may henceforth enjoy the consequence of this discovery: the human body outlined not according to a schematic concept, but captured in the poses it actually strikes.

No one will begrudge this as an artistic phenomenon. The painters of vases in Athens at the end of the sixth century BC certainly knew that they were on to something new and pregnant with possibilities. On another of his vases, Euthymides even has the cheek to challenge a rival painter: next to the drawing of a man seen from a three-quarters view, he writes *hos oudepote Euphronios*, translatable, in effect, as 'I bet you couldn't do this!'. And we may be sure that if we could recover some of the murals that we know once decorated the temples and public places of Classical Athens, we should see on a large scale the fresh areas of expression opened up by the device of foreshortening. But does that freedom of expression have anything to do with political circumstances?

Two considerations initially incline one to deny the connection. Firstly, it is not the case that before democracy arrived, Greek art was static. The statues of young men and women that we know as *kouroi* and *korai* may have conformed to a standard type and standard function, but their Archaic format does not preclude a steady refinement of appearance in the direction of naturalism. Kritian Boy does not appear out of the blue: he stands at the end of a series of statues whose production ranges over two centuries. And developments in naturalistic representation appear to occur quite readily under a tyrannical regime (as Athens was for most of the sixth century BC).

The second consideration is a technical one. The change from black-figure painting, in which detail was engraved, to red-figure painting, in which detail was sketched or painted, arguably encouraged vase painters to be more ambitious in their draughtsmanship. If it is significant, that particular technical development pre-dates democracy: it happens around 520 BC. But with regards to technical advances in sculpture there is no doubt at all. The hollow casting of lifesize bronze statues from prototypes moulded in clay was a technique established in the early sixth century BC or thereabouts. Inevitably, that technique offered sculptors a sort of release. Bronze figures, being lighter and less brittle than solid marble, could be wrought in less schematic poses than their marble equivalents. The experiments facilitated by bronzeworking techniques undoubtedly yielded 'action' statues such as Myron's well-known Discobolus, or the Tyrannicides of Kritios and Nesiotes (see Chapter 5).

So there we have a down-to-earth explanation of the Greek Revolution: no matter what politics prevailed, the catalyst of change was the technical empowerment of Greek artists.

Though few would deny the influence of bronzeworking developments on Greek sculpture generally, many will feel dissatisfied with this as a comprehensive explanation. What, we might ask, encouraged the technical developments? As we have seen, the recourse to Winckelmann's idealizing *Freiheit* seems simplistic. But to discount entirely the link between style and democracy is unwarranted; it merely needs some rephrasing. That is, we should allow for a measure both of political self-definition in the art of Classical Greece and of self-consciousness: an awareness on the part of Greek artists that if they did *not* work within democratic circumstances – or at least if they were working outside the Greek-speaking world – then they might be doing things differently.

A passage from Plato's most mature work, the *Laws* – composed around the middle of the fourth century BC – is worth quoting here. The situation, as usual with Plato, is a dialogue. Discussion has come round to the place of music in the ideal city Plato is proposing. Plato's spokesman gives an example of how music should be regulated: the Egyptians, he says, have got it right. Then he applauds the 'rightful rules' (*kala schemata*) the Egyptians also apply to their art: 'If you inspect their paintings and reliefs on the spot, you will find that the work of ten thousand years ago – I mean that expression not loosely but in all precision – is neither better nor worse than that of today; both exhibit an identical artistry' (*Laws* 656d, trans. Taylor). It is obvious from the context (and our knowledge of Plato generally) that this comment is intended as a compliment to the Egyptians. The response it draws in the dialogue is not 'How boring!' but rather: 'What a marvellous system of government!'.

This Platonic observation is valuable. Plato was a dissenter who had very little sympathy with democracy as a system and he mistrusted artists who attempted to duplicate nature. To fudge the difference between truth and fiction, the real and the unreal, was in Plato's eyes the project of a scoundrel. What he sees in Egypt is the alternative: autocratic rule by the pharaoh, and artists turning out entirely predictable art. And, excepting the notorious interlude of Akhenaten – the renegade pharaoh who built his capital at Amarna towards the end of the Eighteenth Dynasty (*c.* 1350 BC) and appears to have flouted many of the conventional proportions of Egyptian art – we take Plato's point. Over three millennia, the conceptual rules governing figurative and landscape representation in Egypt remained remarkably stable. As one Egyptologist has expressed it, 'invariance in form and production was the means by which an Egyptian craftsman successfully maintained himself as a specialist'.

If that is the case, then the strength of Plato's example is reinforced. For the Classical Greek artist it was precisely his variance, not invariance, of form and production that gained commissions and enabled his own social advancement. It would be overly romantic to label Pheidias, Polykleitos and the other well-known 'names' of Classical Greek sculpture as Bohemians. As we shall see (Chapter 3), the competitive stakes in the field of artistic skill, *techne*, were considerable; the virtue or vice of jealousy, or competitiveness (*eris*), was overtly nourished among the community of artists and craftsmen.

It is not whimsical to speak of a general contribution from artists in fifth-century Athens, particularly, towards a process of democratic self-definition. That is to say, the process whereby the young democratic community made itself an identity and declared itself different from neighbouring peoples and powers. The jaded Plato unwittingly helps us understand what this might involve. A foreign country, and an alien system of government, may be known by its art. In that case, antipathy towards that other place, that other system, can be very directly expressed: you consciously hone a different style, and an alternative set of symbols, to state your own values.

The historical fact is that no sooner was the world's first democracy created than it was threatened from outside. By 510 BC, when the last tyrant was expelled from Athens, the armies of the Persian empire had already occupied parts of East Greece and were *en route* for Attica and the Peloponnese. We need not rehearse here the heroics of the battles – Marathon, Thermopylae and Salamis (see Chapter 6) – that prevented the Persians from colonizing Greece; but we should register that in 480 BC, the Persian commander Xerxes and his officers occupied and vandalized the Athenian Akropolis. They smashed up much of the art around them in this temple-complex turned barrack-house, leaving debris which the Athenians, on their return to the city, piously buried. Archaeologists have gained a marvellous stratum of material from this *Perserschutt* (as its German excavators called it). But there was one statue which the Persians did not ruin, rather they kidnapped it as a token of their brief triumph over Athens: the Tyrannicides, set up in the marketplace as the very first piece of 'democratic' art (see Chapter 5 for a fuller discussion).

The Persians got their come-uppance about 150 years later: when Alexander the Great took the Persian city of Susa, he is said to have recovered the Tyrannicides and restored them to Athens. Whether or not that is true, the entire episode is instructive for those looking for art laden with ideological connotations. The figures of the Tyrannicides are classified by specialists as exemplars of the early Classical 'Severe Style', and in terms of modelling and posture they are easily inserted into the general context of the Greek Revolution. But this was a work of art literally voted into existence, and set up for public appreciation in the centre of Athenian

democratic activity. The stylistic identity of the figures reinforces their political stance: just as Athenian democracy is opposed to the Persian way of government, so the Tyrannicides are opposed to the world of Persian images.

'Europe was not born when Greek galleys defeated the Persian hordes at Salamis, but when the Doric studios sent out those broad backed marble statues against the multiform, vague, expressive Asiatic sea. . . .' This poetically phrased explanation by W.B. Yeats may sound bizarre, and it remains difficult to quantify how far Greek artists were aware of a stylistic rivalry with the Persians. We do know, however, that a number of Greek craftsmen worked on the site of the great Persian capital at Persepolis; and one theory for the motivation of that expensive Athenian building programme we call the Parthenon is that it was done to compete with Persepolis. The broad design of the Parthenon frieze may even have been directly provoked by knowledge of the decoration of the huge reception hall, or Apadana, at Persepolis. Yet while there may be conceptual similarities between the two projects, in no way are they stylistically twinned. Trailing around the reliefs of the palaces of the Persian kings, seeing one scene of tribute and subordination after another (*ill. 10*; see also *ill. 98*), or counting the thousandth identical archer in the service of the king, any Western visitor to Persepolis will sympathize with Lord Curzon's famous judgment: 'all the same, and the same again, and yet again'.

No one is suggesting that the art of Egypt and the Near East was retarded or childlike. Indeed, those who explain the two-dimensionality of such art tend to stress how rational and consistent it is. In terms of figurative representation, this rationality can be variously defined: it is a way of turning all bodily protrusions into profiles; or cutting sections through three dimensions; or simply an art in which frontal images take priority.

10 Section of a relief from the Throne Hall of Xerxes at Persepolis, dating from the mid-fifth century BC, showing a procession of client states bearing tribute to the king.

Above all, it is conceptual art, which some Orientalists link to the cognitive workings of languages that make space for 'inalienable things' – parts of the human body, for example, which categorize the genus of humankind, and which are linguistically fixed and invariable. The easiest way of explaining the nature of this conceptual vision is to examine a typical Egyptian picture of a building (*ill. 11*), in which the artist, thanks to the priority of concept over perspective, is able to give us both a ground-plan and an elevation of the building he has in mind.

Greek painters, as far as we know, never mastered the devices of perspective as cleverly as their Renaissance successors, though their fondness for playing illusionistic tricks is richly documented. By the fifth century BC, however, it is clear that Greek artists generally were obsessed with the possibilities of three-dimensional representation; and were also very probably aware that in this respect they had nothing in common with their counterparts in Persia, Egypt and other neighbouring cultures. The likelihood that this sense of self-definition showed itself in the planning and style of the Parthenon is a topic for discussion later (Chapter 6); for now, we may cautiously conclude that at least one ingredient in the Greek Revolution was the battle of three-dimensional (Greek) art against two-dimensional (Oriental) styles.

And it leads us to the promised consideration of a further factor. As already noted, Gombrich's account of the Greek Revolution goes beyond a purely political explanation. In *Art and Illusion*, Gombrich argued that Egyptian art remained two-dimensional because it was always concerned with the *what* of a subject rather than the *how*. And Greek art, he claimed, was propelled into its revolutionary three dimensions, and all its miraculous great awakenings, by one primary factor: it was above all narrative art, and 'narrative art is bound to lead to space and the exploration of visual effects' (*Art and Illusion*, 118). Is that necessarily – or actually – so?

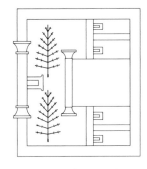

11 Drawing of an Egyptian relief of a palace, Eighteenth Dynasty, in which the artist has combined both plan and elevation.

Narrative, truth and consequences

Coming as it did on the threshold of the 1960s, Gombrich's exposition of the illusionistic necessities of narrative art must have made sense to many readers perplexed or disenchanted by art that was abstract or primitivist or childish. Gombrich offered a rekindling of excitement in the direction of art that deceived the eye into wondering whether it was art at all, of art still innocent of photography, and artists valued for what Gombrich labels 'Pygmalion's power': the power to 'bring alive' the creatures of the imagination.

Gombrich proposes that the Greek commitment to narrative was a cause of the Greek Revolution. He declares that in Egyptian art, and the Mesopotamian cultures, 'there are no mythological cycles telling of the exploits of gods and heroes' (*Art and Illusion*, 109). But this is hardly so. Even on the basis of a superficial acquaintance of Egyptian art, one could cite a number of complex mythological narratives: the reliefs of Queen Hatshepsut's temple on the West Bank of Thebes (Luxor), for example, telling of specific and generic episodes in dynastic history, such as the expedition to the equatorial land of Punt; a folktale-studded papyrus in Moscow, dated to the nineteenth century BC, known as *The Shipwrecked Sailor*; and all the eschatological cycles of Isis and Osiris. And there is no shortage of narratives in the Near East. If the act of storytelling were in itself an impulse to realistic art, why were the manifold narratives of the Old Testament not convincingly rendered – as they would be, for instance, by Rembrandt? (The answer that Judaism is not a culture with artistic traditions may be pragmatically true, but that will not hold for the Egyptians.)

Gombrich believes that the Greeks made images to 'match' reality as closely as possible. Yet as we shall see, that very much oversimplifies the range of Greek images. At the centre of the Greek Revolution, Athens in the fifth century BC, it is not possible to define Athena, the city's patron goddess, by any single image of the 'real' Athena: she is an archaic wooden statuette, clad in a peplos (Athena Polias, 'of the city'); an over-lifesize brazen warrior (Athena Promachos, 'frontline fighter'); and the colossal golden goddess in the Parthenon (Athena Parthenos, 'the virgin'). Not one of these images, in fact, corresponds to Homer's Athena, or the Athena who will appear on the fifth-century stage (e.g. in the opening scenes of Sophocles' *Ajax*). So Gombrich's proposal that Greek artists were bound by their figurative extension of narrative to produce convincingly 'lifelike' protagonists cannot comprehensively cover all the effects and intentions of Greek art.

This is not surprising to anyone who considers the development of narrative techniques in Greek art, and specifically sculpture. Gombrich's idea that Greek artists set out, contemporaneously with Homer (i.e. around the eighth century BC), to give their viewers the *how* rather than the *what* of a story, looks misleading in the light of surviving monuments. The earliest known pedimental decoration is a case in point. On the western front of the temple of Artemis on Corfu (*c.* 600–580 BC; see *ill. 64*), the Gorgon Medusa takes centre stage, dominating the entrance. Perseus, who, according to the already established mythology – as recounted in Hesiod, *Shield of Herakles* (216ff.), and *Theogony* (270ff.) – decapitated the Gorgon, is nowhere to be seen. At first sight, quite rightly so, since Medusa is still in possession of her head. But on either side of her we can make out the figures of a youth and a flying horse. These can be none other than

Medusa's son, Chrysaor, and equine offspring, Pegasus – which emerge from her decapitated body. There is, in short, an act of anachronism here: a sculptural programme within a restricted space which sacrifices continuity of action to a synoptic vision of events. Although it is probably too early here to talk of 'canonical' mythologies, such a sculptural programme must assume, on the part of its viewers, familiarity with the story: the sort of familiarity, in fact, which would subsequently excuse Greek artists the necessity of continuous narrative styles in the Egyptian or Assyrian manner. If most viewers could be relied upon to react to certain diagnostic indicators of a particular story, then they could be left to fill in for themselves such parts of the narrative as space did not permit to the artist. An evocation was enough.

Although we are told about pieces of sculpture in which a more comprehensive narrative technique may have been essayed, such as the seventh-century BC cedarwood Chest of Cypselus that Pausanias saw dedicated in the Heraion at Olympia, which featured a whole complex of stories, interwoven with hexameter verses to assist their interpretation (Pausanias V. 17.5–10), we can accept that the narrative strategies used by Archaic Greek sculptors were mainly either monoscenic or synoptic. The temple on Corfu probably displays both, in fact. In the corners of the pediment are depictions of single moments – Zeus striking a Titan with his thunderbolt; Priam sitting on his Trojan throne, perhaps – which are, so to speak, snapshots of action that preserve its actual unities of time and space. It is a combination of moments, on the other hand, that we see in the central Medusa ensemble, which cannot claim any unity of time, place or perhaps even protagonists (is Medusa also doubling as Artemis, Mistress of the Beasts?). There would be some move towards a third strategy, the cyclic narrative, in which a figure is repeated at various narrative junctures. Particularly suited to the decoration of architectural metopes (thus Herakles and Theseus on the Treasury of the Athenians at Delphi, and Herakles performing his 'Twelve Labours' on the Temple of Zeus at Olympia), this was later extended to mock-epic projects, such as the smaller frieze at Pergamum describing the trials of Telephus. But the sort of uninterrupted narrative flow that characterizes Egyptian and Assyrian reliefs (and eventually Roman too) was not much developed by the Greeks.

So what does realistic representation contribute to these strategies? A great deal, according to Gombrich. 'When classical sculptors and painters discovered the character of Greek narration, they set up a chain reaction which transformed the methods of representing the human body.' This is a reversal of a formula previously suggested by those studying narrative in Greek art, and a persistent analysis of its implications would take us back to the very beginnings of Greek figurative art. Does the story-telling phenomenon that we call 'Homer' generate illustrations for itself? Are pictures a means of communicating with the illiterate? Why are the first figures in Greek art then so conceptual and geometric?

A comparison between late eighth-century BC scenes in Greek art believed to be 'narrative', such as a melée from a giant Geometric Athenian funerary amphora, and an assured contemporary piece of Near Eastern storytelling, for instance the comprehensive relief account of Sennacherib's siege of Lachish (701 BC), from Nineveh (now in the British Museum), makes it hard to see the logic of Gombrich's formula. It is plain from the registers of Sennacherib's campaign that Assyrian artists could tell a story more clearly than their Greek counterparts. So there is nothing inherently special about Greek storytelling, at least in its early days, which demanded realistic representation. But a partial vindication of Gombrich's idea can be achieved if we approach this question from a different direction. Once again, Plato provides a good point of departure.

In Plato's ideal state there would be no place for most writers, artists and musicians. He gives his main reasons for their exclusion in Book Ten of his *Republic*. But earlier, in Book Three, there is an interesting exercise in philosophical censorship which helps to explain Plato's suspicions of artists, and which is relevant to our search for links between narrative and realism. Socrates here draws attention to the fondness in Homer (and other writers, by implication) for *diegesis dia mimeseos* – 'narrative through imitation'. That is, Homer will not relay what his characters say in indirect form; rather, when he puts words into their mouths, 'he does his very best to adapt his own style to whoever is supposed to be doing the talking'. To us, this seems a reasonable literary device. To Plato, it constitutes a form of fraudulence. His copy of Homer, ideally, would be so doctored that all the speeches were conveyed simply in terms of their content: no need for the narrator to go 'playing a part' (*mimeisthai*) – for this is fiction that we are dealing with, so why should it need to be believable?

Sympathetic or outraged as we may be at Plato's stringency, there is an obvious way of relating the sort of *mimesis* he distrusts in literary narrative to the 'imitative' characteristics of the Greek Revolution. In the hermeneutics of storytelling in Greek art, literary genres are often borrowed to furnish artistic categories: so scenes may be described as epic, lyric or dramatic. In sculpture, the dramatic category is perhaps the most striking. A good example of this is the east pediment of the Temple of Zeus at Olympia, carved around 470 BC. A powerful story is being 'enacted' here, resonant both with local legendary interest and also pan-Hellenic ramifications. The fable (or one version of it) goes that King Oinomaus of Elis had a much sought-after daughter, Hippodameia; but he had been warned that he would be murdered by whoever married her. So suitors of Hippodameia were challenged to a chariot race, which they lost

on pain of death; and since the horses of Oinomaus were magically swift, all suitors perished. Until Pelops arrived. Pelops wanted to marry Hippodameia, but also to live: so he conceived the plan of bribing the king's charioteer, one Myrtilos, to substitute the pins holding the wheels of the king's chariot to its axle with wax replicas. As the king's chariot gathered speed, the wax pins would melt, and the king would be thrown from his vehicle.

This duly happened: the king was thrown, and died; Pelops gained Hippodameia. But then he refused to honour the bribe. Accounts differ as to what it was – money, or the favours of Hippodameia herself. In any case, Pelops had the charioteer Myrtilos drowned to silence him. And as Myrtilos was being removed, he laid a curse on the family of Pelops – the house of Atreus.

The local interest here is obviously to do with the origins of chariot racing – an important event within the ancient Olympic Games – and the involvement of Pelops, whose heroic tomb was worshipped at Olympia and who was eponymous to the entire region of the Peloponnese. The pan-Hellenic interest lies in the curse: for the house of Atreus, including Agamemnon, Clytemnestra, Orestes and Electra, would provide a grim cumulus of tragedy for general edification. The fifth-century playwrights who explored the eventual results of the charioteer's curse were as popular in the Greek colonies as they were in Athens: this was the beginning of a cycle of stories that every theatre-going Greek would know.

With all this in mind, why should the sculptural presentation of the chariot race not look curiously like a tableau (*ill. 12*)? It could almost be the actors taking a curtain call: the cast, frozen in mimetic postures, with

12 The east pediment of the temple of Zeus at Olympia, *c.* 470 BC, with Zeus flanked by Pelops and King Oinomaus, and Hippodameia with a chariot group.

13 The seer from the east pediment of the temple of Zeus, Olympia.

no attempt at 'telling the story' in any continuous manner. There is the king, with his wife and daughter; there is Pelops; they all studiously avoid each other. There are the two chariot groups, plus retainers; and in the extremities of the pediment, two sinuous personifications of the rivers that bisect the site of Olympia, the Alpheos and the Kladeos. This is very much a narrative in anticipation: the viewer has to know what will happen – and there is really very little clue to that except in one figure: the old seer (*ill. 13*), who clutches his fist to his face in an almost ham attitude of foreboding. He knows the upshot; he sees beyond the immediate success of the artful Pelops. His gesture betokens the full iterative force of this story.

As Aristotle would explain, in the ninth chapter of his *Poetics*: to be effectively 'cleansing' for those who witnessed it, dramatic tragedy must necessarily blur the boundary between art and life. For the viewers of such drama to feel moved by it, there must be the illusion that 'real people' are participants. Of course, on the Greek stage characters wore masks; and to suspend disbelief is necessary, especially since, in Aristotle's terms, good tragedies come from 'unified stories' (*mythoi*) – stories whose plots are perfectly familiar to the audience. But there must be an essential probability about the actions and words and attitudes of the players. For an hour or two, at least, we must suffer.

The involvement of the viewer is not then so much a consequence of narrative *per se*, but rather the corollary of a culture of enactment. In that sense it is no accident that the Greek Revolution happens in the time and place where dramatic festivals became great public events. When the same myths nourished both theatre and art, we should expect mutual influences. In fact, on the west pediment of Olympia, where Centaurs and Lapiths are

brawling, we may notice direct cross-referencing: for the first time in Greek sculpture, some of the figures involved in serious violence wear expressions of pain or effort, and one of two of the Centaurs, with their furrowed brows and squared mouths, look indebted to the nascent tradition of theatrical masks (*ill. 14*).

A general point should be made here. It is hard to think of an Egyptian or Assyrian relief, complex as it may be, in which any expression of pain is depicted. There ought to be: pharaoh triumphant has myriad victims, many trampled underfoot as they hasten to escape him. Their features, however, are neutral: pity for their plight is not on the artist's agenda. On the other hand, what the Greek Revolution entails is a programme of artistic licence which will culminate in the Laocoon group of the first century BC (*ill. 15*; see *ill. 136*), and incur, *en route*, Plato's disapproval. (The absurd extent of that artistic licence is reached in a story of Seneca's about a painter in the fourth century BC who bought a slave at an auction and slowly tortured his purchase to death in order to sketch the contortions of the man's face: Seneca, *Controversiae* 10.5.)

Centuries later, G.E. Lessing began his meditations, *Laokoon* (1766), with the remark that both art and literature 'present to us appearance as reality, absent things as present; both deceive, and the deceit of both is pleasing'. Lessing would go on to claim priority for literature (he was himself a playwright), which is arguable. It may, however, be that Aeschylus and others did more for Greek sculpture than is ever imagined. In this highly qualified sense, we can admit that the character of Greek narrative contributed towards the Greek Revolution. But it is hardly the whole story.

14 Detail of a Centaur's head, from the west pediment of the temple of Zeus at Olympia.

15 The head of Laocoon, a Roman copy, probably early first century AD, of an original produced perhaps at Pergamum in the late second century BC (see also *ill. 136*).

The cult of beauty: canonical bodies

Kritian Boy (see *ill. 9*) is celebrated for his beauty: he conforms, in fact, to norms of male beauty that have resurfaced in popular Western culture – a taut, but not over-muscled body, a pert bottom, a clean jaw and a rather moody set of features. As we have seen, he was probably an athlete and a victor at the Panathenaic Games. These games – part of a festival staged in Athens at a 'lesser' and a 'greater' level every two years and four years respectively – contained types of competition which deserve the attention of art historians. They belong to a social history which may have had a direct effect on the appearance of statues such as Kritian Boy.

A feature of the democratic organization of Athens was its division into ten tribal voting constituencies, or *phylai*. But this was not only a basis for participation in politics: it also provided a structure for military training and a means for individual and team competitions at various inter-tribal games. The most important of these was the Panathenaic Games; and it is at this all-Athenian meeting that we first get notice of public assessment of physical beauty.

At the Panathenaic Games, each of the ten democratic Athenian tribes would submit representatives to challenge in the sphere of *euandria*, or 'fine manliness'. This entailed tests not only of prowess – one of them seems to have been riding two horses at once, standing on their bare backs – but also of appearance. Quite what criteria were applied to judge a winning effort is not known: but we do know that victors received prizes, such as shields or oxen – and that their fine manliness was celebrated with multiple garlands and ribbons tied to the key parts of their prize-winning bodies (*ill. 16*). We also know that such competitions were not confined to Athens. There was one at Elis in the Peloponnese, also staged in honour of Athena, called the *krisis kallous*, or 'battle of the beautiful'; and another recorded at Tanagra, in Boeotia, dedicated to Hermes Kriophoros (Hermes the Ram-Bearer) – here the prize for the boy displaying the most beauty (*kallisteia*) was to carry a ram around the city in Hermes' honour.

Further evidence for male beauty cults – and they were staged as votive events, on the assumption that a beautiful mortal is pleasing in the eyes of the gods – comes from inscriptions found in Hellenistic gymnasia. These inscriptions suggest a range of contests, whose nuances accommodated not only the strictly beautiful, but also those who tried hard in that direction. So one challenge, the *philoponia*, or 'love of training', evidently rewarded diligent attendance at gymnasium workouts. Another, the *euexia* ('good form') was a pure test of body-building, with marks awarded for bodily 'tone', definition and symmetry. Yet another, the *eutaxia* ('good discipline'), stressed proficiency at military drills.

The social circumstances of these contests and the appraisal of *euandria*

needs briefly sketching. Pederasty prevailed at Athens and other Greek states in a more or less shameless way: that is, although it was governed by its own decorum, the courtship of younger men by their elders, even on the grounds of overtly erotic attraction, was perfectly lawful, and indeed commonplace. And so far as it concerns the art historian, Greek pederasty is important because it patently encouraged the appreciation of male physical beauty. The late fifth-century BC Athenian writer and soldier Xenophon, in the opening passage of his *Symposium*, describes how one youthful victor at the Panathenaic Games is sought after by an older admirer, who sets up a party in the boy's honour: on the entrance of the favoured youth, all present fall speechless as they gaze on his athletic radiance. So many Greek vases, produced for such symposia or drinking-parties, were inscribed with the phrase *ho pais kalos* – 'what a beautiful boy!' – that we must imagine that Xenophon is here describing a common occurrence. But it is clear from this and other accounts (Plato's *Symposium*, for example) that beauty implied more than simply sexual charisma. The beautiful was charged with the good: the Greek phrase *kalos kagathos* is an equation which signifies beauty as a moral quality. So when young Alcibiades crashes drunkenly into Plato's *Symposium*, he makes it clear in his speech to the assembled company that his mentor Socrates, notoriously pug-nosed and stubby-bodied, is exceptional to that rule.

16 Interior of a fifth-century BC Athenian red-figure drinking-cup by Oltos, showing a victorious athlete – his prize-winning body garlanded with ribbons.

A rule it was, nevertheless. In Greek eyes, ugly people were bad people. Nowhere is that clearer than in Book Two of Homer's *Iliad*, where the demagogue Thersites is described as limping, hunched, narrow-shouldered, scrubbily-bearded and 'pointy-headed' (*oxykephalos*). To Homer and his audience, it can be no wonder that this miserable specimen of humanity is railing against the aristocrats fighting at Troy (for the sake of a beautiful woman): from his very appearance Thersites is damned as ignoble, unlovely and a coward. The proper response from the noble ones – and by definition, the beautiful ones – is to beat Thersites back into the gutter where he belongs (*Iliad* II. 211–69).

Greek mythology supports this culture of male, morally invested beauty with stories such as that of Adonis, rewarded for an act of kindness to Aphrodite with eternal youth and endless erotic adoration. Ganymede, plucked from earth by Zeus to become his Olympian cup-bearer on account of his lithe desirability, similarly proves that the gods share human tastes in beauty. But mythology also demonstrates, of course, that women enter into the competitive mode. The Judgment of Paris is the Classical prototype for all modern female beauty contests, and it, too, may have roots in actual Greek practice: we are told by Athenaeus and other anecdotalists that there were, for example, official parades of female pulchritude at Lesbos, in which the women were judged 'as they walked to and fro'. Although the appearance of the female nude in Greek sculpture came later than the male, such contests must have helped generate bodily ideals for the most desirable of all women: not Helen, but Aphrodite (see Chapter 8).

The importance of the ideal of *kalokagathia* – 'good-laden beauty', or 'beautiful goodness' – is something we shall return to when discussing the dedication of *kouroi* at Archaic sanctuaries and cemeteries. In the context of the Greek Revolution, it helps us to understand the process whereby sculptors arrived, around the middle of the fifth century BC, at what was to become recognized as the 'classic' Greek male nude. This was a prototype for so many copies and adaptations, a model so often quoted, borrowed or alluded to (see *ill. 137*), that its retrospective importance is probably swollen beyond its original measure. Because it is essentially an athletic male body that is represented, art historians often mention the effects the practice of athletics must have had on Greek sculptors. The fact that Greek athletes competed and trained naked (a gymnasium is the apposite place to be *gymnos*, naked), causes Kenneth Clark to comment: 'no wonder that [the male body] has never again been looked at with such a keen sense of its qualities, its proportion, symmetry, elasticity and aplomb'. We can propose a more precise question: what if the caliper-led criteria used by judges of the *euandria* and other beauty contests directly influenced the commemorative presentation of the male nude in Classical sculpture?

'Commemorative presentation' is intended to cover all those sculptural commissions which demanded that a male nude figure serve to display a deity (e.g. Apollo), characterize a hero (e.g. Pelops) or immortalize/heroize any one of the following: a victorious athlete, a fallen warrior, a city founder, or a revered ancestor or other deceased male. Kritian Boy, that supposed herald of the Greek Revolution, may, as we have noted, fall into the victorious athlete category; or, if he is Theseus, the hero category. That the same sculptural features could cover this range of possible subjects is highly significant for our understanding of both Greek sculpture and Greek society. In the cities and sanctuaries that the Greek frequented there was, by the mid-fifth century BC, a standing population, as it were, of male nude statues. The Classical male nude was almost oppressively exemplary, then, in several but connected ways. It stood for athletic prowess; and it stood for military commitment and civic virtue. It stood for moral integrity; and it stood for sexual desirability. It stood for personal salvation; and it stood for immortality. One scholar has coined the phrase, 'the reign of the phallus', to describe Athens in the fifth century: whatever the justice of that – the average phallus in Greek statuary is remarkably dainty and unthreatening – it is certainly true that Athens was ruled, in image terms, by the muscular diktats of the fine male nude.

In modern parlance, this amounts to 'body fascism': the imposition of norms for acceptable or successful bodies, brought about largely by a great commercial exposure to paragons of ideal proportions. Kenneth Clark, more engagingly, uses the language of the Greek architectural orders to describe the articulation of the Classical male nude. True, the entablature of the loins on typical fifth-century male nudes such as the Riace Bronzes (see *ill. 91*) is almost monumental, and, pertinently, we do not know if these are the bodies of men or heroes or gods. But why is the effect so powerful? The answer may seem surprising, given what we have so far said about the Greek Revolution. For here we are faced with a canonical body: a body, that is, which appears to go beyond naturalism.

Our survey of beauty contests can only get us so far in explaining how this came about. No record has yet been found of a contest which gives the crucial dimensions of the winner's body. Greek athletes knew about the muscle-building process which modern weight-trainers term 'progressive resistance' – one celebrated figure, Milo, from the colony of Croton, practised lifting with a calf, and kept on lifting as it grew into a fullsize cow – and took matters of sleep and diet very seriously. Sculptors had many opportunities, probably, to witness the reality of a well-muscled torso, complete with six-fold corrugations at the abdomen and that distinctive ridge marking the juncture of thighs and midriff which is known anatomically as the iliac crest. Modern athletes exhibit just such features. But those who look carefully at the anatomy of the Classical nude will note certain features whose definition would, in fact, defy any amount of training. The Riace Bronzes demonstrate two such impossibilities. One is the continuation of the iliac crest around the back of the figure, to divide the rear aspect as emphatically as the front; another is the descent of the spinal cord into a dimple, rather than a pad. Nature never designed humans with these features: this is where the obsession with a symmetrical, highly ordered work of art has overtaken the wish to 'deceive' its viewers with an illusion of reality. The evidence is compounded by anecdotes such as the one relating to the painter Zeuxis: his formula for representing Helen, apparently, was to take five beautiful girls as models and then amalgamate their individual best features to produce a breathtaking superbeauty.

The admission of such formalism in Classical sculpture adds a qualifying gloss to any idea that the Greek Revolution was simply the triumph of naturalism. If sculptors are compromising with real appearances in this way, why should any scholar (for example) make a chronological arrangement of *kouroi* on the assumed basis of anatomical 'progress'?

At the time when the Riace Bronzes were probably produced, *c.* 450 BC, a sculptor called Polykleitos, from Argos, was gaining a reputation for his statues of athletic victors. No original examples of his work survive, though it is clear from both literary and archaeological sources that the Romans admired it almost fetishistically. And it is a Graeco-Roman writer, Aelian, who tells us a nice, if dubious story about Polykleitos – how the sculptor made two statues of the same subject, one of which he executed according to his own principles, the other of which he did in public view, inviting comments and suggested improvements from visitors to his studio. Needless to say, when both statues were exhibited, the one that the public preferred was the one which Polykleitos had made according to his rules rather than their suggestions (Aelian, *Varia Historia* XIV. 8). A principled artist, this Polykleitos. But do we know what his principles were? The task is worth pursuing, given the background of the beauty contests: for it looks as though Polykleitos would have taken a keen interest in what it was that made a winning, relatively 'perfect' human physique.

Our best snippet of information about Polykleitos, and it is no more than that, comes from a second-century AD medical writer, Galen. He is in the course of explaining certain doctrines of a late third-century BC Stoic philosopher, Chrysippos:

> Chrysippos . . . holds that beauty does not consist in the elements [by 'elements' are understood the properties hot, cold, dry, moist] of the body, but in the harmonious proportion of the parts – the proportion of one finger to another, of all the fingers to the rest of the hand, of the rest of the hand to the wrist, and of these to the forearm, and of the forearm to the whole arm, and, in short, of everything to everything else, just as described in the *Canon* of Polykleitos.

Polykleitos it was who demonstrated these proportions with a work of art, by making a statue according to his treatise, and calling it by the same title, the Canon.

(Galen, *De placitis Hippocratis et Platonis* V. 448)

One can more or less make sense of this description of Polykleitan aims. The basic principle is one of continuity, with each section of the body relaying a fraction of itself to the next section: hence Galen's summary of this accumulation as 'and everything to everything' (*kai panton pros panta*). Unfortunately, however, we can do little to reconstruct in detail the ratios that Polykleitos specified in his book. The main difficulty, according to Andrew Stewart, is that we do not know where to begin – where to place our calipers and plumb-lines – but perhaps an even greater difficulty is that we have no original statue by Polykleitos. And although there is archaeological evidence that plaster casts were taken from Polykleitan figures in Roman times, it remains the case that those who try to measure up his Canon from a Roman statue (*ill. 17*) are doing so in vain, because it is increasingly clear that the Romans did not so much copy Greek originals as adapt them, and an adaptation could hardly hope to transmit the unnerving degree of accuracy which (according to the literary sources) the *Canon* required. To the Romans, what was most striking about Polykleitan statuary was its 'four-square' (*quadratus*, or *tetragonos*) appearance; Roman 'copyists' put Polykleitan bodies together almost like building blocks.

17 Measuring a Roman copy of the Doryphoros ('Spear-carrier') – a Greek bronze originally produced in the mid-fifth century BC – in an attempt to establish the Polykleitan Canon.

'A well-made work is the result of numerous calculations, carried to within a hair's breadth.' 'The work is trickiest when the clay is on the nail.' The literary memorabilia of Polykleitos, perhaps culled from his *Canon*, suggest a good deal more than the basic system of ideal human proportions summarized by the architectural historian Vitruvius (in his *De Architectura* III. 1.2–7) and conveniently made graphic by Leonardo da Vinci (*ill. 18*). According to this basic system, a man's foot should be one-sixth of his height, the span of his outstretched hands should equate to his height, and so on. Due to its presumed precision, the aim of the *Canon* of Polykleitos has often been explained in terms of mathematical elegance. Some surmise the influence of the Pythagorean philosophers, who 'supposed the elements of numbers to be the elements of things' (Aristotle, *Metaphysics* 985b), and proportion to be 'the bond of mathematics'. The same influence has also been invoked for the spread of orthogonally gridded Greek town-planning in the fifth century. Others are tempted to see in Polykleitos a Classical Greek answer to the Egyptian canon, which (as Plato saw) had guaranteed a consonance of figurative representation over several millennia.

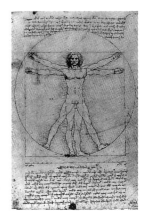

18 'Vitruvian man' from the *Notebooks* of Leonardo da Vinci.

Such guesswork about the intellectual origins of the *Canon* is mislead-ing. It is true that metrology – the science of weights and measures – became important, not least commercially, to the Greek city-states in the fifth century: special buildings must have been set aside for fixing stan-dards, and the well-known metrological relief in Oxford (*ill. 19*) probably once served as a lintel over the entrance to a room where measures were controlled. The adoption of bodily parts (especially the hand length, or *orthodoron*) as units of measurement perhaps encouraged sculptors to look for examples of absolute accuracy or 'perfection'. But the description of the Polykleitan *Canon* as 'anthropometric' – based on measurements of the body, not some absolute, external matrix – must be qualified by its characterization as 'organic', which means that the system was flex-ible enough to accommodate female as well as male figures, young as well as old.

Elusive as the actual *Canon* is, it is probably most accurately evoked by Erwin Panofsky, who reckons that it proceeded on the basis of 'organic dif-ferentiation', and reminds us that it sought, in Galen's words, the defini-tion of what 'constitutes beauty' (*kallos synistathai*). As such, it was never akin to the Egyptian canon, whereby a grid was laid out, and the human form mapped on to it according to the positions where noses, legs and feet *should* be; instead, Polykleitos started with a figure – a successful athlete, perhaps a winner in the *euandria* contest – and tried to work out how the constituent parts of this body, saluted as 'beautiful', related to each other. Thus, says Panofsky, Classical Greek art 'opposed to the inflexible, mechanical, static and conventional craftsman's code of the Egyptians an elastic, dynamic and aesthetically relevant system of relations.' And as Panofsky further points out, the assumptions on which this organic Greek canon rested were not seriously challenged until the third century AD, when the Neoplatonist theories of Plotinus and others, arguing that the soul was reflected in the eyes, caused the sort of distortion of Classical norms that

19 'Metrological relief', probably dating from the fifth century BC, which may once have adorned the lintel of a room where measurements were controlled.

eventually becomes the Romanesque style – in which Thersites, with his cowering shoulders and egg-shaped head, would have at last felt perfectly at home.

The logic of anthropomorphism

A Greek poem, written perhaps in the seventh century BC, describes the following prehistoric scenario. The god Apollo is at large in the Aegean, seeking new sites for his own worship, and new followers to staff those sites. He is protean, capable of assuming many shapes, including zoomorphic: in one guise he is *delfinios*, like a dolphin, and as such he leads a vessel of mariners from Knossos in Crete to one of his chosen sites. He first stages an epiphany at the sanctuary itself, 'amidst the priceless tripods'; then, 'swift as a thought', he shows himself to the crew. The guise he chooses here is anthropomorphic: 'in the form of a man, quick and well-built, in the full bloom of youth, his hair flowing over his shoulders'. He hails the sailors. They are not sure how to respond to this stranger: for all that he is fine and manly, he also resembles one of the deathless gods (*all'athanatoisi theosin*). They settle for nervous badinage; eventually Apollo declares his divine identity and issues appropriate instructions for his cult.

This episode – from the *Homeric Hymn to Apollo* (lines 388ff.) – is loaded with art-historical significance. The Archaic description of Apollo as a young man, long-haired and athletic, has been frequently cited with regard to the appearance of Archaic Greek *kouroi*, who were indeed once called (by their early discoverers) 'Apollos' on that account. But attention is less commonly drawn to the peculiar nature of Greek anthropomorphism revealed by this poetic incident. Apollo chooses to appear to the sailors as a *kouros* – his incarnation is not a supernatural surprise to them; he shares their species, their *ethnos*, their language – and yet they realize from his frame (*demas*) and his stature (*phue*) that he is more immortal than mortal. We have, then, something close to a paradox: a god who takes anthropomorphic shape, yet reserves a measure of divinity. In the terms of that peculiar idiom, this is a case of having your cake and eating it. In terms of art, it is both naturalism and idealization at the same time. And the consequences of this virtual paradox are highly important for the Greek Revolution.

To Muslims, Jews and some Christians, the worship of graven images is an abomination. To the Greeks, the absence of graven images in religious practice was equally repugnant, or at best curious. Herodotus, a tolerant observer, noted that the Persians conducted their cults in an open landscape, worshipping without the paraphernalia of altars, statuary or temples: they do so, he suggests, because 'they do not believe the gods to share the same nature with men, as we Greeks imagine' (*Histories* I. 131). Later writers went further than Herodotus, and condemned iconoclastic cultures as uncivilized. It took sophistication, according to this argument, for the gods to be figured; and as a second-century AD philosopher would put it, 'the Greek manner of honouring the gods recruits whatever is most beautiful on earth [*en ge tois kallistois*], whether in terms of raw materials [*kathara*], human shape [*morphe de anthropine*] or artistic precision [*techne de akribei*]' (Maximus of Tyre, *Orations* II.3, ed. Hobein). *Akribeia* – finesse, precision, skill – is a virtue often ascribed to Greek sculptors in the records of literary approbation, and the artistic employment of rare materials, such as gold, amber and ivory, which made some cult statues double up as treasuries, is an obvious justification for the chryselephantine extravagance which would disgust the Christian inheritors of Greek sanctuary sites. But the most interesting clause of this statement by Maximus concerns human shape. The best human bodies, he is saying, are vehicles of the divine. Such is the basis of ancient Greek anthropomorphism.

The relevance of a deeply embedded religious anthropomorphism to the Greek Revolution will soon become clear: but before we discuss its positive contribution, it is as well to rid ourselves of an oft-quoted and overestimated 'objection' to Greek anthropomorphism. It comes from a late sixth-century BC poet-philosopher called Xenophanes, who evidently disapproved of the manner in which Homer, and others had humanized the gods, in bodies, clothes and speech (and hence motivation). Xenophanes takes a relativistic stand: the Ethiopians, he points out, say that their gods are black and snub-nosed; the Thracians, that theirs are blue-eyed and redhaired. 'If horses could draw', he goes on, 'would their gods not be horsey?' And lions have lion-gods, or oxen have oxen-gods?

Combined with the fragmentary utterances of another sixth-century BC sceptic, the Ionian philosopher Herakleitos (to the effect that praying before a statue is as efficacious as praying to a brick wall), the insider-criticism of Xenophanes has been taken – ever since it was preserved for us by an enthusiastic early Christian iconoclast, Clement of Alexandria – as a record of intellectual doubt concerning anthropomorphism and as suggesting that the production of cult images predominantly satisfied a popular culture. But it is unlikely that Xenophanes represents anything more than an eccentric view. Most Greeks would not have been persuaded by his relativistic argument: yes, Ethiopians and other Africans had black deities, but these were not the inhabitants of Olympus, the all-powerful ones; and as for the idea of horses and animals drawing or sculpting, the point is that they cannot: it is an essentially human attribute.

Herodotus may be considered to confirm this faith in the civilized, humane nature of anthropomorphism, simply by the astonishment, or at least polite bafflement (II. 65), he registers at the Egyptian tradition of worshipping cats, and deities with heads of dogs or cows. The Egyptian extension of anthropomorphism into zoomorphism is, for Herodotus, almost as peculiar as the Persians having no images at all. Thus it is a feature of Greek self-definition, this manner of honouring the gods; and because Greek religion is also highly polytheistic, it becomes a matter of importance to all those frequenting Greek sanctuaries to distinguish one deity from another. If cult statues were aniconic, special guidance was certainly necessary: for example if a particular pine trunk or piece of driftwood were to constitute the seat of 'woody' Dionysos Dendrites. Pausanias tells of some fishermen from Methymna on Lesbos who caught a mask-like piece of olive-wood in their nets: 'the features had something divine about them, yet they were foreign, not the usual features of the Greek gods'; so oracular advice from Delphi was needed to create the recognition that this was Dionysos (Pausanias X. 19.3), and deserved worship accordingly.

Alain Schnapp has argued that one stage of distinction was provided by the various words which in Greek could be used to denote a statue. Unfortunately, neither he nor anyone else has yet established a precise series of definitions to accompany the known Greek terms for 'statue'. *Agalma* is probably the commonest word, and carries the connotation of 'something that brings joy' – to the deity it honours, and to whoever views it (which may be why so many Archaic statues wear a permanent smile). Some philologists (notably Louis Robert) believe that *agalmata* (pl.) were primarily images of deities, though this glosses over the undoubted aspiration on the part of some human representations to be regarded as pseudo-divine, or at least posthumously venerated. Perhaps it is safer to say that *agalma* refers less to the type of image than to the nature of the place where it was dedicated, i.e. sacred.

Kolossos did not originally denote massive dimensions in a statue (though Herodotus used the word for the huge figures he saw in Egypt) but may simply have meant a person's simulacrum or replica. *Idruma*, less commonly used than *agalma*, has the sense of being an object 'set up' or 'dedicated', so that the verb *idrusasthai* can simply mean 'to erect a statue'. (*Aphidruma* seems to refer to a cult statue which replicates a more important cult statue at another sanctuary: the Olympian Zeus, for example, was copied at several other places.) *Andrias*, with overtones of 'manliness', was usually reserved for statues of men (and occasionally women) rather than gods. It was especially suitable for portraits and generated some nice colloquialisms – the fourth-century BC orator Demosthenes impugned one of his enemies, Aeschines, by alleging that when he was small, Aeschines' mother would call him *ton kalon andrianta* – 'pretty little puppet' (with the implication that if Aeschines was treated like a *kalos andrias* as a boy, he would shamelessly exploit his good looks as a man). As *agalmata* may strictly belong to sacred contexts, so *andriantes* may pertain to essentially civic settings.

Baetylia implies a non-figured object of cult: at Aphrodite's sanctuary at Paphos on Cyprus, a large pointed baetyl-stone was worshipped well into Roman times. Technically such cult-objects are 'aniconic', and thus outside any discussion of anthropomorphism, yet the baetyl at Paphos was probably linked with the myth of the birth of Aphrodite and is taken to have been appropriately phallic in its cult context. A *xoanon* or *bretas*, however, denoted a figured object. It may have received its humanoid features accidentally – for instance a peculiar piece of driftwood, or some such – but more often it was a carved image, 'old-fashioned' in both senses of the term. That is, it had been made long ago; or else carved in a deliberately olden, or archaizing, style. As such, its material was usually wood.

Schnapp is right to point out that a 'progressive' view of Greek anthropomorphism, whereby aniconic *baetylia* and rough-hewn or totemistic *xoana* evolve into more sophisticated naturalistic images of deities, is misguided. Yet one finds little philological evidence to support his claim that a dictionary of cognitive associations existed for the various generic ways in which the Greeks referred to the forests of statuary surrounding them. Epigraphical evidence from a site such as Aphrodisias in Asia Minor, for example, reveals a Hellenistic or Graeco-Roman populace happy to trade all sorts of terms around the general concept of public 'images' (*eikones*). The search for definitive terms may intrinsically be a lost cause.

If this system of statue-categories was not consistent, then, it was all the more essential that deities in sculpture were given 'personal' characteristics: an identity that facilitated recognition and encouraged appropriate salutation from their viewers. This might be a local identity, or else pan-Hellenic. As we shall see, the logic of anthropomorphism permitted a certain identity to develop and change. Chapter 8 records the case of Aphrodite, whose appearance as a nude goddess in the early fourth century BC at first seems to have shocked, and then delighted, the Greeks who worshipped her. But it also allowed what some might regard as a lacuna in the consistency of the Greek Revolution: that is, images were not discarded on the grounds that they were 'old-fashioned' or unnaturalistic. On the contrary, some images appear to have gained in the fetishistic power precisely because they had an archaic or archaizing style about them.

Apollo may again demonstrate the force of this. We have seen how he was characterized in the Homeric Hymn as a young man, with hair streaming over his shoulders. So long as Archaic Greek youths wore their hair long, the chances of confusing a *kouros* with Apollo are going to be high. But what happens when hairstyles change, as they do towards the end of the sixth century BC? Well, Apollo may change with them. If the central image on the west pediment of the temple of Zeus at Olympia is Apollo (which seems likely, given the relative scale of the statue), then Apollo proves himself a fashionable young man. But for certain cult purposes, it may have suited the commissioners of Apollo-statues to keep the god looking more or less in keeping with his Homeric epiphany. An early fourth-century BC vase from Apulia records just such an image, colossal and gilded (*ill. 20*); and a rare surviving bronze figure from the Piraeus zone of Athens has been named the 'Piraeus Apollo' (*ill. 21*) simply because it seems to be a consciously archaizing attempt to differentiate Apollo from coeval *kouroi* – who by this time (*c.* 510 BC) would invariably have worn their hair tied up.

20 Apollo in his temple: a detail of an Apulian krater of the fourth century BC.

A cognitive space was certainly reserved for the archaic or the archaizing as a token of venerability. What the Classical Greeks would regard as prehistoric statuary, which they attributed to the mythical Daedalus (see Chapter 3), they admitted to be technically immature: 'If Daedalus were around now, and producing those old-style statues of his, everyone would laugh at him', points out Socrates in Plato's *Hippias Major* (282a). But age invested an image with some divinity. Pausanias would notice this when in his travels he came across 'Daedalic' statues, and one Neoplatonist philosopher, Porphyry, would go so far as to claim that primitive images were 'more divine' than sophisticated statues (*De Abstinentia*, II. 18). Certainly, the creation of the enormous Athena Parthenos statue on the Akropolis (see Chapter 7) did not supplant, in terms of cult importance, the olive-wood image of Athena Polias which had stood there since perhaps the seventh century BC, and had survived even the Persian occupation of the citadel in 480 BC.

Pausanias was travelling in the second century AD, and Porphyry writing even later, but their attitudes should not be dismissed as quaint or nostalgic. We know that sculptors who were otherwise committed to naturalism, such as the fifth-century BC Myron, might take commissions to produce deliberately old-fashioned statues, perhaps in wood rather than bronze or marble. Likewise, there is evidence for fifth-century poets – Aeschylus, for example – being called upon by temple priesthoods to compose paeans and choruses in 'traditional' or out-moded metres and language. Certain types of statuary, in fact, were scarcely affected by the Greek Revolution: the 'Herms', the usually phallic columns of the bearded god of passage that stood at street corners and other places of transit, often presented an archaized aspect; so, too, the statues of Hekate, specially reserved for crossroads. It is almost as if the semiotic, informative function of such statues – to help orientation around the *polis* – prevented any tampering with their artistic treatment.

21 The 'Piraeus Apollo', a bronze original dating from c. 530–520 BC.

Admitting this reserved cognitive space for the archaic in Greek religion, however, does not detract from the overall impulse of anthropomorphism in terms of the Greek Revolution. For at the heart of Greek anthropomorphism is the faith in animated images; the belief that, whether old-fashioned or utterly up-to-the-minute in style, statues in cult contexts were more than representations: they could act and respond. They had, so to speak, a life of their own.

A passage from a Graeco-Roman author denoted as 'Pseudo-Lucian', probably writing in the third century AD, may illustrate what this sort of anthropomorphism might entail in terms of cult practice. He is describing an eastern variant of the Apollo cult, noting that in one temple there is a statue of a bearded Apollo – unusual in presenting the god as a mature man, and unusual in other respects too:

> About his deeds I could say a great deal, but I will describe only what is especially remarkable. I will first mention the oracle. There are many oracles among the Greeks, many among the Egyptians, some in Libya and many in Asia. None of the others, however, speaks without priests or prophets. This god takes the initiative himself and completes the oracle of his own accord. This is his method. Whenever he wishes to deliver an oracle, he first moves on his throne, and the priests immediately lift him up. If they do not lift him, he begins to sweat and moves still more. When they put him on their shoulders and carry him, he leads them in every direction as he spins around and leaps from one place to another. Finally the chief priest meets him face to face and asks him about all sorts of things. If the god does not want something done, he moves backwards. If he approves of something, like a charioteer he leads forward those who are carrying him. In this manner they may collect the divine utterances, and without this ritual they conduct no religious or personal business. The god also speaks of the year and of all its seasons, even when they do not ask . . .
>
> I will tell something else which he did while I was present. The priests were lifting him up and beginning to carry him, but he left them below on the ground and went off alone into the air.
>
> (Pseudo-Lucian, *De Dea Syria*, 36–7)

To the twentieth-century cynic, this will seem like priestly manipulation of gullible worshippers at Greek sanctuaries. And undoubtedly some skullduggery must have gone on. In Copenhagen, there is a bust of the philosopher Epicurus which has a special duct leading to the mouth from the back of the head. Experiments with tubes and funnels have demonstrated that the statue can thus be made to speak by a concealed ventriloquist, and so presumably cajole some credulous supplicant into accepting an oracle or other expensive piece of advice. This is an example from later antiquity, but such tricks must have gone on earlier. Cult statues moving, sweating, bleeding or weeping are numerously documented, and could easily have been engineered in similar ways – tubes, perforations, and so on – to the Epicurus bust.

At the Spartan temple of Artemis Orthia, a notorious ritual took place:

Spartan boys submitted themselves to public flogging on a competitive basis, to see who could hold out the longest and thus become the 'altar-winner' (*bomonikos*). Ancient in its origins, the ritual eventually became a Roman tourist attraction, and a theatre was built around the altar to accommodate spectators. Pausanias, when he witnessed the event (III. 16.7–11), noted that the priestess supervising the whippings held an archaic image or *xoanon* of Artemis. If the thrashing was thought to flag, the image 'drooped' – a sign for the tempo and effort of the flogger to be stepped up. What is interesting here is how a statue (or statuette, in this case) is deemed to be an agency: Artemis registers, she *feels*, what is going on in her precincts, and preserves her ancient taste for the spilling of human blood.

'Some of the gods whom we honour we see clearly, but of others we set up statues as images, and we believe that when we worship these, lifeless [*apsychous*] though they be, the living gods [*empsychous theos*] beyond feel great goodwill towards us and gratitude.' Plato thus struggled to account for the image-making machinery of Greek cults (see his *Laws*, 931a). Commentators assume that by 'gods . . . we see clearly' he means the stars, but how can one clarify the rapport he postulates between 'lifeless' statues and 'living gods beyond'? Most Greek worshippers must have preferred to accept what their own language implied: that a statue served as the 'seat' or *hedos* of a deity, and the temple it stood in could properly be regarded as the god's home or *oikos* (no matter, incidentally, that a god could have more than one image, and more than one home: spontaneous ubiquity is a sign of divinity, in Greek eyes).

Veneration of animated status can occur even beyond the strict confines of Greek religion. When Graeco-Roman travellers visited Egyptian Thebes (modern Luxor), they paid special homage to the so-called 'Colossi of Memnon' because the two enthroned figures were reputed to 'speak'. Modern guidebooks explain this phenomenon as a sibilance emitted by a crack in one of the figures as the stone heated up in the morning. In ancient times this was said to be the voice of Abyssinian Memnon, slain at Troy, enjoining his mother Eos (Dawn) to staunch her tears (the dew). Back in Greece proper, the fifth-century poet Pindar describes a fantastic Archaic bronze temple of Apollo at Delphi, whose frontage featured six sirens or 'enchantresses' (*keledones*). These creations, he says, were capable of singing. And, still in the realms of literary fantasy, Homer liked to imagine the smith-god Hephaistos making dogs and lions from gold, silver and bronze, and giving them life (*psyche entheis*), so that they could serve as effective guardians – for the palace of King Alcinous, for example (*Odyssey* VII. 91–2).

Yet this amounts to more than travellers' tales and poets' dreams. There is no doubt that statues, since they were considered animated, could

monitor, applaud or punish human behaviour; and that they were also regarded as having prophylactic powers. Greek art and literature are packed with examples of such credence. Cassandra clutching at a statue for protection after the fall of Troy (*ill.* 22) is a common vignette on Greek vases, and Aeschylus, in his *Seven Against Thebes*, dramatizes the effort made by the Theban women to save their city from a siege by appealing to the 'regiment' (*strateuma*) of the city's statues (*archaia brete*). It is true that in this particular play, the account of the women's action is flavoured with misogyny – trust the likes of womankind (*gynaikeion genos*), complains the King of Thebes, to suggest such a futile strategy – but men surely also held this faith, that cult images were talismans that both protected and needed protection (hence the evacuation of the Athena Polias statue from Athens to the island of Salamis in 480 BC, when the Persians invaded).

Greek religion was reciprocal in its nature. Before a statue of a deity you made your offerings and said your prayers: you expected some goodwill in return. The statue, therefore, must have ears and it must be capable of sensing the many vanities of human wishes. In this respect, a statue, to be credible, must appear to have sensory powers. This is why anthropomorphism ultimately has so much responsibility for the Greek Revolution. But at the same time it generates some odd results. We shall encounter later (Chapter 8) the unfortunate consequences visited upon young men who became infatuated with statues of Aphrodite. Though in Greek terms this was regarded as bizarre (*para phusin*), it must also have gained sympathy. We are told about one pilgrim to Delphi who, having removed a statue from its base and spent a night with it, is not punished. Instead, he leaves a wreath behind 'as the price of the intercourse', and Apollo expresses satisfaction through his oracle (see Athenaeus, *Deipnosophistae* 606). Why indeed should the priesthood object, since it is in their interests to further belief in the animated, responsive powers of cult images? The art-historical consequence of all this is that the primary and popular Greek criterion for judging the worth of a statue becomes: how far is it lifelike?

Artists blatantly exploited that criterion. Plato's disapproval of artists stems precisely from his suspicion that they were out to confuse the public by blinding them to the differences between truth and fiction and creating virtual realities which would in the end disorientate their viewers. Hellenistic art history is packed with anecdotes about the painters and sculptors in Plato's time who notoriously succeeded in creating illusions: the painter who painted a bunch of grapes, and watched birds peck at his picture; the painter who invited a rival into his studio and asked him to pull back a curtain to reveal a masterpiece – and the rival, fooled, tries to pull back a painted curtain, and so on. Almost exactly the same stories would be resuscitated for new applications in the art history of the Italian Renaissance. Hence, therefore, the numerous plaudits for a statue of a heifer made, we learn, by Myron (of Discobolus fame). Here is a selection of responses recorded in *The Greek Anthology*:

> I am Myron's little heifer, set up on a base. Goad me, herdsman, and drive me off to the herd.
> A calf died beside thy heifer, Myron, thinking that the bronze had milk inside.
> In vain, bull, thou rushest up to this heifer, for it is lifeless. The sculptor of cows, Myron, deceived thee.
> The lead and stone hold me fast, but otherwise, thanks to thee, sculptor Myron, I would be nibbling lotus and rushes.

No trace of this statue remains, and none of the great number of epigrammatic compliments it received actually describes its appearance; as Simon Goldhill has noted, they simply dramatize a response. Myron apparently received similar reactions to his statue of a sprinter, with Hellenistic wits suggesting that the figure be chained to its base, lest it run away. That advice was taken seriously by some curators of statues, for Pausanias several times records seeing chains holding a statue to its base.

In Hellenistic Alexandria, grand carnival processions were staged whose centrepieces were mechanized statues, engineered to participate in interactive displays. For one Alexandrine procession or *pompe*, a statue, 3.6m (12 ft) high, was designed of Nysa, nurse of Dionysos, which could rise automatically, pour a libation of milk, and then sit down again. And

Hellenistic literature connives in the enterprise, parodying popular judgments of the sculptor's art. In Theocritus' *Idyll* XV, for example, ladies visiting a temple are aroused to almost sexual ecstasies when they see how 'lifelike' (*empyschous*) are the figures on a tapestry, especially the lovely young Adonis; and in the fourth *Mime* of Herodas, two ladies, with suspiciously disparaging names ('Kynno' and 'Kokkale') and heavily rustic accents, talk us through some temple statues ascribed to the sons of Praxiteles – absurdly, and remorselessly, in terms of how the statues look like they need a bite to eat, how you can almost hear them talking, and so on.

Again one is struck by an element of misogyny here, and of course a sophisticated intellectual audience is supposed to laugh at such naivety. But it would be rash to dismiss the credence in animated statues as some sort of popular gullibility. To judge from the results of the Greek Revolution, the degree to which images could be animated was a matter for very serious consideration.

Conclusion: 'Pygmalion's power'

Our search for the causes of dynamic stylistic change in Greek sculpture has explored the traditional explanations, and also advanced along routes of analysis less frequently taken. It is time to attempt a conclusion.

In his influential essay, on 'The Work of Art in the Age of Mechanical Reproduction', written in 1935, Walter Benjamin claimed that the key to analysing the social history of art was to appreciate art's aura. By 'aura' Benjamin meant 'the unique phenomenon of a distance, however close [an object] may be' – a cultic function, an authenticity derived from the 'contextual integration of art in tradition'. The aura of a work of art, in Benjamin's terms, is 'that which withers in an age of mechanical reproduction'. If we take this concept of aura as crucial, then we are bound to place particular stress on the demands of anthropomorphic cult practice when explaining the Greek Revolution. And this is not simply because most Greek sculpture once stood in what were variously, but definitely, sacred spaces. It is also because the sculptor was conceived of as an essentially vicarious agent: through him came glimpses, or even revelations, of the divine.

Gombrich describes the enterprise of the sculptors of the Greek Revolution as a display of 'Pygmalion's power' – the power to bring things alive by assiduously representational or naturalistic art. A reconsideration of the Pygmalion story will help clarify how far this power is bound up with the aura of Greek sculpture. Following the Roman poet Ovid, who tells the story best (*Metamorphoses* X. 243–97), we encounter Pygmalion as a sculptor by profession (in other versions, he is an ancient King of Cyprus). He is a bachelor, confirmed in his view that no living woman is good enough for him. So he makes an ivory statue of the most beautiful woman he can imagine (in other versions it may be specifically a statue of Aphrodite), and then prettifies it with jewelry and fine clothes; pampers the idol, to the point of lying her beside him in his bed; and prays all the while to Aphrodite to make his creation come alive. Aphrodite grants his prayer, giving Ovid the opportunity of describing a particularly erotic metamorphosis as the ivory turns sensuously to flesh beneath the wondrous explorations of Pygmalion's touch, and on the miraculous new complexion 'the bruises of passion' are inflicted. Immediate consummation is achieved; nine months later, a daughter called Paphos will be born to the pair. The ideal has become flesh; art has 'come alive'.

The myth of Pygmalion has fascinated artists and all those with creative imaginations ever since, for obvious reasons, including the nineteenth-century English Pre-Raphaelites: Edward Burne-Jones painted a memorably vapid rendition of it (*ills 23* and *24*). As a myth, it can also be read in a rather negative way: once Pygmalion's creation comes alive, as Jas Elsner comments, 'it is no longer artistically marvellous: the gap between appearance and reality that made its mimesis an artistic *tour de force* disappears'. And one can quote sentiments reflecting disappointment that statues of beautiful women are *not* proper substitutes for the real thing: Aeschylus gives us a telling glimpse of the brooding Menelaus after his wife Helen's abduction – 'the grace [*charis*] of fair-formed statues [*eumorphon de kolosson*] is hateful to him: and in the hunger of his eyes, all passion of love is lost [*errei pas'Aphrodita*]' (*Agamemnon*, 416–19). If statues could be conjured into life, the Trojan War might never have happened.

Nevertheless, 'Pygmalion's power' is as good as any other way of encapsulating the determination of sculptors to reconcile the ideal with the natural. This is what ultimately explains the Greek Revolution. Its motivation was what we would call 'religious', and that remains a very general motivation, since religious activity in ancient Greece can scarcely be distinguished from the everyday strategies of social, political and even economic business. But the underlying basis for the stylistic dynamism of Greek sculpture is the conviction that the divine and the mystical are not beyond the human imagination to comprehend. The state of true transcendence was unthinkable. Images of greater things made them part of the facts of the world.

23–4 *Pygmalion: the hand refrains*, and *Pygmalion: the soul attains*, by E. Burne-Jones (from a series 1869–79).

3

DAEDALUS AND THE WINGS OF TECHNE

It is accepted that societies and cultures live in a state of equilibrium . . . For any significant change to take place . . . innovations must be linked in a deviation-amplifying mutual causal system: the innovation produces effects which favour the further development of the innovation . . . When the structure of the subsystems is such that marked change can occur in them (for instance when a technological threshold such as the invention of metal casting, or the sowing of grain, can be surmounted) a cultural 'take-off' is possible.

Colin Renfrew, *The Emergence of Civilisation* (London 1972), 43

The gynaecology of Greek art

It is commonplace to use the terminology of procreation in both art history and archaeology. Many accounts of Archaic Greek sculpture are framed in terms of 'seeds' being 'sown', techniques 'hatched' or 'conceived', forms 'born', and so on. To anyone surveying those books claiming to explain the 'birth' of Greek art generally, the gynaecological metaphor must soon lose its usefulness: for the claimed parentage is often less a matter of forensic certainty, and more an area of political correctness or ethnic propaganda. Thus Turkish scholars claim ancient Anatolia to have been the indispensable supplier of motifs, monsters and other decorative devices; Jewish scholars are perhaps inclined to stress the role of the Phoenicians, not only as commercial transmitters of Eastern objects; Egyptologists insist that only a knowledge of the 'Egyptian canon', and Egyptian stone-cutting techniques, could have enabled the Greeks to progress from figurines to monumental statues; and staunch philhellenes argue that Minoan and Mycenaean sites yield all the necessary precedents and prototypes for the figurative styles we now generally salute as 'Greek'.

To locate a time and place for 'the birth' of Greek sculpture is probably a misguided enterprise. As long ago as 1774, the German philosopher J.G. Herder argued (against his contemporary Winckelmann, whose view of the absolute 'perfection' of Classical Greek statuary we have already encountered) that it was futile to hold up Greek art against Egyptian and claim superiority for Greece. Protesting against Winckelmann's complaint of 'lack of movement' in Egyptian statues, Herder defends the suitability of these Egyptian figures for their own social circumstances. 'They're supposed to be mummies!' cries Herder ('Mumien sollten sie sein!'): why expect them, then, to demonstrate 'action' or 'movement'? Egypt under the pharaohs has, in Herder's language, its own cultural centre of gravity: art does its job perfectly well, according to local expectations.

Herder's protest establishes a sort of relativism; a suspension of absolute judgment, to which we must ultimately resort if we do not want to join in the game of locate-the-birthplace. It does not imply a blanket denial of foreign factors in the shaping of early Greek sculpture (or later Greek sculpture, come to that); nor does it release us from the task of deconstructing the literary carapace of inventiveness and originality that the Greeks created for themselves. But it does shift the emphasis of inquiry away from what is now commonly called 'Orientalizing' as a period of Greek history, and towards the process of Greek self-definition in art. In this way, without slighting civilizations which are chronologically senior, we can account for the appearance of the first Greek sculptures in primarily Greek terms: that is, looking to the archaeology of Greek sanctuaries and early Greek city-states to tell us why sculptors were first motivated to try their hand at that risky and laborious business, the large-scale shaping of marble.

The pseudo-economic analysis of this process of innovation and change would invoke a 'multiplier effect': that is, a tendency for innovations to spread themselves in ways that may never have been foreseen by those originally responsible for screening or introducing such innovations. So changes in vase-painting (for example, using a freehand brush to paint detail formerly etched through a black glaze) may have affected techniques of relief sculpture; or techniques of making bronze or wooden statues may have directly inspired new ways of cutting stone. In that sense this chapter must be regarded as seriously incomplete, since our evidence for certain categories of Greek art – wooden sculpture, large-scale painting, chryselephantine statues and even hollow-cast bronzes – is either non-existent or patchy. But this should not deter us from creating a non-diffusionist account of how innovations made progress in the hands of Greek sculptors. It is easy enough, on the basis of technical analysis, to attribute this or that innovation to a precedent outside Greece: for instance, to demonstrate that the claw chisel, so important to the development of Archaic Greek marble sculpture, had already been used by the Egyptians on their granite. But a tool's utility is conditional: only an exploration of how the claw chisel might suit the purposes of *Greek* sculptors will tell us why, in the sixth century BC, it became useful to them. To deny diffusionist approaches is not a display of Classical arrogance. And before we go any further, we must dismantle the Greeks' own extravagant claims to artistic independence.

Daedalus: the invention of the arch-inventor

By his works he is known: the works were *daidala*, and he was Daedalus; and 'Daedalic' is the usual denomination for the earliest style of Greek sculpture. If only it were so simple.

The first thing to acknowledge is that while he is generically eponymous to the 'first' Greek statues, Daedalus has a truly mixed reputation. One scholar has registered 'the hint of treachery which often accompanies the glamour of *daidala* in the earliest literature'. This resonance can be sensed into Roman times and beyond, as the name of Daedalus continues to be evocative of tricks, ingenuity and a particularly shrewd sort of arrogance (thus it was Daedalus who fashioned wings for the first airborne humans, but his son Icarus who tried to fly at an impossible altitude).

The flight, now best-known of Daedalic exploits, occurs in the mythical context of an escape from King Minos in Crete. Daedalus, without Icarus, thereby arrives in Sicily, where his clever energies are soon harnessed for all sorts of useful projects: hot baths, dams and other proto-feats of civil engineering. Apart from providing a rather obvious metaphor for the process of Greek colonization in the West, this legendary amalgam of artist, engineer and aviation specialist inevitably tempts us to liken Daedalus to Leonardo da Vinci. But there is a single and substantial difference. The works and notebooks of Leonardo survive, whereas for Daedalus there is not a single fragment of archaeological attestation. There is no such thing as the historical Daedalus.

Some ancient writers thought there was. That diligent tourist Pausanias tells us on several occasions that he came across statues, especially in the remoter sanctuaries of the Peloponnese, which he (or his local informants) believed were made by Daedalus. Pausanias, however, tends not to use the phraseology of *daidala* for olden statues; his preferred term is *xoana*, by which he usually means wooden cult images. His eye can detect that their execution may be primitive, or primitivist; but both despite this and because of it, he sees that they are venerable works, even if not actually made by prehistoric sculptors (for example, he tells us that one *xoanon* he saw on the island of Aegina was by Myron, more often celebrated as the fifth-century BC author of the Discobolus). The aesthetic equation of 'old-looking' with 'divine' then applies to those few statues Pausanias accredits to Daedalus, which he thought he saw at two sanctuaries in Boeotia: Lebadeia and Thebes.

The latter encounter may be reckoned typical of a naif art history which allowed Daedalus to take his place among the 'names' of Greek sculpture. Pausanias, in the course of his tour around Thebes, comments on what is to be seen at the sanctuary of Herakles. First there is the 'official' cult statue of Herakles 'the Champion' (*Promachos*, literally 'frontline fighter'), carved in marble by two local sculptors. Then there is a *xoanon* of Herakles, which the Thebans claimed was by Daedalus – 'and I thought so too', adds Pausanias – and dedicated (*anetheken*) at the sanctuary by Daedalus himself, in gratitude to Herakles. This local lore is a cue for a story, a variation on the usual myth: Daedalus, escaping from Crete with his son Icarus, devises the first boats to be powered by sail (easily fleeing from the oar-driven ships of King Minos). But Icarus is a poor hand on the tiller, and is lost overboard somewhere off the island of Samos. The boy's body is feared lost: but Herakles finds it, and does him the honour of burial. Hence Daedalus thanks Herakles with a statue.

Why this statue should have been dedicated at Boeotian Thebes is not at all clear, but Pausanias makes no comment on that. How the 'historical' Daedalus operates in the same chronological ambience as the hero-god Herakles is also not clear, but it fails to worry Pausanias. He passes on to the rest of the sculptural decoration of the sanctuary: temple gables showing selected Heraklean Labours, by Praxiteles; and two colossal figures of Athena and Herakles, commissioned by Thrasybulus *c.* 403 BC and executed by Alkamenes. Thus Daedalus slots unquestionably into the general run of Greek artistic genius: his distance as a forefather accordingly diminishes.

In conflating myth and history around the name of Daedalus, Pausanias is only following a Graeco-Roman tradition which saluted Daedalus as a *protos heuretes*: a 'first finder' of all sorts of tools and techniques, whose name could be blessed by those subsequently dependent upon such innovations and dodges. When Pliny the Elder, compiling his compendious *Natural History* in the mid-first century AD, came to catalogue all the world's inventions, he accredited Daedalus as the discoverer of the saw, the axe, the plumb-line, the drill and two types of glue (*two* types of glue is a nice touch of Pliny's supposed knowledgeability in handicraft matters). By Pliny's time, Daedalus functioned as a virtual patron saint of Roman craftsmen, particularly carpenters (Pliny's list of Daedalic discoveries is classified under *fabrica materia*, 'making things', but looks more concerned with woodwork than sculpting). Other writers in the Roman ambience, such as Diodorus Siculus (late first century BC), extended the genius of Daedalus to large public works, and stressed his all-round capabilities: Daedalus was therefore characterized by his *philotechnia*, his general 'love of craft'.

The mythical traditions upon which Pliny and Diodorus were drawing must remain ultimately obscure, and are certainly difficult to trace beyond the eighth century BC. Homer knew about Daedalus, and located his epic home as Crete (*Iliad* XVIII. 592), but the Cretan connection may considerably pre-date Homer, if the experts in Linear B script are right in reading a reference to Daedalus in one of the Knossos tablets (KN Fp 1.3). This tablet mentions one *da-da-re-jo-de* among a list of recipients of small amounts of oil. Other recipients listed include the local cult version of Zeus, and 'all the gods'. In this context, *da-da-re-jo-de* should be a derivative from the personal name *Daidalos*, and so a cult chapel to Daedalus – a *Daidaleion* – may have existed at Knossos around 1300 BC.

Be that as it may, there is little doubt as to where and when the mythical incorporation of Daedalus within the Classical Greek literary tradition took place. As Sarah Morris has meticulously demonstrated, it was in fifth-century BC Athens that Daedalus became 'a sculptor, an Athenian, a relative of Hephaistos, a protégé of Theseus, and the hero of a local community'. Daedalus, for the Athenians, was not only purloined from Crete to become one of them (hence one group or *deme* of Athenian citizens was known as the *Daidalidai*); he was also popularized in Athenian culture as the paradigmatic clever artist – a pioneer, in a sense, of 'the Greek Revolution', of the enterprise to make artificial figures lifelike and mobile. 'This likeness by Daedalus – it does everything but talk!' exclaims a band of satyrs in a play by Aeschylus. Philosophical opinions, Socrates says in one of his dialogues (*Meno* 97d), are like the statues (*agalmata*) of Daedalus: 'if they're not fastened up, they play truant and run away'. A (lost) comedy by Aristophanes was called *Daidalos*; its plot appears to have hinged on the mischief caused by statues deserting their bases. And serious-minded Aristotle briefly pondered just how it was that Daedalus got this reputation for 'mobile' statues: could it be that he made them hollow and filled them with quicksilver?

The background to this fascination – half-approving, half-suspicious – of 'lifelike' statuary, and its attribution in the first place to Daedalus, is a general Greek perception that in other countries statues are not done like this. We have already discussed Plato's comments on Egyptian art, which imply this much; and when Socrates, in the reference mentioned above, refers to wandering statues by the 'Athenian' Daedalus, he comforts his perplexed interlocutor by saying: 'Ah, perhaps they don't make statues like this where you come from?' (Meno is Thessalian). So we can see the self-defining element in this mythology.

But there is also a sense in which the myth of Daedalic ingenuity serves a further Greek cultural need: what we might call the *Eureka!* mentality, the faith in making historic individuals eponymous to perceived 'discoveries' or 'inventions'. As often as not these individuals – like Archimedes in his bath – make their discoveries as much by accident as by design: hence

Pliny (in his *Natural History*, XXXV. 151) allowed the 'first terracotta sculpture' to be created when a Greek potter, one Boutades of Sicyon, moved by his daughter's distress at her boyfriend's departure, drew an outline round the boy's shadow, filled it with clay, and fired the clay into a lifesize keepsake. It is not enough, in Greek myth-history, to impute an innovation to a process or a gradual development: names of individuals (preferably Greek) must be found on which to hang that exclamation, '*Eureka!*' – 'I've found it!'

Yet another purpose of the mythical Daedalus was to define artistic status in Classical Greece. Peripatetic, cunning, loyal only to his own ingenuity, half-worshipped, half-mistrusted by his contemporaries, Daedalus reflected the ways in which artists of the fifth century BC were popularly perceived. The myths of Daedalic activity help to explain the curious position artists occupied in Greek society. They were, as their work amply demonstrates, great experimenters; they could also win handsome commissions, presumably to their own enrichment; yet they were always of essentially non-aristocratic standing. Their rank was what the Classical Greek citizen would have seen as *banausic*: artists were grubby-fingered, they laboured and sweated for a living; they did not attend to the well-manicured political duties of better individuals. As the second-century AD Greek writer Lucian, perhaps recalling his own career choice, would put it: one might have become a sculptor, and a successful sculptor at that – 'but even if one had become a Pheidias or a Polykleitos, and produced many great works [*polla thaumasta*], everyone may have praised one's skill [*techne*], sure; but no one would ever have wanted to change places. However successful, the sculptor is always a rude mechanical [*banausos*] – a manual labourer, who knows nothing else but working with his hands' (Lucian, *Dream* 9).

Still, despite their banausic status, artists earned reverence. When a mythographer records that Daedalus was the 'first to represent the gods' (*deorum simulacra primus fecit*: Hyginus, *Fabulae* 274), he charts not only a pioneering artistic ambition, but also the means for an artist to gain public veneration. The artist displayed skill, *techne*, by his representation of the divine; he also thus demonstrated a semi-divine status, since to be able to represent the gods he must also have seen them, if only in his mind's eye. Hence the near-magical attributes in literary anecdotes concocted around Greek artists, which would later pervade the Renaissance hagiographies of Giotto, Michelangelo et al.: the artist was a vehicle for divine communication, therefore a 'divine maker' (*deus artifex*).

Pausanias has an interesting observation to make in this respect. He notes, in the course of describing a religious festival at Plataea called the *Daidala* (IX. 3.1ff.), that Daedalus 'the Athenian' actually got his name from a type of wooden cult image. Pausanias knows this type more usually as a *xoanon*, but in these parts (Plataea and Boeotia) it is also known as a *daidalon*. From his description of the festival, it is evidently an image carved from an oak tree, which will eventually be burned at a sacrificial altar. But what is significant is the etymology of the name 'Daedalus': it is rooted, according to Pausanias, in the production of the oldest cult images in the Greek world.

From the various descriptions of these old cult images in Pausanias and other writers, it is clear that we have effectively lost the origins of large-scale Greek sculpture. The reason being that prehistoric Greek sculpture was made from wood, which rarely survives at all, let alone entire, in the archaeological record. Pausanias himself lists the following as trees generally used for *xoana* or *daidala*: ebony, cypress, cedar, oak, yew and lotus: he adds juniper as an exception, and we should add olive as an oversight on his part. It is apparent from some of his descriptions (e.g. of the *xoanon* of Aphrodite at her sanctuary near Megalopolis, in the central Peloponnese: VIII. 31.6) that additions in stone could be made to a basically wooden figure – such as hands, face and feet; and that these statues were often gilded or painted, or both. But apart from saying that statues like this look 'old' (*archaios* or *palaios*) or have 'something venerable [*entheos*] about them', Pausanias leaves us with no firm identikit for reconstructing a typical *xoanon*. The *xoana* were made out of wood – did that make their shape columnar, or plank-like? That would depend on whether it was a tree trunk or a prepared plank that was carved. And why should we assume that wooden sculpture means less articulated human forms? Egyptian wood sculpture from 2500 BC onwards made dextrous use of tenon joints to produce extended limbs for wooden figures, and the limewood sculptors of Gothic Europe achieved dramatic folds and gestures with figures taken from a single block.

An intimation of just how much is lost to us, and how insecure any statements about the origins of Greek art must remain, has recently appeared from excavations at the site of Palaikastro, at the eastern tip of Crete. The charred remains of a composite statuette, which its excavators describe as a 'chryselephantine kouros' (*ill. 25*), are enough to demonstrate the extent of sophisticated craftsmanship in the Late Minoan period (*c.* 1500 BC). Standing almost half a metre high (20 in), the figure is mainly made from pieces of hippopotamus ivory, jointed together with wooden dowels, and has a head of serpentine. It is embellished with rock crystal (for the eyes) and gold (traces of golden sandals have been found). It would have slotted into a base by means of two drilled pegs at its feet. The ingenuity of its construction is impressive and its pose is striking: the left leg advanced, and arms bent at the elbow, with hands raised as if to give (or receive) some votive accolade – or perhaps, in a Minoan setting, to grasp the horns of a bull. Details are sensitively worked – including the veins on the hands – and

25 A Late Minoan ivory 'kouros' found at Palaikastro, Crete, dating from around 1500 BC.

26 *(above)* An ivory statuette of Hera (front and side views), from Perachora (Corinth), dating from the late eighth century BC; the carving is very frontal, lacking a full profile view.

27 *(right)* The Auxerre Goddess: a 'Daedalic' sculpture of the early seventh century BC, probably originally from Crete.

although the context of recovery fails to define the statue's identity or purpose, the excavators may be right to label it vaguely as a 'youthful deity'. Such figures probably also existed on a much larger scale: at Knossos, Arthur Evans thought he had come across the remains – bronze locks of hair, with a mass of charcoal – of a colossal wooden statue measuring some 2.8 m (9 ft) high (*Palace of Minos*, Vol. III, 522). How much of the body of this supposed figure was worked is unknown: it was possibly nothing more than a draped column.

The Palaikastro 'kouros', with its advanced left leg, may well have more claim to Daedalic authorship than any other extant statue. But the term 'Daedalic' has already been hijacked to describe a style of sculpture that prevails at a later period, and not only on Crete (though Crete looks like its earliest home); and while no scholar seriously supposes that the mythical Daedalus had anything to do with sculptures labelled 'Daedalic', we are bound to indulge this misnomer – it has lodged too long in the parlance of Classical archaeology.

'Daedalic' covers a variety of media and dimensions, ranging from small anthropomorphic pots to large pieces of architectural sculpture, but its stylistic characteristics can be easily summarized. First, it depends on a frontal approach from its viewers. There is no depth to Daedalic figures: faces are mask-like, and bodies plank-like. Typical, in its absence of a full profile view, is the ivory mannikin of Hera from the Corinthian sanctuary of Perachora (*ill. 26*). Second, the style is formulaic, or mannered. Faces are turned into triangles; hair into blocks (the 'judge's wig'); and detail is rendered according to essentially pictorial conventions. Looking at one of the best-known examples of this style, the limestone 'Auxerre Goddess', probably from Crete (*ill. 27*), we may wonder if the gesture of this statuette is not in fact a hand on heart but rather is to be read as extending forward in supplication: for the rules imposed by frontality would demand that an arm extended at the elbow be carved as lying across the body. (In which case, the figure must be deemed more likely a votary than a goddess.)

The plank-like form of this and other Daedalic pieces encourages the hypothesis that they may be translations of wooden cult *xoana* into stone, bronze and terracotta; and the seventh-century BC dating of such pieces means that they are often claimed as the oldest of Greek sculptures. As we have seen, their attachment to 'Daedalus' is unfortunate. But we can put some substance into the claim for Daedalic statuary to be considered as 'Greek'. Its points of production were once identified as predominantly 'Dorian' Greek sites – Corinth, Rhodes, Crete and Sparta – but where Daedalic statues were made is less important than where they were found. The fact is that they travelled. They were displayed at burgeoning seventh-century sanctuaries: of Zeus at Olympia; of Hera at Argos and Perachora; of Apollo at Delphi and Delos, to name the most obvious. These were places where Spartans, Argives, Corinthians, Athenians and so on shared and developed what they had in common: Greekness; these were places in which sculptures appear that can properly be called 'Greek'. On this basis, a frontal, non-naturalistic style does indeed characterize the earliest large-scale Greek sculpture known to us: so we should perhaps be forgiving to those scholars in the past who, sympathetic to the self-defining mythology of the Greeks, allowed this style to be known as 'Daedalic'.

R.J.H. Jenkins, whose monograph *Dedalica* (Cambridge 1936) did much to spread the use of the term 'Daedalic' in this sense, claimed that 'our earliest large Greek statue in stone' was made *c.* 650 BC. He was referring to Nikandre, a votive female figure now in Athens but found on Delos and probably made on Naxos; she stands 1.75 m (5¾ ft) high. Now, having consigned 'Daedalus' and 'Daedalic' to their rightful places, we should address the nitty-gritty of early Greek sculpture: the *techne*, the skill or the knack of making it.

Techne: limestone and marble

If Greek stone sculpture did indeed develop out of a tradition of wooden statuary, then it is no surprise that the medium of the first 'Archaic' Greek figures should be limestone. Limestone – which the Greeks called *poros*, or *porinos lithos* – is found in soft or hard varieties, and in its softer varieties it can be worked with tools very similar to those used in carving wood, such as gouges, knives and scrapers. Soft types of limestone are considerably easier to carve than marble, and therefore easier to extract too. The mass of most limestones is not actually much less than marble, but perhaps enough to make their transportation easier. So *poros* may have been attractive to pioneer sculptors wanting to make a transition from wood to stone; and it remained attractive, despite the exploitation of marble, to those dedicants of statues, or indeed builders of temples, whose budgets were tight.

Allowing for the fact that finished carving would then be brightly painted (the polychromy of Greek sculpture is a feature addressed at the end of this chapter), it remains the case that soft limestone takes less detail than marble, and will not sustain the same degree of hard polishing. The material contrasts between the two stones are conveniently exemplified by some of the metopes, carved *c.* 480 BC, from Temple E at Selinus (Selinunte) in Sicily (*ill. 28*). Here, the sculptors wanted the females involved in their mythological vignettes (e.g. the goddess Hera, or an Amazon) to strike the viewer as female; that is, to display pale, fine complexions. Had they been painters, they would have painted female flesh parts with a thick white compound; as it is, they have added to the main limestone relief 'spare parts' in marble, as far as possible reserving the

28 Figure of Hera, on a metope from Temple E at Selinus; early fifth century BC. The face and neck are carved from a piece of marble, inserted into the limestone of the relief, dramatically demonstrating the different qualities and durability of the two stones.

marble for those areas of the female form not covered by drapery. The relative qualities (and durability) of marble and limestone are thus clearly exposed.

There is no doubt that marble was publicly perceived among the Greek states as a superior material for sculpture by the mid-sixth century BC. When, towards the end of the sixth century, there was rivalry at Delphi between two political dynasties, the Peisistratids and the Alkmaionids, the latter were able to express some sort of overt superiority by 'upgrading' the Temple of Apollo (as recounted by Herodotus, V. 62). From the finds at Delphi, this alleged political manoeuvre seems to be attested by a change in materials used for pedimental decoration. The sculptures of the west pediment of the temple were carved from tufa from Parnassus; those of the east pediment were in marble from Paros. The endowment of marble was plainly an expression of conspicuous commitment to Apollo and his oracular favour.

We might go further, and claim the use of marble as one of the self-defining characteristics of Greek sculpture. As Nicholas Penny has noted, the deployment of white marble for much later European sculpture makes Greece look very much like a basis of Western art in this respect. There are a great many figures from sanctuaries in Archaic Cyprus that can truly be described as 'Egyptianizing' or otherwise 'Orientalizing' in style and here is the place to point out that the material of those figures is invariably limestone – Cyprus, like Egypt, has no marble – which may be (in the sixth century BC) a fair reason for setting such statuary somewhat aside from the mainstream of Greek production.

So what of the earliest attempts to use marble? A rather optimistic theory is sometimes advanced by prehistorians of the Aegean, that Cycladic figurines produced in the third millennium BC constitute the forerunners of Greek marble statuary. It is true that a few of these figurines approach the dimensions of 'figures'; also true that their places of manufacture are those islands on which monumental marble-working, both architectural and sculptural, is generally recognized to begin towards the end of the seventh century BC. However, provenances for these prehistoric images are rarely certain. It is supposed that they mostly lay in graves, but there is no evidence that, after an interval of some two thousand years, they were ever on view to the seventh-century inhabitants of those same islands. The stone used for the figurines was probably collected without quarrying (even today, swimming off the shores of Naxos, ones notices plenty of sea-polished lumps of marble which might invite the shaping hand), and was fashioned by a mixture of scraping and abrasion: scraping with obsidian, abrasion with the locally abundant emery. The result is now saluted for its 'breathtaking simplicity of form', and seductively displayed at the Goulandris Museum in Athens, but its connections with the efforts of the seventh and sixth centuries are improbable. The use of island marble; of added paint for facial details; of abrading materials like emery; and the application, perhaps, of a basic system of proportions are all more likely explained by coincidence, rather than distant influence over the millennia.

We should turn to a more decisive technical factor: quarrying. An incidental phrase from a fifth-century BC historian will illustrate its importance. Thucydides, describing a passage of the Peloponnesian War in 425 BC, tells how Athenian troops landed rather unexpectedly at Pylos, and improvised a garrison there. 'Having no iron tools', says Thucydides, they simply gathered loose stones (*lithoi logades*), and piled them up, as well as they could fit them together. The explanation of the lack of tools is necessary for his audience. Thucydides implies that if tools had been to hand, the fortification blocks would have been properly quarried.

This brief reversion to a state of nature, in which stone cannot be quarried because iron tools are not available, again raises questions of indebtedness. It is generally supposed (without direct testimony) that Greek quarrying techniques came from Egypt: and indeed the modes of extraction seem to have been superficially similar. The Egyptians of the Old and Middle Kingdoms generally used a bronze punch to stun their rocks (granite, porphyry, assorted sandstones; rarely alabaster, and never marble); the Greeks would prefer an iron pick, hewing a trench around a potential block before levering it out. That the Egyptians also trenched around an intended piece is shown by an abandoned obelisk of Queen Hatshepsut (who ruled 1490–1468 BC) at Aswan: this was granite, and a fine index of how large a single piece of that stone could be extracted.

Both Greek and Egyptian methods must have relied on a preliminary matrix of measurements. It is not clear, however, that Greek sculptors applied the Egyptian canon of cubits to their extraction of marble. Michelangelo, who understood quarrying, would see a block and then imagine a statue; likewise, if he had a statue in mind before he had found the block, he might spend many months quarrying in order to find the right stone. Extracting marble might be said, then, to be more romantic than mathematical. Certainly its early sculptors were proud of being able to extract very large pieces and work them into shapes: the colossal Apollo which the Naxians dedicated at Delos in the sixth century BC boasted (in the quaint first-person fashion that adds force to a belief in animated statuary), 'I am from one stone, statue and base' (*to auto litho emi andrias kai to sphelas*).

Marble quarries were opened up in various parts of the Greek world: on the Cycladic islands of Naxos and Paros, and the northerly island of Thasos; at Doliana in the Peloponnese; and at Pentelikon and Hymettos in Attica. Eventually, some of the busiest quarries were connected with large

29 Unfinished colossal statue of Dionysos, *in situ* in a quarry at Apollonas, on Naxos, where it was abandoned, probably when a crack appeared.

Graeco-Roman communities in Asia Minor, such as Ephesus and Aphrodisias. But our concern here is with the earliest evidence, which probably comes from Naxos.

Traces of marble quarrying are to be found at several Naxian sites; the earliest appears to be the village of Apollonas. The name is misleading since the half-finished statue abandoned in the quarry above the shore-side settlement is most certainly not Apollo (*ill. 29*). This figure would have stood 10.66 m (35 ft) high if it had been erected. To what stage of the quarry's chronology it belongs is open to speculation, but a reasonable guess is somewhere between the mid-sixth and mid-fifth centuries BC. It was clearly intended to wear a beard; perhaps as an image of Hermes, or more likely Dionysos, who was legendarily (via Ariadne) connected with the island (and the early coinage of Naxos features a tell-tale Dionysiac vessel, the *kantharos*). But for present purposes, the eventual subject is irrelevant. What is important is that it was to have been a colossal statue, and that whoever was entrusted with the job of extracting the statue's raw material from the quarry was also entrusted with carving the figure to within a centimetre (in some places) of its intended finished surface.

The stages of the operation can be simply retraced. Having identified a potential block, the masons cut a trench around it wide enough for them to stand in while working on the basic shape of the statue. They then used metal punches to strip the block of as much stone as possible, prior to attempting to move it. This involved a sure knowledge of what the statue was going to look like when it reached its ultimate polished appearance. Then came the trickiest part of the process: levering away this shaped piece from its bedrock, having probably 'honeycombed' the underlying stone. And it was apparently at this stage that something went wrong with the Naxian Dionysos: it may have been the fissure that is visible today across the upper part of the torso of the figure. The enterprise went no further; thousands of man-hours were wasted.

The reason for removing so much stone from the block prior to its attempted transport was presumably logistical and economical. The density of marble (at least 2.7 tons per cubic metre) makes it a formidable prospect to lug around. The Naxians, as is clear, became well practised at moving it, and in dimensions even greater than this failed Dionysos, though the quarries at Melanes, in the interior of the island, show by further discarded statues that accidents could happen in transit too. But the chief interest of this process of extraction is, so to speak, vocational. In modern terms, the stonemason or quarryman holds one job; the sculptor another. This is a division of labour which Italians in the sixteenth century marked by defining one job *tagliapietra*, and the other *scultore*. Michelangelo was probably unusual in the degree to which he supervised, or even participated in, the quarrying stage; but he did not allow others to have any hand in preliminary fashioning or roughing out. He would take the block back to his studio, and had various methods of his own for subsequently 'releasing' the statue within it.

On Naxos, no such division of labour can have prevailed. Modern conceptions of the distinction between 'stonemason' and 'sculptor' – the one categorizing a 'craft', the other an 'art' – have led scholars to suppose that there was some prevalent canon which enabled a statue to be roughed out in the quarry, then sent elsewhere to be finished off, by a separate workforce; but this seems highly unlikely. The Naxian Dionysos conforms to no other surviving 'type', whether in terms of its scale or its subject: so how can the (unartistic) quarrymen have known what the (artistic) sculptor had in mind? As we shall see, the isolation of the Greek sculptor as a hermetic genius, lonesomely meditating his next aesthetic shock, is dangerously anachronistic. It is far more sensible to imagine the sculptor (or more likely, sculptors) of Archaic statuary doing as much work as possible prior to transport. No 'workshop' is really required for such sculpture, and what suits a marble-cutter best is to have his block lying flat on the ground, or slightly off horizontal, for as long as possible – it makes wielding a mallet much less wearisome. Such *in situ* work also allowed sculptors to discover flaws in a block before going too far with it.

The stages of carving an Archaic marble figure from a single block of marble can be simply described as follows:

1 Sketch or incise the *profile* of the intended figure on opposite sides of the block (as in the would-be equine statue in limestone from Sparta, in the British Museum, *ill. 30*);

2 Partially carve the profile;

3 Sketch or incise the *front* view of the intended figure;

4 Partially carve this front view. The result so far will look roughly shaped (*ill. 31*), but can be then improved by:

5 Rounding off and cutting into interior space (e.g. between arms and legs), with some preliminary smoothing. Transport may not be contemplated until this stage, as evident from the abandoned *kouroi* on Naxos (*ill. 32*). Finally:

6 Definition of forms (e.g. hairstyles, facial features), addition of incised details (e.g. markings of abdominal muscles), and fine polishing of surface. A light- or reddish-coloured wash was probably applied to nude figures, or any exposed flesh parts: there is no evidence that the Greeks appreciated the glare of 'raw' marble, and carved clothes were vividly painted.

Carving a relief is a simpler proposition, with only the front view to concentrate on and a reserve of solid stone to work against. Its stages may be readily understood by comparing two limestone metopes from the east side of the early (*c.* 550 BC) Heraion at the Foce del Sele sanctuary near Paestum, in South Italy. They come from a series illustrating a skirmish between Herakles and Centaurs which the sculptors never finished off, so one is only a shadow, or rather the half-carved form, of a Centaur (*ills 33* and *34*).

Roughing-out of figures was generally done with single-pointed tools – picks, pick hammers and pointed chisels of varying weights. The introduction of the claw chisel to Greece – an iron chisel with teeth, used at an angle to the stone – is dated to the first quarter of the sixth century BC, and may have speeded up the finishing process. Various types of drill were also developed during the sixth century, and dexterity with such drills – mostly

30 An unfinished marble statuette from the temple of Artemis Orthia at Sparta; sixth century BC. The profile and some details have been incised in the block.

31 *(above)* An unfinished figure from Mount Pentelicus in Attica; sixth century BC. The shape has been roughly carved from the block.

32 *(left)* A *kouros* at Melanes, on Naxos; sixth century BC. The statue lies where it was abandoned, apparently in the middle of transporting it from the quarry.

powered by bow-devices or straps, and incorporating drill-bits as large as 20 mm (⅘ in) – is extravagantly displayed on the draperies of the later sixth-century marble 'maidens', or *korai*, dedicated on the Athenian Akropolis (see *ill. 59*). These *korai*, along with some of their male counterparts, also demonstrate the structural devices by which Archaic sculptors freed themselves from some of marble's monolithic tyrannies: using separate pieces of marble for the head or legs, for example (*ill. 35*); or making statues more spatially ambitious with separate arms neatly inserted at discreet junctures of flesh and drapery (*ill. 36*). No glue was required for fixing these pieces. Metal dowels might be inserted for added strength, and the joins sealed with a light cement, but basically the technique relied on extremely snug-fitting socket-and-tenon joints.

Archaic Greek sculpture is sometimes applauded for its 'direct carving',

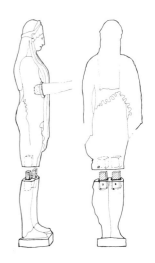

33 *(top left)* Limestone metope of a Centaur from the Heraion at Foce del Sele, Paestum; sixth century BC.

34 *(top right)* An unfinished limestone metope from the Heraion at Foce del Sele, Paestum; sixth century BC.

35 *(centre)* The method of joining different parts of an Athenian marble *kore*; c. 525 BC.

36 *(right)* A marble torso from the Akropolis, the arms of which were added separately and are now lost; early fifth century BC.

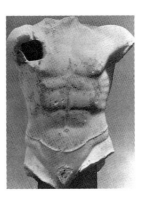

by whimsical admirers who begrudge artists the use of copying or pointing machines. But, in fact, it is unlikely that Archaic sculptors commenced
carving without a model of their intended piece, of at least one-third its
scale, if not 1:1. The two bovine youths found at Delphi, usually known
as Kleobis and Biton (see *ills 76* and *77*), may possibly not represent the
two brothers of these names found in Herodotus – there are epigraphic
doubts about this identification – but one thing is sure: they are sculptural
twins, difficult to distinguish from each other, and are probably both
'copied' from a single model (or else one from the other).

What developed in the fifth century BC was a method of 'pointing-off'
to transfer measurements from a model to the stone being carved. This
practice, which would be refined in later Greek and Roman times, is
usually betrayed by knobs or nodules left on apparently finished statues –
small points of reference left on the surface of the stone, from which the
statue could be checked against its prototype. The pedimental sculptures
of the Temple of Zeus at Olympia (*c.* 460 BC) bear traces of such measuring points. Later, we find references to *paradeigmata*, *proplasmata* and
typoi as essential stages in the sculptural process; and Pliny says that the
models of the bronze sculptor Arkesilaos actually fetched higher prices in
the Roman art market than the finished works of some other sculptors
(*Natural History* XXXV. 155).

Models for 'Daedalic' statuary were probably made of wood. Later on,
terracotta would be the preferred modelling medium. In this respect, it is
perhaps misleading to emphasize, as some scholars do, the 'plastic' impact
of bronze sculpture upon marble-working, which may be characterized as
essentially 'glyptic' – that is, a process of stripping away and cutting into
a material, rather than building it up. But despite the ingenuity of tenon
joints, and before the Hellenistic practice of making group compositions
out of single large blocks of marble, it is true to say that bronze sculpture
offered, to the exponents of the Greek Revolution, more excitingly 'lifelike' possibilities than marble, limestone or any other stone. It is to the first
essays in bronze that we now turn.

Techne: bronze and terracotta

In Book Eighteen of Homer's *Iliad,* Thetis, mother of Achilles, visits the
smithy of Olympus, seeking special armour for her son. Homer, who has
little to say about Daedalus, enjoys himself with a portrait of Hephaistos,
the grimy maestro of the gods. Again, we see the fastidious 'civilized'
Greek mixture of distaste and admiration for skilled labour exemplified by
the marginality of Hephaistos: lame, sexually frustrated, consigned to
sweat, dust and toil, and consequently asthmatic, he is nevertheless a figure

of immense power. Thetis comes across him in his workshop putting the final touches on *automatoi*: wheeled tripods which have their own momentum (compare the 'walking' statues of Daedalus). Hephaistos may be physically disabled and psychologically twisted, but his consort here is specified by Homer as 'Grace' (*Charis*), and what he makes for Thetis is dominated by a wonderful shield – five concentric layers of bronze, teeming with figurative detail.

Actually, Homer has only a vague idea of what bronzeworking entails. He is clear that this armour is made of bronze (*chalkos*), but his vignette of Hephaistos is a high-temperature farrago of crucibles, funnels, tongs and hammers, all stoked up by the smith-god's magical (automatic) bellows. It looks suspiciously as though Homer is conflating bronze with iron, for bronze – an alloy of copper and tin, with the proportion of tin governing the extent of malleability – is frequently hammered cold, and with light tools. It is iron that is forged red-hot. But as a poet, Homer is more fascinated by the end result of all this din and effort. His enchantment with the complex figurative scenes Hephaistos works upon the Shield of Achilles can be measured by a register of virtual sound effects emitted from this creation. Hephaistos depicts people singing, cattle lowing and a stream that babbles: no wonder we forget that this is supposed to be a utilitarian object.

But metal armour was primarily a thing of beauty and prestige in Archaic Greece. The earliest bronze body-armour must have been a good deal less protective, and more restrictive, than multiple-layered hide; yet it glittered, and impressed an enemy. Herodotus tells us how the Egyptian pharaoh Psammetichus (Psamtik I, 664–610 BC) was so taken by the East Greek 'men of bronze' (*chalkeoi andres*) pirating around the Nile Delta in the seventh century that he hired them as mercenaries. Perhaps they were wearing corselets of the sort discovered in several Late Geometric graves, made from hammered bronze plates to close-fitting and 'sculptured' specifications. The best-preserved example, from Argos, and dated to about 720 BC, was shaped for a trim athletic warrior, whose pectorals were properly accommodated, and whose abdominal muscles were also marked on the corselet. The art of the armourer is here very close to the art of the bronze sculptor.

In fact, early Greek bronze statuary was made using essentially the same technique as body armour – *sphyrelaton*, which simply means 'beaten' or 'hammered'. The resulting objects, known as *sphyrelata*, were sometimes beaten from a single disc of bronze, just as bronze vessels could be; but more often they were composite: plates shaped from both back and front by hammering were then slightly overlapped and riveted together. A late eighth-century BC statue, perhaps of Apollo, from Dreros in Crete, about half lifesize, was put together from over thirty separate pieces, and the riveted seams are mostly not visible to anyone viewing the statue from the front. As Denys Haynes points out, the elements of shared decoration, as well as construction, reveal the hand of a sculptor who knows how to make armour (or an armourer who has turned to sculpture).

It used to be supposed that a carved wooden core-figure was essential to such figures, arising from the religious practice of embellishing or 'enriching' wooden cult statues with bronze exteriors; but in fact a freehand technique is far more plausible, allowing sculptors to work on bronze plates both from the inside out (repoussé) and from the outside in (chasing). The statue from Dreros (plus two female companions, discovered on the same altar) has neither a wooden core, not inner armature of any sort. Provided scale was kept reasonable, none was structurally necessary. An inner lining of bitumen was enough to provide extra weight and durability. The head of a winged deity from Olympia, made in the early sixth century BC, shows how delicate hammered bronze could be, especially with added inlaid details (*ill. 37*).

Among the range of *sphyrelata* are the great ceremonial tripods, dedicated at various Greek sanctuaries from the ninth century BC onwards, with protomes – figured 'extensions' – rising from their rims (usually gryphons or similar beaky creatures). The Heraion on Samos is particularly rich in these objects, with over two hundred protomes so far recovered. It is evident that during the seventh century BC a major technical change took place, whereby the protomes were no longer hammered into shape, but cast.

This is a nice case of the intersection of archaeological and ancient literary testimonies. The Greek claims for the 'invention' of bronze-casting are, of course, ultimately as unfounded as their claims to be the first makers of stone statues – bronzes had been cast in Egypt and the Near East long before, in the third millennium BC – but one place dominates the confused literary account of where in Greece bronze-casting was first practised. This is Samos. Two individuals, Rhoikos and Theodorus, are also sometimes singled out, though archaeology has failed to attest to their existence. What archaeology has supplied, however, is evidence that on Samos, in the late seventh century BC, hollow-cast bronzes began to be produced: first the gryphon protomes, which would have been difficult to attach had they been solid cast, then independent statues – *kouroi*, horsemen, and so on.

Solid-cast bronzes had been perfectly simple to make. Beyond much earlier examples from Crete, vast numbers of solid cast figurines have been found at sanctuaries which were becoming popular in the eighth century BC: at Olympia, especially, but also Delos, Delphi and Dodona. These votives were probably made in temporary workshops set up for particular festivals and ceremonies. The solid-casting technique involved making a

37 A *sphyrelaton* – a hammered bronze – of a winged goddess, from Olympia; sixth century BC.

figure in wax, which was then given a clay 'coat', leaving an aperture; the figure was fired, turning the clay to terracotta and the melted wax poured out via the aperture. Into the now-hollow figure was poured molten bronze. Once the bronze was set, the clay jacket could be chipped off, and all that was then required was smoothing or minor engraving and chasing. The wax model was lost, of course, but beeswax, when warmed, is a pliable and easily-shaped material, and another miniature horse or ox might be made within minutes.

Solid bronzes beyond a small scale are very rare. Apart from being prodigal in the use of metal, and producing heavy statues, there are technical risks in solid-casting large pieces. As it cools, bronze contracts, and releases gases and bubbles: cracks and disfigurements occur more frequently as scale increases. On behalf of the ambitious Archaic Greek sculptor in bronze, then, we might identify sympathetically three technical desiderata: first, to cast lifesize hollow figures; second, to cast them in separate units (so that if one part went wrong, say the arm of a statue, it did not involve a recasting of the entire figure); and third, to cast duplicate figures – that is, to devise a method of casting that did not entail the destruction of the original model (duplication was not only economical, but also useful for constructing groups).

Why was the island of Samos so significant in the development of casting techniques? The answer is, for once, straightforward. Samos was unusually rich in Near Eastern and Egyptian *objets d'art*. The extent of this richness may be readily gauged by comparing the votives from the Samian Heraion with those from a geographically comparable sanctuary, such as the Athenaion at Lindos on Rhodes. Quite why Samos enjoyed such exotic traffic is still a perplexing question, but it is clear from the deposited orientalia (most of it now published) that local bronzeworkers on Samos were exposed to numerous examples of eighth- and seventh-century BC hollow-cast bronzes from Egypt, which would have encouraged them to develop their own methods of producing such statues.

Unfortunately, no Greek author ever recorded these methods: we have no ancient equivalent of the Italian sixteenth-century bronze specialist Benvenuto Cellini's overweening account of how he cast his masterpieces. On the basis of archaeological remains, scholars continue to debate precisely how hollow casting was achieved in Greece. Their explanations are often clouded in technical obscurities, and in any case a good deal of improvisation doubtless went on in the ancient Greek foundries. The following scenario for the making of a *kouros* statuette from Samos (*ill. 38*) should be taken as a simplified, and non-definitive, account.

Standing only 28 cm (11 in) high, this figure appears to have been made from two moulds: one for the back and one for the front. These moulds may be called 'intermediate': they will have been taken from an original figure made of clay, or perhaps carved from ivory or wood, and they give negative images of the desired bronze version. In fact another *kouros* of exactly the same dimensions and style as this one has been found at the Heraion, implying that indeed there was a single original from which both statues were ultimately produced. The intermediate moulds would be lined with wax – this is the wax lost in the 'lost-wax' (*cire perdue*) method – and a 'core' created within. Such a core would be a slurry of sand and plaster, or liquid clay, perhaps. Once the core was set, with the wax adhering to it, the outer intermediate moulds could be removed. Around the waxed core was constructed a network of 'gates' and 'vents', with a main funnel. This structure of wax rods looks messy and complex but was only there to conduct molten bronze around the core figure (flowing from the base upwards), and provide ventilation for gases. Around the core figure, and incorporating this system of funnel, gates and vents, was added a coarse clay exterior coat (known as 'the investment mould'). Pins would stabilize the core model to this outer clay blanket: these were essential, since once the clay was fired, and the wax ran out, only these pins would support the core within its mould.

All that remained was to heat the bronze and pour it in. The gap created by the lost wax might vary (thicknesses of bronze range from 2 to 25mm,

38 A small bronze *kouros* from Samos; late sixth century BC.

but average at around 5mm (i.e. a quarter of an inch). The outer mould would then be chipped off. If the statue were being made piecemeal – as most Greek hollow bronzes were – it would also be possible, once the bronze had cooled, to hack out the inner core too. The statue was now more or less complete; it remained to assemble the constituent parts, either with socket joints (similar to those encountered in marble) or by a sort of welding that involved pouring molten bronze around the areas to be joined; and add such detail as was possible when the bronze was cold. A fifth-century Athenian cup (*ill. 39*) shows the assembly and finishing stages of some large bronze statues, involving not only beating out, but also scraping. Intriguingly, the tools being used to smooth the surface of the bronze look very similar to the strigils used by athletes to tone and depilate their bodies after exercise. Also from Athens comes an example of what the clay mould of a bronze *kouros* would have looked like (*ill. 40*).

39 A detail of the 'Foundry Cup', an early fifth-century BC Athenian red-figure *kylix*, depicting the process of manufacturing bronze sculptures.

It has been noted that on really fine fifth-century bronzes, such as the pair from Riace, most of the final detail was already determined by the wax model. Gazing at the sinews of one of the Riace figures, and meditating on the fiery technical hazards that haunted most of the stages of casting large-scale bronzes, we may appreciate once more that competitive mentality which the Greeks called *eris* – a word which at its strongest implies outright strife – catalysing the bronzesmith's art.

The maker of terracottas, the *koroplastes*, was less honoured among artists. It was a relatively simple business. From a master model, or *patrix*, of any material, moulds were taken (mostly in clay, sometimes plaster). A single mould would produce reliefs and plaques; with a double mould, either solid or hollow figures could be produced, by simply lining the mould with wet clay (which shrinks on drying, and is therefore easy to coax out of the mould). In central Greece, terracotta figures were mostly small scale, and often served as children's toys, or as rather downmarket votive offerings. One would call these mass-produced, which in terms of quantity they were; however, it is worth noting that surprisingly few duplicates are found, implying a quick turnover in moulds.

40 A clay mould for the lower half of a bronze *kouros*, from the Athenian Agora; mid-sixth century BC.

In the Western colonies, however, and in Hellenized Etruria, terracotta statuary was taken more seriously. Literary traditions (e.g. Pliny, *Natural History* XXXII. 152) record that a seventh-century aristocratic exile from Corinth, called Demaratus, came to Italy with three craftsmen (*comitatos fictores*) who specialized in terracotta shaping and painting. It is around this time that the production of terracotta statues and architectural components – anthropomorphic antefixes and gutter-mouldings, for example – begins in Etruria, and hardly looks back. During the late sixth and early fifth centuries BC, complex pedimental groups (the temple decorations from Pyrgi are good examples) and confident essays on Greek themes, such as the reclining *kouros* from Cerveteri (*ill. 41*) were achieved. In South

Italy, especially Sicily, marble statuary would eventually make its presence felt; however, here, too, the terracotta-makers achieved a lightness of touch which can be a relief from solid stone sculpture. The dancing or 'fleeing' girls in Reggio (*ill. 42*) are exemplary of such lightness.

The colour on ancient terracotta sculptures survives more persistently than the colouring of stone, but we should not let that deceive us. As William Gell observed of the Greeks: 'no nation ever exhibited a greater passion for gaudy colours'. This passion did not confine itself to terracottas alone: all stone sculpture was painted, and notice of that paintwork must necessarily cap any discussion of the techniques of Greek sculpture.

41 Reclining terracotta figure from Cerveteri, Etruria; early fifth century BC.

42 Dancing maidens: a late sixth-century BC terracotta relief from South Italy.

A note on polychromy

The excavators of Greek sculpture have had to break the news, unwelcome to some, that the Greeks were passionate about painting their statues. This information had dawned on students of Greek architecture in the eighteenth century, but as late as 1862 we find Charles Newton, publishing his finds from Halicarnassus, rather deploring the vulgarity of colours employed on the Mausoleum frieze. There is a natural antipathy, inherited from the Renaissance, towards the notion of obscuring the translucence of white marble. But there is no doubt that polychromy was an important finishing touch to Greek sculpture, from its earliest manifestations onwards.

The olden wooden *xoana* were certainly painted. Many, standing outside and exposed to the elements, needed paint for protection. Marble has a lesser requirement for paint as a prophylactic, but in the glare of bright sunlight, statues (and buildings) in marble are almost impossible to appreciate. The Roman architectural writer Vitruvius tells us of a waxing and oiling process (called *ganosis*) devised by the Greeks to prevent solar damage – flaking and fading – to the paint on statues (*De Architectura* VII. 9.2–4). It has also been established that the Parthenon and other marble temples were treated with an organic wash that had the effect of toning down this blank, over-whiteness of raw marble; and it is clear that even nude statues such as Kritian Boy were treated.

This makes sense in the context of the Greek Revolution: Kritian Boy was painted the colour of a sun-tanned youth for the same ultimate reason that he was given inlaid eyes – to add to his verisimilitude. Gentler tints would have been reserved for the flesh parts of female statues, since women spent most of their time indoors. But clothes were a riot of colour. The Acropolis *korai* have provided many instances of this glorious paintwork, and new photographic techniques reveal that the textiles on statues such as the 'Peplos *kore*', whose painted drapery visible at the time of excavation has been restored on her cast in the Cambridge Museum of Classical Archaeology (*ills 43* and *44*), may themselves have been invested with complex painted figured scenes such as chariot-racing. It seems that the statue was *re*painted at intervals, evidently quite short ones. The evidence may go so far as to attest a division of skills at this stage, with some later sources (e.g. Pliny, *Natural History* XXXV. 133) suggesting that the art of the painter (*grapheus*) was germane to a really fine statue.

Limestone statues were brightly painted (hence the 'Bluebeard' figure from one of the Archaic temples or treasuries on the Acropolis: see *ill. 67*); terracottas, too, called for the sort of artwork usually associated with vases. About bronzes we are less well informed. Late references to 'rosy-cheeked' bronze statues (e.g. Callistratos, *Ekphrasis* XI. 435K) imply at least the tinting of flesh parts, and hair too was probably enriched with painted detail. Statues were sometimes gilded to enhance their value, but never deliberately patinated. Metallic gleams may have retained their own aesthetic premium: there was no point in giving statues like the Riace bronzes (see *ill. 92*) inlaid copper lips unless, presumably, the particular metal could be perceived and thus appreciated.

43–4 A cast of the 'Peplos *kore*' from the Akropolis, Athens, dating from the mid-sixth century BC, with a restored and painted version, giving some impression of what it originally would have looked like.

4

SACRED DECORATION

With the aid of ancient literature and illustrations the expert may be able to restore in his mind's eye the activities in house or market, the visitors who entered the temple with their offerings, the long processions which led to it at the festivals, and the varied disarray that filled now empty spaces. But the best-trained imagination has its limitations. Take, for instance, that altar-stone outside the temple – it rises grey and worn, with flowers in the crevices and round about, amid grass and aromatic bushes gay with butterflies and bees: here the Greeks heard the bellowing of frantic cattle, watched the flies blacken the widening carpet of blood, and smelled a reek that was fouler than in any slaughter-house.

A.W. Lawrence, *Greek Architecture* (Harmondsworth 1973), 289

The economics of idolatry and the archaeology of cult

The sanctuary of Artemis at Ephesus in Asia Minor was in antiquity one of the most prodigal of sanctuaries. Endowed already in the sixth century BC with a temple of unusually large dimensions, its success only seemed to attract more donors, including Alexander the Great and several generous Roman emperors. The cult of Artemis as fostered by the Greeks was not altogether new: it blended with a tradition of worshipping the Mother Goddess practised in Anatolia since prehistory. And the cult statue of Artemis at Ephesus looked grotesquely ancient: a simple wooden *xoanon*, festooned with amber globules that gave her the appearance of being super-fertile and ultra-matronly. Marble copies of the image render the amber globules as so many breasts, and to anyone not persuaded of the truth of anthropomorphic representations, this goddess (*ill. 45*) must have seemed not only bizarre in her nature, but also downright licentious. (There is a view that the supposed breasts were bull scrota, but the point about fertility stands.) It is not surprising that the Jews and Christians who visited Ephesus deplored the sanctuary.

St Paul came to Ephesus in around AD 54, and spent a little over two years in the area. The New Testament (Acts 19) records how he disputed with

Greek philosophers there, ministered to the sick, preached to both Greeks and Jews in the area, and organized bonfires of their books: thus 'the word of the Lord', as Acts notes with satisfaction, 'increased and prevailed'.

But not without controversy. A certain Demetrios, a silversmith (*argyrokopos*) who specialized in making miniature silver shrines of Artemis, convened a meeting of his fellow *technitai*, and pointed out the threat that this preacher was posing to their livelihoods. A part of Paul's message, Demetrios rightly saw, was that 'there are no gods which are made by hands' (*ouk eisin theoi oi dia cheiron ginomenoi*): and if his message continued to gain ground, not only would they all be out of business, but the great goddess Artemis, who was worshipped not only in Asia but in the wider world, would be insulted. Demetrios succeeded in raising an uproar: crying 'Great is Artemis of Ephesians!', the Ephesian craftsmen rushed across to the theatre on what appears to be a collective accord to lynch Paul.

45 Artemis of Ephesus: an engraving of the Wilton House copy of the cult statue.

Partly by virtue of Paul's discretion in lying low, and shortly afterwards slipping away to Macedonia, but mostly by the calming invocation of Roman law, the situation was defused. Paul was judged legally blameless of either 'temple robbery' (*hierosylia*) or blasphemy. Yet anyone coming to this episode with an archaeological acquaintance of Greek religion will sympathize with Demetrios and his fellow workers. They were right: the Judaeo-Christian hostility towards the fabrication of divine images would, eventually, destroy their handicraft and bring about the eclipse of their goddess.

Many readers of this book will belong, like its author, to a broadly Judaeo-Christian background; or at least, if we would prefer to define it thus, to a tradition of scientific rationalism. As such, we are not well placed to understand the nature of religious belief at Ephesus. We are likely to take a cynical view of the operations of Demetrios and his fellows, or the priesthood which encouraged their presence: we may imagine simple pilgrims to Ephesus being fleeced at every angle of the sanctuary, cajoled into believing that the great Artemis would heal their limbs, gratify their desires, punish their enemies or make their crops grow – just so long as they parted with cash for votives or souvenirs. Like Paul, we will consider this a brazen case of manipulation: we may go even further, and condemn it in Marxist terms as the mass administering of opiates by a cunning and controlling class of priests-cum-politicians.

There is no denying that Greek sanctuaries were places where a great deal of what one might call 'business' was conducted, with an exchange of valuables both in cash and in kind. Often in rather remote areas, they generated a sector of service crafts and industries, and promoted communities which would not otherwise have existed. Curiously, they may be seen to have functioned in ancient times rather as many function as tourist destinations today: attracting, on a seasonal basis, large numbers of visitors for whom food, lodging, entertainment and gifts have to be supplied. (Despite St Paul, Ephesus now probably enjoys just as big a turnover as it ever did.)

But this is to banalize ancient society by treating it according to our own predominantly secular standards. Who is to say what Artemis did or did not do for those who respected her image? In his valuable book *The Greeks and the Irrational*, E.R. Dodds drew attention to the many instances within Classical culture – ostensibly so close, so familiar to us – where we modern rationalists would find ourselves nonplussed, bemused or even disgusted by ancient Greek behaviour. And in no place would this have been more likely (as the epigraph to this chapter implies) than a Greek sanctuary. So it remains a problem for any Classicist to explain why, during the fifth century BC, two developments could take place simultaneously in the Greek world: the genesis of that 'rationalistic' and largely empirical medical method we know as Hippocratic; and the expansion of the cult of Asklepios – the healing god who visited his pilgrims at Epidauros in their dreams and healed supernaturally. To dismiss one development as 'intellectual' and the other as 'popular' is too easy, and misleading: Hippocrates himself allegedly operated in the Asklepeion on Kos, and the inscriptions relating to cures at the sanctuaries of Asklepios may describe 'scientific' treatments in patently supernatural terms. Traces of what some would call a 'primitive' or even 'savage' mentality are none the less evident in the predominantly *religious* domain of all ancient Greek medicine. 'We owe a cock to Asklepios': the very last words of Socrates, a philosopher not known for his primitive mentality, can only be understood if we sympathize with a society that valued its ritual substructure.

The extent of this problem as it may affect our treatment of 'sacred decoration' is nicely illustrated by an anecdote of Western antiquarianism. In the Fitzwilliam Museum at Cambridge there is the upper part of a colossal caryatid (*ill. 46*). It is in a battered state, and most visitors to the museum pay it little regard. This is a pity, for a great deal of trouble was taken to transfer it from its original Greek site to Cambridge (where the vestibule of the University Library was its first lodging). The original Greek site was Eleusis in Attica, where since at least the sixth century BC a cult to Demeter – the 'Mysteries' – had been instituted. The statue was first recorded and identified as Ceres (Demeter) by Sir George Wheeler, on his travels with J. Spon in 1678. To say 'first recorded and identified' is to write from an academic perspective, however. Although the statue was weathered, it was by no means lost or obscure to those living in its vicinity. Another scholar-tourist, Edward Dodwell, visiting Eleusis in the late eighteenth century, reports the figure 'in its full glory, situated in the centre of a threshing-floor', and tells us that the local farmers 'were impressed with a persuasion that their harvests were the effect of her [i.e. Demeter's] bounty'. Previous attempts by French antique-hunters to remove the statue had failed: having been dragged to the port, 'Demeter', according to the locals, had flown back to her proper place.

'Like the virgin of Loretto', sardonically comments E.D. Clarke, the man who eventually succeeded in transferring the statue from Eleusis to Cambridge. His strategy for wresting it away from its poor credulous keepers was simple and ruthless:

> I found the goddess in a dunghill buried to her ears. The Eleusinian peasants, at the very mention of moving it, regarded me as one who would bring the moon from her orbit. What would become of their corn, they said, if the old lady with her basket was removed? I went to Athens and made an application to the Pacha, aiding my request by letting an English telescope glide between his fingers. The business was done.

(W. Otter, Life and Remains of Rev. E.D. Clarke, London 1824, 505)

Neither an 'enlightened' English scientist – Clarke would become a Professor of Mineralogy at Cambridge – nor a Muslim governor – the Turkish 'Pacha' referred to by Clarke, who would later allow Lord Elgin to take 'one or two pieces of stone' from the Athenian Akropolis – could care very much for residual Greek faith in sacred statues. (Irritatingly, Clarke went back to Eleusis a year after his removal of the fertility-bringing goddess, and claimed that despite her absence there had been a bumper harvest.) We may find ourselves similarly inclined to dismiss such phenomena as the workings of the primitive mind, which we would rather not imagine lingering in Classical Greece – so often considered as the cradle of science, mathematics and rationality.

It is true that some ancient tension can be shown to have existed between what we would call 'magic' or 'superstition', and the development of scientific or 'rational' inquiry. The Pre-Socratic philosophers of the sixth century BC have been described as apparently 'ignoring with astonishing boldness the prescriptive sanctities of religious representation'. Geoffrey Lloyd has established that in the arena of ancient Greek medicine, relations between 'faith-healers' and the Hippocratic physicians should be described as 'adversarial', at least in terms of the respective rhetorical positions adopted by either side; and the Greeks perhaps betray a basic unease with the protocols of established cult when they create an ambivalent meaning for the word *deisidamonia*, which can signify either a healthy 'respect for the gods' or an unhealthy 'superstition'.

The complexities of the social psychology involved here are beyond the scope of this book to explain. (We have only to think of the mystical cult that was associated with the philosopher-mathematician Pythagoras to

46 A caryatid from the Propylaea at Eleusis; probably second century AD.

realize that the boundaries between rationality and religion cannot be drawn precisely.) What concerns us is religious iconography: the means whereby metaphysical beliefs were externalized. The architectural development of the Greek temple makes 'sacred space' relatively easy to identify in the period that concerns us, but we remain surprisingly ill-informed about the day-to-day cult functions of the great Greek sanctuaries. This is partly due to our reluctance to take seriously the many dedicated images those sanctuaries contained.

Aristotle may have defined man as a political animal, but Wittgenstein's definition is more important here. 'Man is a ceremonious animal.' We have already seen (Chapter 2) just how far the logic of anthropomorphism could extend – that is, to a proper state of transubstantiation, as deities revealed themselves in wood, stone and metals. We must then treat idolatry not as a primal error, condemned by Mosaic law, but as a sincere means of religious communication. In the tolerant phrase of another philosopher, Thomas Hobbes (1588–1679), it is 'the worship by signs of an internal and real honour'.

Accordingly, if we consider again what St Paul sought to achieve at Ephesus, we must recognize that his attack on idolatry was aimed at the very heart of Greek religious practice. The production of votive statues served a protocol established in the Near East since at least the early third millennium BC: of dedicating an image to record and perpetuate a prayer. It may be ambiguous whether such an image represents deity or votary, but that does not matter – the worshipper leaves in the temple a visible, tangible form of imprecation.

When such statues – or more likely, statuettes – are excavated *en masse*, the effect can be disconcerting to the modern mind. Certain sites in Cyprus have yielded large ensembles of such votive terracottas, in particular the sanctuary at Ayia Irini, where over two thousand statues and statuettes have been recovered. Contemplating such assemblages set up in museums more or less as they were found – placed in a semicircle around an altar and arranged according to size, we should remember that even in the smallest dedications, there is power gained from repetition, like a rosary or oft-repeated formula of prayer (*ill. 47*). And we know from various Greek sources that votive dedications carried strong social, not to mention economic, indicators: a 'love of honour' (*philotimia*) was thereby made evident in places where both gods and mortals would notice it. Greek worshippers harboured no desire to do good by stealth: ostentation was an essential facet of personal piety. No wonder that Theophrastus, compiling his satirical character-sketches in the fourth century BC, would include a stock figure of 'Petty Pride' (*Mikrophilotimia*), who, 'should he have cause to dedicate a bronze finger or toe in the temple of Asklepios, is sure to polish it, wreathe it, and anoint it every day' (*Characters*, XXI).

The enthusiasm of dedicants caused some practical problems. From the Asklepeion at Rhodes comes a third-century BC inscription which says:

> No one is permitted to request that an image be raised, or some other votive offering [*anathemata*] be set up in the lower part of the sacred precinct . . . or in any other spot where votive offerings might block the passage of visitors.

Like any other religious practice, the custom of dedicating votives was open to manipulation, self-seeking and hypocrisy. Doubtless there were Greeks who found some sanctuaries excessively zealous in their turnover of images, or repellently eager to lighten the purses of their visiting devotees. But the archaeologist of cult is required to show more charity than St Paul. Votives should be appreciated for what they are: the best relics of faith and belief that we have.

47 Some of the votive terracotta statues and statuettes found at the sanctuary at Ayia Irini, Cyprus, rearranged in a museum.

Votive occasions and votive sculpture

Probably the greatest oversight of many historians of Greek art is to forget the fact that most of what we call Greek 'works of art' were fashioned for dedication *ex voto*. Once in museums, and detached from their original dedicatory inscriptions, these votive objects are too easily absorbed into an art history that stresses the skills of those who made them, while ignoring the pieties of those who commissioned them. It is true that public credit may have attached to certain votive gifts on the grounds that they were made by the most highly regarded artists of the day. To achieve a votive memorial with maximum artistic *akribeia*, or finesse, may have been as valuable as having it executed in solid gold. But some survey of the occasions and motives for these offerings is essential to understanding a very large proportion of extant Greek sculpture.

Before we commence that survey, several further comments on general votive purposes are in order. All sorts of objects might be dedicated at a Greek sanctuary, though here our attention is focused on those involving sculpture. Whatever the object was, germane to the act of its dedication is a reciprocal religious mentality. Benefits between deity and devotee are traded on a strictly mutual basis. Many formulae employed for votive dedications have a pseudo-contractual tenor to them, even when in verse, as in the following epigram addressed to a goddess of childbirth, Eileithyia, requesting an easy labour (*eulochos*): 'Come again, Eileithyia, answering the call of Lycainis, alleviating her birth pangs and producing a trouble-free delivery. Just as you have now received this as thanks for a daughter, so will your fragrant temple receive something else in thanks for a son' (Callimachus, Epigram LIV).

Votives are therefore usually made in a spirit of gratitude for past favours, or else on a conditional basis. By establishing a reciprocity of favours, in Walter Burkert's words, 'the insecure future is psychologically mastered'. With this in mind we may now survey the occasions when votive dedications were made, and give some examples of the statuary thus generated.

Tithes and first-fruits. Any deity might be rewarded for ensuring a good harvest, or invoked to do so in the future, by dedicating a share of the produce – the first-fruits (*aparchai*). Demeter's cult was particularly appropriate for such dedications, given the mythology which evolved around the abduction and seasonal return of her daughter Persephone. At Eleusis, therefore, we find sculptures which articulate gratitude in these mythological terms. Best-known is the relief, now in Athens, which shows Demeter and Persephone briefing a boy, Triptolemos, before he sets off on an airborne mission to instruct mankind in the skills of agriculture (*ill. 48*).

48 A relief from Eleusis, of c. 440 BC, showing Demeter and Persephone with Triptolemos.

(opposite)

49 Reconstruction by C.R. Cockerell of the interior of the temple of Apollo at Bassae in the mid-late fifth century BC.

50 A detail of the Gigantomachy of the north frieze of the Siphnian Treasury, Delphi; late sixth century BC.

51 The Nike of Paionios, Olympia; fifth century BC.

War. Deities were likewise given a cut of the spoils of war, or else enjoined by gifts to take one side or another (as any Greek familiar with the *Iliad* would know, the Olympians did not stand aloof from human quarrels). Trophies might be set up to display captured arms and armour, or else sculptural representations made of such booty-stacks. The inventories of the Parthenon reveal that the temple was cluttered with shields, missiles, spears, breast-plates, helmets, greaves, swords and bridle-bits. A nineteenth-century reconstruction of the temple of Apollo at Bassae, showing trophies standing between interior columns (*ill. 49*), is not at all fanciful. In the more open spaces of a sanctuary, visitors would also see the prows of ships, festooned with naval regalia, and perhaps incorporated into statue-groups.

Treasuries – small temples, mostly endowed at the pan-Hellenic sanctuaries by city-states with something to prove – might also be erected as thanksgivings for success in war, and consequently serve to display captured booty. This function is important to remember when assessing their sculptural decoration. Of the treasury of the Megarians at Olympia, Pausanias relates: 'in the gable of the treasury is wrought in relief the battle of the gods and the giants, and above the gable is a shield with an inscription stating that the treasury was dedicated by the Megarians from the spoils of the Corinthians' (VI. 19.2). It is hard to resist interpreting the gable as a sculptural allegory for Megara's triumph over Corinth. The Gigantomachy theme was played out, too, on the north frieze of the Siphnian Treasury at Delphi (*ill. 50*), which had a Trojan combat on its east side (the remaining two sides, showing a rape and an assembly of gods, may refer to causes of war). Although a highly specific political allegory has been suggested for the Gigantomachy here – encouraged, perhaps, by the representation of the giants in more or less contemporary military costume – we may be content to view such imagery as being generally suitable for a sanctuary such as Delphi, packed with military memorabilia, and with the treasuries of some eighteen city-states competing for attention. As Herodotus notes (III. 57), the Siphnians, thanks to a one-tenth tithe from their gold mines, 'furnished a treasury at Delphi as valuable as any to be found there'.

Other tokens of military success might involve an aggrandizement of victory by casting it in legendary terms. We shall encounter this on a large scale when dealing with the Athenian votive memorials after the battle of Marathon (in Chapter 6). A lesser, but typical, example is the memorial at Olympia mentioned by Pausanias (V. 26.7) dedicated by the citizens of Heraklea Pontica who, having vanquished a barbarian tribe in their Black Sea environs, celebrated this victory by dedicating sculptures showing selected labours of Herakles (their mythical founder). We may also notice the monument set up at Delphi by the Spartans after their naval victory

52 *(opposite, left)* The Delphi Charioteer; *c.* 470 BC.

53 *(opposite, right)* The Motya Charioteer: a marble figure found on the island of Motya, off Sicily, which probably belonged to a group dedicated to commemorate a chariot-victory. The holes are for metal attachments; *c.* 470–460 BC.

54 *(above)* A relief of an athlete crowning himself, from Sounion in Attica; fifth century BC.

55 *(below)* Athena and Nike crowning an athlete, on a relief of *c.* 440–430 BC.

over Athens at Aegospotami in 405 BC, which showed the Spartan commander Lysander, along with his admirals, his pilot and his soothsayer, surrounded by, presumably partisan, deities: Zeus, Apollo, Artemis, the Dioscuri – and Poseidon, conferring a crown upon Lysander. (The inclusion of the soothsayer in this group is a significant token of the role of cult in military affairs.)

At Delphi, too, stood the bronze palm tree commissioned by the Athenians after a victory over the Persians at the River Eurymedon in 469 BC. In the description of Pausanias (X. 15.4) this had not only fruit in its branches, but a gilt Athena and two of her owls – plainly symbolizing an Oriental victory for Athens. And, of course, there were the manifold *Nikai* – winged personifications of victory, often in gold, which served as generic images of triumph when borne aloft as decoration of a temple gable, or cradled in the hand of a powerful deity, but became specific emblems of commemoration when they were set on individual bases or pillars. Such was the nature of the most memorable victory-figure recovered from Olympia, the Nike of Paionios (*ill. 51*). Its sculptor, Paionios, might feel justly proud that he had won the commission to make it, but even more important (according to the inscription at the base of a pillar which raised the Nike to breezy heights) was the fact that the Messenians were celebrating their part in the capture of Spartan Sphacteria, during the Peloponnesian War (in 425 BC). In the same precincts at Olympia stood a statue of Zeus erected by the Spartans at least a century earlier, on the occasion of a war with Messenia. The inscription at the base of that statue (see Pausanias V. 24.3) may be taken as typical of votive formulae on such monuments: 'Receive, O prince, son of Kronos, Olympian Zeus, a fine statue [*kalon agalma*], and be propitious to the Lacedaemonians [Spartans]'.

Games. 'War minus the shooting', as George Orwell describes them, games were contested so fiercely by the Greek city-states that fatalities were not unusual. Prizes were varied, including tripods, crowns, amphorae, jumping weights and equine accoutrements, all of which were available for votive display. But vast quantities of sculpture were also generated. Such sculptures were initially humble enough: at Olympia, miniature clay or bronze figures of horses and chariots dating to the eighth and seventh centuries BC have been recovered by the thousand. But such offerings quickly grew in scale. The well-known charioteer figure from Delphi (*ill. 52*) is a thanksgiving for victory in a race, around 470 BC, from one of the Deinomenid tyrants of Syracuse (Polyzalos, or his brother Gelon); and a similarly dressed marble figure found on Motya, near Sicily, seems to have been part of a comparable chariot-victory dedication (*ill. 53*).

Successful athletes appear to have been granted, as an intrinsic part of their prize, the right to dedicate statues of themselves. The distinction some scholars try to make between what counts as truly votive and what is sheer self-promotion is probably false: the athletes have gladdened the gods by their performance, and have earned the right to express a personal sense of achievement. They are also suggesting, by having 'portraits' of themselves set up in a sanctuary, that their victory was at least partly the result of divine favour. So, quite apart from the many descriptive images of sprinters, boxers and discus-throwers that once populated Greek sanctuaries (and city centres, in some cases), and whose production seems to have provided certain sculptors with full-time employment (the fifth-century BC Myron, for example), we see many commemorations of the act of athletic acclamation itself. The athlete may (with a misleadingly modest bow of the head) crown himself (*ill. 54*), or else receive his crown from a Nike, or a deity, or both together (*ill. 55*). In the case of a team event, such as martial ('Pyrrhic') dancing, or a relay race with torches (the *lampadedromia*), a votive plaque might be dedicated, showing some or all of the winning squad.

Illness and calamity. Most of the Olympians could be importuned on matters of personal health and safety: all that was required was to coin a suitable sobriquet. Hence Apollo *Alexikakos*, 'repeller of harm'; Artemis *Soteira*, 'saviour'; Athena *Hygeia*, 'health[giving]'. Pausanias reports (I. 24.8) that there was a statue near the Parthenon, made by Pheidias, of Apollo *Parnopios*, 'Locust', so-called because when Attica was plagued with locusts, the god promised their riddance (and apparently kept his promise). But specialized healing cults also evolved, and a votive statuary of healing can consequently be documented.

A fourth-century BC relief from Athens, set up by one Lysimachides, is exemplary of such votives (*ill. 56*). In fact, it exemplifies two types of votive sculpture. First, the dedication of modelled parts of the body. We see Lysimachides hauling an outsize model of his own leg, probably made of terracotta, which bears the obvious signs of his distress: a severe case of varicose veins. That he is adding it to a stock of similar dedications is indicated by the pair of feet in the background. The size of the leg may be intended to convey the seriousness of the complaint, the status of its donor or else the miraculous nature of the cure. The relief itself performs the second votive function of recording, presumably in gratitude, the original dedication of the model leg.

Lysimachides was cured of his varicose veins at a small shrine towards the Areopagus in Athens, raised in honour of a presumed 'hero-physician' called Amynos. About Amynos we know little, but he was evidently in the same sort of cult mould as Amphiaraus, about whom we are better informed, and Asklepios, whose cult became widespread in the Classical

56 A fourth-century BC relief dedicated by Lysimachides, in thanks for a cure, brought about in turn by the dedication of a model of the afflicted part shown here.

period. Both Amphiaraus and Asklepios were of heroic rather than Olympian status: in very vague terms, they were remembered as being great healers once upon a time in Greece. Asklepios may be styled the patron saint of ancient Greek doctors, who often named themselves *Asklepiades*, 'son of Asklepios': in his central cult centre at Epidauros stood a chryselephantine cult statue of him, which spawned multiple copies. Votive reliefs make the healing techniques of Epidauros explicit. Ostensibly they consisted of 'thaumaturgy' – healing by dreams. Invalids spent a night, or longer, at the sanctuary in a custom-built dormitory (the *enkoimeterion*). While they slept, the god visited them and effected his cures. Even more bizarre to modern readers is the fact that a number of dogs roamed around the sanctuary, whose saliva was believed to have healing properties. But we may wonder, for instance, when studying a votive relief from the Asklepeion in Piraeus, whether the detailed inscribed records of 'miracle' cures, and the art that commemorates such miracles, are not simply conniving in another 'aura of enchantment'. This relief shows us a bearded figure, plausibly 'Asklepios' (but perhaps one of the temple's medical staff), 'laying hands' on the patient (but perhaps actually conducting an operation), with the patient apparently 'sleeping' (but perhaps under an anaesthetic). Supernatural or rationalized, it may not matter to the other figures standing by the bed: they are the patient's family, and all they care about is an effective cure.

We may cap our notice of healing votives with the observation that the concept of plain good luck does not exist in ancient Greek terms: 'fortune' is divinely constructed, and therefore narrow escapes from death or disaster require acknowledgment. So it was that the poet Arion, having been robbed and thrown overboard by rapacious Corinthian sailors, was escorted safely to the mainland by a dolphin. He duly donated in a shrine at the port of Taenarum, where he landed, a bronze figure of a man on a dolphin's back. Herodotus (I. 24) mentions this, and the dedication was later seen by Pausanias (III. 25). While the story itself may strain our credulity, the act of grateful dedication is entirely consonant with Greek practice.

Rites of passage. Puberty, coming of age, marriage, childbirth, death: all these are reflected in the votive accounts. Despite their abysmal record of fidelity (at least according to the poets), Zeus and Hera were patrons of wedlock. Aphrodite might receive dedications hopeful of consummation, and the sculptural development of her lusty cult is important (see Chapter 8). But above all, the benefit of children was what most worshippers sought. Both Hera and Artemis served the function of the nursing deity or *kourotrophos*; and a goddess called Eileithyia might intervene specifically to ensure an uncomplicated childbirth. Hestia, goddess of the household,

Leto, mother of Apollo, and the generally bountiful Demeter, are among other ensurers of *kalligeneia* ('fair offspring').

The image of the child at its mother's breast would appear to be a simple one, but of the Greek *kourotrophos* figure it has been claimed that 'nowhere in the world, either before or after, has any other art explored so extensively and for so long the possibilities of form, content and symbolism in the group of the child-bearer'. It is true that Greek sculptors turned many variations around this basic theme. The figure might be male, cradling the infant Dionysos, and in which case weaning the babe on to a bunch of grapes (such is the fourth-century BC Hermes 'of Praxiteles', dedicated in Hera's temple at Olympia). Or it might be a symbolic maternal relationship embodied: the statue attributed to Kephisodotus, of Peace (*Eirene*) nurturing the cherub Wealth (*Ploutos*), was one such. This was erected on the Areopagus perhaps in association with a new cult of Eirene introduced to Athens in 375 BC and particularly apt for Athens after the disasters of the Peloponnesian War.

One of the most tender monuments of Archaic Greek sculpture is probably a variation on the *kourotrophos* theme: the fragmentary relief of mother and child from Anavysos in Attica (*ill. 57*). Its original context is not clear: if space is allowed for the seated figure of the mother, it looks too wide to be a grave *stele*. The child's eyes are not closed, as they might seem, so it may not be a memorial of premature death (as it is usually listed). A mythical nursing scene may be intended, perhaps Demeter and her adoptive son Demophon, but the scene stands as a generic, yet closely observed epitome of the infant-nurturing relationship.

We shall look more specifically at funerary monuments in the next chapter as their inclusion here might overstretch the sense of the term 'votive'. But one grave-marking statue should be mentioned here, because its dedication poignantly refers to a rite of passage unfulfilled. This is the marble girl (*kore*) from Merenda, also in Attica, who must have served as the tombstone for a woman who probably died young, and certainly unmarried. The inscription on her base draws the viewer's attention to 'Me, marker [*sema*] of Phrasiklea. I will forever be called maiden [*kore*], and be known to the gods as such in lieu of marriage'. The poignancy is heightened by two possible translations of this girl's name, both equally to her credit, as either 'Famous-for-her-thoughts', or else 'Conspicuously-of-good-report'. Since her statue is slightly over lifesize, and she is shown wearing a crown, the chaste Phrasiklea must have been honoured with posthumous adoration.

58 The 'Potter relief' from the Akropolis; c. 510 BC. The craftsman is seen holding examples of his trade.

Official honours and social progress. It was not unusual for someone elected or appointed to office to set up a votive sculpture in gratitude for advancement. The city magistrate, the gymnasium superintendent, the athletics trainer, the priest and the priestess – all might celebrate their term of office with a statue or a plaque. Equally, a trader or craftsman enjoying good business might indicate (and perhaps further promote) his success by means of a conspicuous dedication. Thus, from the Athenian Akropolis, we find a potter (Euphronios or Pamphaios may be his name) dedicating a relief of himself *c.* 510 BC (*ill. 58*). It shows him holding two of his own drinking-cups or *kylikes*, partly to define his metier, but probably also as a memorial of two cups actually left at the sanctuary for Athena's benefit. Earlier in the sixth century another potter, Nearchos, commissioned a *kore* on the Akropolis, expressly as a share of profits (*aparche*): *Nearchos anetheken [ho kerame]us ergon aparchen t'ath[enaiai]*, reads the principal line of the statue's base. It is rather perverse that this should be known now as 'Antenor's *kore*', after the sculptor responsible for making it (mentioned in the second line of the dedication).

We know from that inscription and a number of others that men could dedicate 'maidens' on the Akropolis and elsewhere, and not necessarily to a female deity (one *kore* was dedicated to Poseidon by a fisherman thankful for a bountiful catch). So it is probably wrong to think of them as portraits of priestesses, though their garb and gestures sometimes suggest as much, and there is certainly a tradition within Greek sanctuaries of commemorating female sacerdotal servants. There are undoubtedly erotic touches to the representations of the Akropolis *korai*, most particularly in

59 *Kore* from the Akropolis, dating from the late sixth century BC.

60 The Moscophoros or 'Calf-bearer' from the Akropolis; c. 560 BC.

the way that they tug the side of their skirts, pulling them tight around their legs and backside, and the manner in which long strands of plaited hair are allowed to define pert breasts (*ill. 59*). Perhaps we should understand the image of the *kore* as a surrogate 'lovely girl' in the service of the host sanctuary. This would not be the only situation where Greek males liked to define their ideal woman as both devout and sexy at the same time.

The religious calendar. Although the nomenclature and the order of monthly cults and observances at Athens are more or less known, about many details – and the religious calendars of other cities – we remain surprisingly uninformed. We know enough about the cult of Demeter to recognize, for instance, that a votive figure carrying a piglet will have been connected with Demeter's worship; and a case for relating the frieze of the Parthenon to the procession of the Panathenaic Festival can arguably be sustained. But we cannot be very precise in identifying the occasion that generated one of the earliest, and finest, dedications on the Akropolis – the Moscophoros or 'Calf-bearer' set up around 560 BC by one Rhombos (*ill. 60*). Rhombos may have won his calf as a prize at the Panathenaic Games (which are supposed to have been first codified in 566 BC); or perhaps he is bringing the beast for sacrifice, having culled it from his own herd (some claim that he is wearing a herdsman's cloak); or he may have won the right, by a show of athletic strength, to carry the calf around in some special procession. The motif of man carrying a calf or sheep on his shoulders is known from other sanctuaries – many simple bronze versions of such a figure have been recovered from a sanctuary of Hermes at Viannos, in Crete, and an unfinished colossal 'Ram-bearer' has been found on the island of Thasos. But none other is as wonderful as the Athenian Moscophoros, even if his precise significance eludes us.

Many further examples of references in the votive-sculpture record to feast-days could be gathered: not only memorials of the religious act itself, of which a plaque from Gela is typical (*ill. 61*), but also numerous models of whatever animals, fowl, fruit or cakes were dispatched on this or that occasion. Some accompanying inscriptions make it plain that these were not always commemorative of an act, but in themselves constituted its performance: thus to dedicate a terracotta piglet may have passed muster for the real thing.

The votive register also gives iconographic articulation to certain religious initiations that would otherwise remain obscure. The Mysteries at Eleusis, for example, can be partially explained by reference to votive reliefs recovered from the sanctuary.

Propitiation and atonement. An athlete caught cheating today may be banned from further competition. An athlete caught cheating or bribing at the ancient Olympics was bound to express penitence through a votive statue. It is a measure of the ancient unscrupulous will to win that a good many of these punishment-statues, showing Zeus hurling his thunderbolt, were once to be seen at Olympia, complete with pious inscribed injunctions ('victory comes from strength and speed, not money'). The sculptural type has survived in figurines, and in a fifth-century BC bronze from Artemision, which despite its marine provenance probably shows Zeus rather than Poseidon (*ill. 62*).

Political misdemeanours were similarly open to the expression of repentance through statuary. Plutarch tells us that when the fifth-century BC general Themistokles held office as overseer of the Athenian water supply, he used the collected fines from those caught diverting water to dedicate a bronze *kore* to Athena.

So much for votive occasions, and their results. If only more Greek sculpture had stayed in contact with its inscribed or painted sentiments of dedication we should be able to construct a far more satisfactory picture of individual motives behind sculptural commissions. But there is also a

61 A woman carrying a goat, probably as a sacrifice, on a late Archaic terracotta relief from Gela, Sicily.

62 A bronze statue of Zeus from Artemision; *c.* **470 BC.**

wider perspective on the process whereby sanctuaries became crowded with images. We may broadly call this perspective 'political' – though that means less in ancient Greece than in a society where secular and religious powers are more clearly distinguished.

Religious instruction, propaganda and 'peer polity interaction'

It may readily be imagined that the construction of a Greek temple was a major political and financial commitment. To decorate that temple was to pile additional costs on an already hefty bill. In some parts of the Greek world – the Sicilian and South Italian colonies, in particular – temple architecture might be left unadorned, to speak for itself. But otherwise the pressure to buttress architectural statements with sculptural props was evidently there; and in certain circumstances, a virtual decorum – a set of artistic expectations – of temple decoration seems to have prevailed. No temple erected on the Greek mainland during the fifth century BC is without one of the following sculptural subjects: the Gigantomachy (Olympian deities against primal Giants); the Centauromachy (the tribe of Lapiths against Centaurs); or the Amazonomachy (Greeks fighting female warriors from the East).

In very broad terms, most temple decoration can be described as religious instruction – the prescriptive articulation of the thoughts instilled in worshippers at a given temple or altar. What Paul Veyne has called 'the

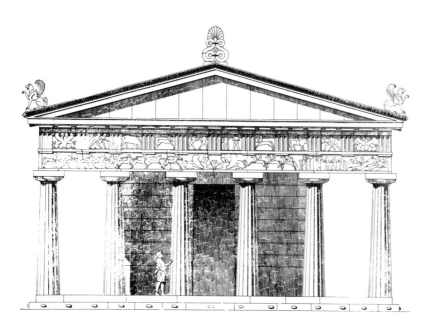

63 A reconstruction of the sixth-century BC temple at Assos; the frieze illustrates some of the exploits of Herakles.

constitutive imagination' of the Greeks is thus exposed, though we can only hope for glimpses of its workings. To categorize the programmes of friezes, pediments and metopes as instructive in this sense is generally straightforward. The Centauromachy and other combats become emblematic of right triumphing over wrong, civilization over barbarism, divine order over impiety, and so on. In the case of an early decorated temple at Assos, in the Troad, put up around 550–530 BC (*ill. 63*), the recipient of such instruction was shown Herakles fighting a sea-monster, Herakles fighting Centaurs, and perhaps Herakles enjoying a banquet with King Eurytos, or else Herakles assumed to Olympian heights. The complex mythology of Herakles, with all its triumphs and trials, must here be deemed to say to all who arrive before the temple, 'follow Herakles'. Elsewhere, we may find temple decoration that is not so much prescriptive as *pro*scriptive: the metopes from the Heraion at the Foce del Sele, near Paestum (the Greek colony of Poseidonia) contain, among other scenes, what has been called a 'sinners' cycle': images of mythological miscreants being punished in the Underworld, such as Sisyphus, Tantalos and Tityos. We are a long way yet from the iconography of damnation as displayed in some Romanesque cloister, but a Greek priest may well have used the example of Sisyphus as the basis for some homily or chastisement. The function of sculpture to illustrate such moralities was natural enough on a temple wall. When it comes to public messages in Greek sanctuaries, the

64 The relief pediment from the temple of Artemis, Corfu, with the Gorgon Medusa in the centre; c. 570 BC.

interests of priests and politicians might very often be identical. So should we be looking for more than simply moralizing themes in temple sculptures?

The problem here is that no Greek author ever informs us about political symbolism in temple sculptures. That does not mean that none ever existed, but it does make it a matter of pure academic speculation to 'decode' such symbolism. It is unlikely that programmes of temple decoration were free from political bias, but also unlikely that we shall recover the nuances of propagandistic intent. Some attempts to interpret political imagery are, however, broadly plausible.

The earliest attempt at pedimental decoration is a case in point. When the limestone temple of Artemis on Corfu (Korkyra) was built in about 600 BC, its western pediment was used to present a medley of scenes carved in very deep relief. We have already noted (in Chapter 2) how tricky it is to interpret these particular scenes as having any narrative or even thematic unity, and in fact no definitive explanation can be given for one vignette in the corner of the pediment that shows an enthroned figure being threatened (even the sex of the enthroned figure is unclear). But the central scene is recognizably the Gorgon Medusa (*ill. 64*), and, in fragmentary state, her offspring – the monstrous boy Chrysaor and the flying horse Pegasus. The Gorgon was a creature who dealt in fear, and her appearance in the centre of a temple pediment may be described as 'apotropaic' – turning away evil,

65 The remains of a
limestone pedimental group
from a sixth-century BC
temple on the Akropolis,
Athens, showing Herakles
being presented on Olympia.

or else instilling a decent measure of fear and reverence in those approaching the building. So it is perfectly understandable why, when the legend of
Perseus decapitating the Gorgon demanded that her children be born *after*
she has lost her head, our sculptors here preferred to let her keep it. While
it might seem ironic that the Gorgon herself was made of stone (since that
was the effect her gaze had on humans who encountered it – literally
petrify them), this was nevertheless a head worth conserving for the
frontage of a sacred place.

But there may well have been a political motive here too. Corfu was a
Corinthian colony, established by a branch of a tightly knit aristocratic
ruling group at Corinth known as the Bacchiads. During the seventh
century BC, the Bacchiads at Corinth were displaced by a tyrant, Cypselus.
The incomplete histories we have of the tyranny of Cypselus and his son
Periander suggest that a part of their foreign policy was to assert control
over those Bacchiads in Corfu. It may be that the Cypselids accordingly
endowed the island with a large temple and commissioned a pedimental
symbol of central Corinthian power. What makes this theory attractive is
the fact that the numismatic hallmark of Corinth, from earliest coins
onwards, is the image of Pegasus. Legend connected many of the adventures of Pegasus with Corinth, so an image of his extraordinary genesis
was an appropriate means of reminding the colonists on Corfu of their
Corinthian loyalties. It is also worth noting that temple decoration in
another Corinthian colony, Sicilian Syracuse, also seems to favour Gorgon
images: Medusa, by her maternal association with Pegasus, thus became
not only religiously apt for a Corinthianizing temple, but also politically
correct.

A second example, or series of examples, comes from Athens. Again it involves a sixth-century tyrant. Perhaps we should not be surprised to find traces of propaganda from tyrants: it might be said to come naturally to them. And in the case of Peisistratos of Athens, a detailed chronicle of what appear to be propagandistic exercises has been assembled (mostly by John Boardman). Patterns of imagery on vases imply a particular interest in Herakles during the Peisistratid tyranny, and certain scraps of circumstantial evidence – that Peisistratos had a bodyguard armed, in Heraklean fashion, with clubs – can be cited as support of the idea that Peisistratos used Herakles as an *alter ego*. (It was a reasonable mythological choice for a despot, as many Hellenistic kings would later prove.) One advantage of posturing as Herakles lay in the hero's unusual status: despite his semi-divine parentage, Herakles began his life as a mortal and was only later assumed to Olympian ranks when, with Athena as his ally or *epikouros*, he received his apotheosis. We are told that Peisistratos once staged his own mock-apotheosis, by riding into Athens in a chariot co-piloted by a girl dressed up as Athena (the girl's name, Phye, 'size', connotes an intrinsically imposing figure); and among the confusion of debris assigned to the Peisistratid period of temple- and treasury-building on the Akropolis, it looks as though we may have some sculptural references to the greatness of Herakles/Peisistratos. One pedimental scene shows the presentation of Herakles to Olympus: nervously, but resplendent in his lion's-scalp head-dress, our doughty hero approaches the relatively massive central figure of Zeus enthroned (*ill. 65*). Another pedimental angle shows Herakles wrestling with the sea-monster, Triton (*ill. 66*); perhaps an allegorical allusion to the amphibious expedition Peisistratos launched against the nearby state of Megara; and yet another corner-piece contains a very curious three-headed monster known as 'Bluebeard' (*ill. 67*). The name comes from the navy paintwork that survives on the triple beards, and we are otherwise at a loss to produce a pedigree for this hybrid. To shrug one's shoulders and say that it must be 'Oriental' is an inadequate response. So a possible political explanation must be welcomed, and it has been proposed that the three bodies of the bearded conglomerate represent three political factions in sixth-century Athens, which Peisistratos is said to have

66 *(below left)* Herakles wrestling with Triton: a detail of the sixth-century BC limestone pediment from the Akropolis.

67 *(below right)* 'Bluebeard', a triple-bodied monster from the sixth-century BC limestone pediment from the Akropolis.

reconciled under his tyranny. These factions are historically recorded as the 'People of the Shore', the 'People of the Hills' and the 'People of the Plain': Peisistratos, one from 'the Hills', brought them together. And if we look closely at our triple-bodied monster, we find that each of the constituent figures holds an attribute: a bird, a sheaf of grain and what appears to be a wave. Could these attributes be symbolic, respectively, of the Hills, the Plain and the Shore?

Those who think such proposed allegories too sophisticated are obliged to come up with better explanations. So far, it should be said, sceptics of political propaganda in Archaic Greek temple decoration have failed to produce such alternatives. There is more general agreement about symbolism in temple decoration in the fifth century (see Chapter 6), and few would dispute the claim that Hellenistic monarchs sprinkled art under their patronage with their own dynastic agenda. But the problem with the Archaic period is simply the paucity of historical sources. Any iconological construct must look weak when based on no more than a sentence or two in Herodotus.

There is, however, another way of approaching this political aspect of sacred decoration: that is, to draw upon the terminology of 'peer polity interaction'. Though this phrase is resonant of archaeological theories which sometimes seem to complicate rather than elucidate the processes they are supposed to explain, it has already been applied with good results to patterns of Greek temple dimensions. ('Peer polity interaction', for our purposes, denotes the common activities of the city-states within the Greek ambit: their alliances, their mutual military rules, their symbols). Anthony Snodgrass has demonstrated how comparative measurements of Greek temples betray rivalries between competing city-states: if the temple at Ephesus erected *c.* 550 BC covers an area of 6017 sq. m (64,678 sq. ft), then the temple-builders at Samos *c.* 530 BC make sure that their area is 6038 sq. m (64,995 sq. ft), thus trumping the Ephesians. The colonists in Sicily can likewise be shown to have deliberately increased temple sizes as a form of one-upmanship; and the erection of treasuries at Olympia and Delphi seems also to have entailed a form of peer polity interaction – as Snodgrass says, with intentions of which the participant states must have been perfectly conscious. Even when barbarian powers made donations at Greek sanctuaries (as did Croesus of Lydia at Ephesus and the Etruscans at Delphi), the process of interaction was palpable.

'Interaction' includes all sorts of emulation, conflict and communication, but here we shall consider its purely symbolic workings. And indeed, Colin Renfrew's original promulgation of the peer polity interaction model included an example of the process which directly concerns an important category of Greek sculpture: the *kouroi*, as we designate the series of standardized Archaic figures of male youths recovered from

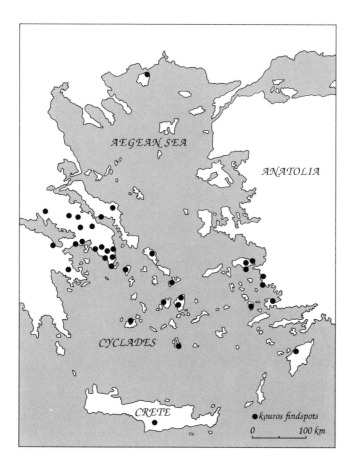

various Aegean sites (see Chapter 5). A map of the *kouros* findspots (*ill. 68*), though it excludes some important finds from western Greek colonies, shows a basic clustering of the *kouros* type as not only a Greek, but a predominantly Ionian Greek phenomenon (they are remarkably rare in the Dorian Peloponnese). It does not show local weightings, of course, nor does it explain the variety of contextual meanings that a *kouros* statue might assume, but to claim that this distribution shows the 'extent of symbolic interaction' among the Greek city states in the sixth century BC is probably reasonable. It has been estimated that there were twenty thousand *kouroi* once in existence. Even when fragmentary, they are instantly recognizable as Greek rather than Egyptian (despite resemblances of pose); and even more significantly, they can be recognized as 'standard' *kouroi* even when their stylistic development is sufficiently dynamic for a close chronology to be devised around them. Whatever else they were – we

68 The distribution of *kouroi* in the Aegean (certain finds beyond the Aegean are not shown).

shall look at their meanings more thoroughly in the next chapter – they must be admitted to carry symbolic value.

We may appreciate that value by contemplating a selection of statues excavated from a site which is off the map, but nevertheless illustrates nicely the process of symbolic interaction. This is the polity of Naukratis, in the Nile Delta. 'Polity' allows us to escape a number of ambiguities in the Greeks' own classification of Naukratis – it is termed both a city, *polis*, and trading-post, *emporion* – and equal ambiguities left by a hurried late nineteenth-century excavation of the site. But finds from Naukratis more or less support the account of it given by Herodotus, who describes the proper settlement there as a concession from the pro-Greek pharaoh whom the Greeks knew as Amasis (Ahmose: 570–526 BC). Amasis also granted traders frequenting Naukratis the right to erect altars and temples. Of these sanctuaries, says Herodotus (II. 178) the most prominent was the Hellenion, 'founded jointly by the following cities: of the Ionians, Chios, Teos, Phocaea and Clazomenae; of the Dorians, Rhodes, Knidos, Halicarnassus and Phaselis; of the Aeolians, just Mytilene. . . Apart from this the Aeginetans have founded by themselves a sanctuary of Zeus, the Samians another of Hera, and the Milesians one of Apollo.'

Naukratis was discovered in 1883 by the Egyptologist Sir Flinders Petrie. How he located the site is highly significant. At an antiquities bazaar in Giza, near Cairo, Petrie was offered an alabaster statuette of a male warrior figure. He immediately recognized it as non-Egyptian: to be precise, as Carian work. Where might Carian statuary have come from? Since Herodotus lists two Carian cities, Halicarnassus and Knidos, as those with Naukratite interests, Petrie thought he might be on the Naukratis trail. He snapped up the figure, and asked where he could get more like it. Eventually he was led to a site in the Delta near Nebeira, where, as he memorably describes it, his feet crunched over a carpet of exposed Greek pottery.

The chances of clarifying the nature of Naukratis are now slim as most of the site is inundated. But the means by which Petrie found the site surely illuminate the process of symbolic interaction among the Greeks. Naukratis must have had a very curious status: a busy place of transit, with relatively few long-term Greek residents, it was watched over by a substantial garrison of Egyptians. Greek traders came and went, and said their prayers at various altars. What these traders wanted was symbolic assurance that, in a strange land, among powerful and suspicious barbarians, they were ensconced among Greek-speakers, and protected by Greek deities.

The numerous dedicatory inscriptions from Naukratis reveal partisan loyalties: Apollo will be hailed, presumably by visitors from Miletus, as *Milesios* or *Didymaios*; he is never *Naukratitos*. But there are also dedications to 'the Greek gods' generally, a formula which echoes the pan-Hellenic oath quoted by Herodotus (V. 49: *pros theon ton Hellenion*). And as far as we can tell from the highly dispersed statuary of this sacred enclave at Naukratis, it looks as though 'Greekness' was asserted in symbolic form too. Petrie's alabaster statuette was not unique. Naukratis has yielded further votive sculptures which would have comforted any Archaic Greek visitor feeling homesick. Thus, there are the usual memorabilia of sacrifices such as the kid goat offered to Aphrodite. Another statue records the donation of what appears to be a large leg of mutton (*ill. 69*). And there are *kouroi* too – not of marble, since none was locally available, but where possible using alabaster or white sandstone, and trying as best they could to look like the sort of *kouroi* that might have been encountered at Didyma or Delos (*ills 70* and *71*). This is what is meant by symbolic interaction: statues serving as badges of Greekness, signalling a cultural unity even though a political 'nation' of Greece itself did not exist.

Conclusion: the endowment of Olympia

We should try to draw together some summary of the nature and range of 'sacred decoration'. As intimated in the Introduction to this book, it is rather misleading to entitle a chapter as such: the quantity of Greek sculpture that does not in some way or other qualify for the general function of having decorated a sacred place must be extremely small. But it may be wise to end with an evocation of how it was that Greek sanctuaries came to be great galleries of sculpture, and there is no better example than Olympia.

Like most Greek sanctuaries, Olympia has Bronze Age origins. Prior to the eighth century BC it may have been a place where agricultural festivals were staged. If horses were being traded at such meetings, then horses would be tested by racing them, and that may be how the games began. The later Greeks imagined that the Olympic games commenced in 776 BC – perhaps a little too early, on the basis of the archaeological evidence, but not far wrong. From about 700 BC there is evidence that small votives, and prize tripods, were being made at the site. Thanks to its neutrality, it became a pan-Hellenic point of rendezvous: early participants at the sanctuary (and associated games, presumably) included Arcadia, Messenia, Argos and Sparta. The Peloponnesian popularity of the site was furthered by the adoption of an old Bronze Age tumulus as the supposed burial place of Pelops; and when the Temple of Zeus was constructed in 470 BC or thereabouts, one choice for pedimental decoration was the tale of how Pelops had challenged a local king to a chariot race (see Chapter 2).

The first temple at Olympia was dedicated to Hera. Its pedimental decoration was in cedarwood, and showed the exploits of Herakles.

(opposite)

69 Votive figure from Naukratis, Egypt; sixth century BC.

70 *Kouros* figure from Naukratis, Egypt; sixth century BC.

71 Statuette of *kouros*-type from Naukratis, Egypt; sixth century BC.

According to mythology, it was Herakles who first instituted the games and so all participants were encouraged to think of themselves as following the Heraklean way. We see the hero at his best on the twelve metopes of the Temple of Zeus: he wrestles with colossal bulls, and his weightlifting involves supporting the entire globe (*frontispiece*), but he is also Everyman, and the choice of labours here seems designed to appeal to athletes from all over the Greek world. Six of the labours take place in various parts of the Peloponnese; two in the West; one in the East; one in Crete; and one in the Thracian North (the remaining one is in Hades). Several of the metopes make it plain that Herakles cannot achieve what he does without his sponsor Athena. Take the scene of his holding up the world: Atlas, who normally does that job, has abandoned it in order to fetch the golden apples of the Hesperides; Herakles, a smaller man, needs a cushion or two to make up the height (or soften the burden). He thinks he may be holding the globe alone: but we, the viewers, can see that Athena, as usual, is lending a helping hand. She is his ally, his *epikouros*.

No wonder, then, that when Pausanias arrived at Olympia he counted no less than seventy altars in the sanctuary. Athletes competed by the grace of Zeus, and for the gladness of Zeus: there is no victory without divine assistance, and some truth in the description of Greek sport as 'the ritual sacrifice of physical energy'. Yet athletes also competed for themselves and their cities. Olympia became part of a circuit (*periodos*) of sanctuaries where games were held (Nemea, Isthmia and Delphi were on the same circuit); and what was a circuit for the athletes was also a circuit for the sculptors too. Athletes sought victories, and victories sought sculptors. City-states interacted with each other, and interaction required expressive symbolism. In short, the sanctuary became a marvellous monumental host of dynamic athletes – and dynamic art (*ill. 72*).

72 A reconstruction of the sanctuary of Olympia, thronged with statues dedicated by victorious athletes.

5

HEROES APPARENT

The bodies were there, the belief in the gods was there, the love of rational proportion was there. It was the unifying grasp of the Greek imagination which brought them together. And the nude gains its enduring value from the fact that it reconciles several contrary states. It takes the most sensual and immediately interesting object, the human body, and puts it out of reach of time and desire; it takes the most purely rational concept of which mankind is capable, mathematical order, and makes it a delight to the senses; and it takes the vague fears of the unknown and sweetens them by showing that the gods are like men, and may be worshipped for their life-giving beauty rather than their death-dealing powers.

Kenneth Clark, *The Nude* (London 1956), 22

Of the great and the good

If Greek culture could be characterized in a single word, then a strong contender would have to be 'heroic'. Greek literature and Greek religion are both permeated by heroes and hero-worship: so, too, is Greek sculpture. Before we acquaint ourselves with the resulting images, it is worth sketching a profile of what may tentatively be called the typical Greek hero. This necessarily blurs some distinctions of status that would once have existed, but it is based on the same conceptual basis as most Classical Greeks onwards, at least, would have been familiar with since childhood: that is, the delineation of heroism by Homer.

The Homeric hero loves life, though he is bound to die, and quite often by a violent death. While alive, however, his appetite for meat, wine, women and fighting is excellent: he indulges no half measures. Even if he is wounded, it is either slight, or fatal. And in his intensely physical world, he strides large. A common Homeric device for letting us know the distance between us and these heroes is to describe one of them easily tossing a rock which 'nowadays two of the best men in a city could scarcely heave on to a waggon' (*Iliad* XII. 445). So heroes are not only strong and well formed, but they are big, which can be an important element in recognizing them in sculpture.

73 A reconstruction by
C.R. Cockerell of the west
pediment of the temple of
Aphaia, Aegina; c. 490 BC.

The Homeric hero is, moreover, usually 'god-like' (*theoeides*). King
Priam says of his son Hector: 'he was a god among men, and he seemed
to be the child not of a mortal but of a god' (*Iliad* XXIV. 258–9).
Agamemnon's appearance is described in terms of a series of divine points
of comparison: 'in eyes and head like Zeus who delights in thunder, in
girdle like Ares, in chest like Poseidon' (*Iliad* II. 478). Plainly these com-
paranda only make sense to an audience used to visualizing their gods; it
may consequently be rather difficult, in iconographic terms, to distinguish
a hero from a god.

Homer knew about hero-cults as eighth-century BC religious institutions: in his description of the funeral games of Patroklos (*Iliad* XXIII) he
seems to be imagining the beginnings of a hero-cult in the contest (*agon*)
held to commemorate Patroklos. And his warriors are very well aware of
the honours they may receive in the event of their death. Here is one of
Homer's most attractive characters, the Lycian ally of the Trojans,
Sarpedon, enjoining a fellow-Lycian to come out and fight in the front line:

> 'Glaucus,' he said, 'why do the Lycians at home distinguish you and me with
> marks of honour, the best seats at the banquet, the first cut off the joint, and
> never-empty cups? Why do they all look up to us as gods? And why were we
> made the lords of that great estate of ours on the banks of Xanthos, with its
> lovely orchards and its splendid fields of wheat? Does not all this oblige us now
> to take our places in the Lycian van and fling ourselves into the flames of battle?
> Only so can we make our Lycian men-at-arms say this about us when they
> discuss their Kings: "They live on the fat of the land they rule, they drink the
> mellow vintage wine, but they pay for it in their glory. They are mighty men of
> war, and where Lycians fight you will see them in the van."
>
> 'Ah, my friend, if after living through this war we could be sure of ageless
> immortality, I should neither take my place in the front line nor send you out to
> win honour on the field. But things are not like that. Death has a thousand pit-
> falls for our feet; and nobody can save himself and cheat him. So in we go,
> whether we yield the glory to some other man or win it for ourselves.'
>
> (*Iliad* XII. 310–28, trans. Rieu)

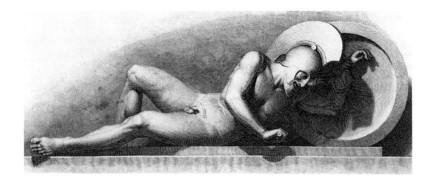

74 Engraving by C.R. Cockerell of the dying warrior from the east pediment of the temple of Aphaia, Aegina.

75 Detail of dying warrior from the east pediment of the temple of Aphaia, Aegina.

This impressive exhortation of *noblesse oblige* from Sarpedon says more about the Homeric concept of heroism than might many pages of scholarly prose. And it should be completed by noting what happens later on in the *Iliad* (XVI) when Sarpedon meets his death at the hands of Patroklos. His body on the battlefield is in danger of mutilation, so Zeus commands Apollo to speed down, lift the corpse to safety, anoint it with ambrosia, and then send it to Lycia, where the kinsmen of Sarpedon 'will give him burial, with a barrow and a monument, the proper tribute to the dead'. So Sarpedon, as he himself forecast, will be heroized when dead: though his death is terrible, and an experience which pitches him into coldness and darkness and the spheres of the bloodless shades, it is also a blessing. Sarpedon, as a hero, thereby becomes glorified and immortal (*athanatos*).

The concept of a 'beautiful death' (*thanatos kalos*) was a powerful ideology in societies where it was normal for most male citizens not only to train regularly for the eventuality of war, but also to have first-hand experience of battle. They needed no war artists or film crews to show them the realities of bloodshed. At their drinking parties or *symposia*, men who trained and fought together craved the ennobling entertainment of epic poetry such as Homer's. And of course, the sculptors were not unmoved by this ethos. If we glance at two of the most ambitious sculptural attempts to depict heroic combat, from the early fifth-century BC pediments of the temple of Aphaia on Aegina, we see an overall effort to convey the clash of arms, and the tumult of battle (*ill. 73*); and in detail, palpable sympathy for the heroic way of death (*ills 74* and *75*). It is essentially unrealistic, insofar as the warriors are without clothes or body armour; yet there is a vivid interest in the postures of life deserting the heroic body. We may remember the immediate reaction of the Achaean warriors when Hector is finally despatched by Achilles: prior to any acts of vengeance, they register the 'beautiful death' of their enemy and 'they gazed in wonder at the stature [*phue*] and awesome appearance [*eidos agetos*] of Hector' (*Iliad* XXII. 370).

'Say not that the good die'

In Book One of Herodotus, the early sixth-century BC Athenian law-giver Solon, a man of almost proverbial wisdom, is asked to nominate people he considers to have been supremely happy. Among his candidates are two young men from Argos, Kleobis and Biton. Athletes of prowess and prize-winning renown, their greatest test of strength occurred when their mother was due to celebrate a festival of Hera at the Argive Heraion, which lies some way from Argos proper. The team of oxen due to take their mother by waggon to the sanctuary failed to materialize on time: so Kleobis and Biton harnessed themselves to the cart and dragged it along, with their mother aboard, for a distance of 5 or 6 miles, until the sanctuary was reached. Solon continues the story:

> 'After this exploit, which was witnessed by the assembled crowd, they had a most enviable death – a heaven-sent proof of how much better it is to be dead than alive. Men kept crowding round them and congratulating them on their strength, and women kept telling the mother how lucky she was to have such sons, when, in sheer pleasure at this public recognition of her sons' act, she prayed the goddess Hera, before whose shrine she stood, to grant Kleobis and Biton, who had brought her such honour, the greatest blessing [*tychein ariston*] that can fall to mortal man.
>
> 'After her prayer came the ceremonies of sacrifice and feasting; and the two lads, when all was over, fell asleep in the temple – and that was the end of them, for they never woke again.
>
> 'The Argives had statues made of them, which they sent to Delphi, as a mark of their particular respect.'
>
> (Herodotus I. 131, trans. de Selincourt)

This account comes in the course of an unlikely conversation between Solon of Athens and Croesus, the fabulously rich king of Lydia. Its purpose is to puncture the inflated egotism of Croesus, who thinks that his wealth should qualify him as the happiest man in the world. But to advocate fatal acts of piety as a route to happiness is not as perverse as it might sound. The idea that the good man (*aner agathos*) does not die, but instead lapses into a 'holy sleep' (*hieros hypnos*) is echoed in Greek elegiac literature. This is not merely a matter of semantics or poetic postures, rather it sets up genuine intimations of immortality. One could read the story of Kleobis and Biton as a tragedy glossed as a triumph, a 'blessing' (an inadequate translation of the Greek *makarismos*) in disguise: did the poor boys die of exhaustion at the end of their heavy duties? And yet it is suggested that divine ordinance brought about their end, in response to a prayer, which makes it not so much of an end as an apotheosis, or assumption.

At any rate, they were heroes ever after, and the Argives, not otherwise known for their enthusiasm for producing *kouroi*-figures, went to the trouble of dedicating images of Kleobis and Biton at Delphi. Our previous encounters with the concept of 'peer polity interaction' will help us explain why pieties on behalf of Hera, performed at Argos, should be celebrated by statues at Apollo's sanctuary of Delphi: with these statues, the Argives are sending out messages to other city-states about what it takes to be an Argive citizen. And from excavations at Delphi (from near the Athenian treasury, to be precise) has come a pair of statues, which have been identified as the *kouroi* that Herodotus mentions (*ills 76 and 77*).

The identification is not absolutely certain: on the thigh of the figure deemed 'Kleobis' some claim to be able to read (albeit very faintly) the name *Polydeukes*, and therefore take the boys to be the Dioscuri; and the inscribed base of the figures is incomplete and ambiguous. Still, the Argive brothers remain good candidates for these statues. Though it is not always clear from photographs, the figures are (unusually for *kouroi*) wearing ankle boots, which may be suggestive of a hike across the Argive plain; and each of them could justly be described as a bovine type (*boupais*) in terms of physique. The slightly flexed elbows of the figures seem to recall a tugging motion. In short, they are just how one might imagine the statues of Kleobis and Biton to have been, if one takes Herodotus to be relating a story set in the early sixth century BC.

The statues of Kleobis and Biton are akin to many other Archaic funerary monuments, as we shall discover, insofar as they are memorials of brave young people set up by their parents. They are also counted as *kouroi*. *Kouros* signifies youth and manhood, sometimes also warrior status. Etymologically, it is related to a word (*koros*) that signifies a seedling, or shoot of a plant. The memorial statues we know as *kouroi* embody what some take to be an aristocratic ideology of *kalokagathia*, 'beautiful goodness', but they also embody a more specifically heroizing sentiment. The Homeric Hymn to Demeter tells how the goddess had plans to raise an adoptive son, Demophon, and steeped him in ambrosia – the divine nourishment for this 'young sprout' (*neon thalos*), which soon had everyone marvelling at 'how full in bloom he came to be' (*hos pro-thales teletheske*). And more than this: he would grow up as a *daimon*, a god or demi-god, of whom ordinary mortals would declare, 'to look at him is to gaze upon the gods' – and whom they would duly feel inclined to worship.

So the debate often encountered regarding the significance of the *kouros*-type – whether such statues were intended as 'gods' (especially Apollo) or mortals is misleading. Whether the *kouros* is set up as a votive offering in a sanctuary, or a marker (*sema*) or memorial (*mnema*) in a funerary context, its intentions are always heroizing. We have already seen (in Chapter 2) how closely the poetic descriptions of Apollo correspond

76–77 (opposite and above) Kleobis and Biton, twin *kouroi*, dedicated as funerary monuments; c. 570 BC.

with the appearance of the *kouroi*. Even when hairstyles change, and dandy young men of the later sixth century BC prefer to tie their hair up, we should not be deceived: they are still in fact 'unshorn' (*akersekomes*), like Apollo. But a specific resemblance to one god or one demi-god (the hero is often 'half-god', *hemitheos*, in Greek parlance) was not the expectation. It was the conjuring of a generic heroic look that was important.

The *kouros* may seem rigid in his stance. In fact, with the left leg slightly advanced, and those broad shoulders, the figure is like a wound-up spring ready for action. When, in the thick of battle, Menelaus prays to Athena for extra strength, Homer is quite specific as to where she instils it: in his knees and shoulders (*Iliad* XVII. 569). Neither standing nor walking, the *kouros* suggests the perfect 'nimble-footed' or 'swift in knees' (*laipsera gouna*) readiness of the Homeric hero. Sometimes the scale of the statue may be increased to colossal, but that is unusual. It is the standardized form of the *kouros* which makes it so readily assimilated (as intended) to the epic world of Menelaus, Achilles and Hector. Even when a man dies old, it is in this bloom of youth that he wants to be remembered. The actual circumstances of death may directly relate to the Homeric ambience. One Attic *kouros*, erected around 530–520 BC, stood on a base that declared: 'Stay and mourn at the tomb [*sema*] of dead Kroisos, whom raging Ares destroyed one day as he fought in the foremost ranks [*promachois*]'. And on a grave relief from Megara, now in the J. Paul Getty Museum in California, dated to around 480 BC, an infantry soldier (*hoplite*) named Pollis declares not only that he was 'the beloved son of Asopitos', but that his death occurred because he was 'not a coward in the line of battle'. Both Kroisos and Pollis, then, lived up to the Homeric ideal.

Perhaps the best way of understanding the nature of this heroizing ethos is to see how it could be parodied, as in the *Clouds* of Aristophanes, written for an Athenian audience in 423 BC. This comedy is best known as a satire on the teachings of Socrates, but it includes a nice sketch of the Athenian notion of 'the good old days', when men were men and did not spend their days in idle philosophizing. The spokesman for this nostalgia, 'Mr Right' (*dikaios logos*), invokes the values of the veterans of Marathon, the *Marathonomachai* (line 986) as his moral touchstone. There is much talk (as there always is in such debates) of strict discipline and plenty of fresh air; a vigorous, no-nonsense homosexuality is also entailed. But when it comes to describing the physical specimens that this old educational system (*paideia*) produced, Mr Right could almost be describing a *kouros*: if you were brought up in those days (the battle of Marathon was in 490 BC), you were likely to have 'a glowing tan, a manly chest, broad shoulders [*omous megalous*], a modest tongue, beefy buttocks [*pygen megalen*] and a dainty prick [*posthen mikran*]' (*Clouds*, 1011–14). By contrast, the chicken-ribbed, pasty-faced, pathetic minnows of today (continues Mr

Right) are so ashamed of their puny bodies that when it comes to doing a Pyrrhic dance, they have to try and cover themselves up as best they can with their shields.

We know about the Pyrrhic dance as an event of the Panathenaia: a votive slab in the Akropolis Museum shows two groups of such dancers who display the taut musculatures of which Aristophanes' Mr Right would approve. And, of course, they are naked. This brings us to a concept which is so often misunderstood or thoughtlessly invoked by modern scholars that it deserves a brief discussion by itself.

78 'Hockey-players' on a late sixth-century BC Athenian statue base.

'Heroic nudity'

If Thucydides be a fair index, the Greeks considered nakedness, in certain circumstances, a characteristic of their civilization. Thucydides (I. 6) says that it was the Spartans who set the example first, competing naked at games, and stripping off to anoint themselves and practise gymnastic exercises. As already noted, to go naked, in Greek, is to be *gymnos*: a gymnasium, therefore, is a public space where nakedness is to be expected. Non-Greeks, as Thucydides implies, are shyer in this matter – or else they live in climates less conducive to the removal of clothes.

To say that nakedness is 'civilized', at least when practising sports, does not however explain the term 'heroic nudity'. Undoubtedly, there are scenes in Greek sculpture where the action naturally calls for the depiction of naked male bodies: the Pyrrhic dance, for one; and, on an earlier relief, the lads apparently playing an archaic version of hockey (*ill. 78*). But this does not seem to qualify as 'heroic nudity': it would be better to call it 'gymnastic nakedness'.

'To be naked is to be oneself.' John Berger's well-known dictum seeks to establish a difference between nakedness and nudity which may be useful here. Berger proceeds:

To be nude is to be seen naked by others and yet not recognized for oneself. A naked body has to be seen as an object in order to become a nude. (The sight of it as an object stimulates the use of it as an object.) Nakedness reveals itself. Nudity is placed on display.

To be naked is to be without disguise.

To be on display is to have the surface of one's skin, the hairs of one's own body, turned into a disguise which, in that situation, can never be discarded. The nude is condemned to never being naked. Nudity is a form of dress.

(J. Berger, *Ways of Seeing*, Harmondsworth 1972, 54)

Berger's distinction was formulated with the tradition of European oil-painting in mind; with some thought also of modern stereotypes of advertising and pornography. But we may be inclined to agree that the nakedness of the *kouroi* is sufficiently formal to be considered as nudity. The almost fetishistic way in which some Classical archaeologists have scrutinized the anatomical details of the *kouroi* might suggest that the sculptors of *kouroi* thought about nothing else but getting the naturalistic features of the male body right, but this is a dangerous assumption. It is true that if one compares *kouroi* a little under a century apart (*ills* 79 and 80), sculptors have made something like anatomical 'progress': the earlier *kouros*, with its ribcage outlined by a single hoop, and a triangular groin, is virtually geometrical. But of course, the later, more 'accurate' figure is still an ideal: however widespread the practice of athletics, however punishing the regime of military exercises, men do not easily achieve torsos like this. It is the sort of ideal which, in the mid-fifth century BC, would develop into the 'canonical' nudes of Polykleitos.

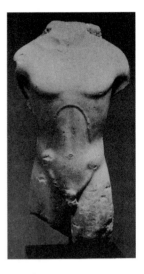

79 A *kouros* torso; *c.* 550 BC.

As we saw in our previous notice of Polykleitos (Chapter 2), some social basis may lie behind the 'beautiful-and-good' (*kalos k'agathos*) ethic, in the form of beauty competitions. Some also see the regularly muscled sculpted Greek torso as a sort of pseudo-armour (the so-called *cuirasse esthétique*), inherently aggressive because of its military overtones. Feminists go further, and declare it to be symptomatic of a misogynistic and 'phallocentric' regime – the difficulty with this, though, is that the genitalia of Greek nudes are hardly threatening (to be endowed with a large penis was a sign of bestial or barbaric nature: satyrs, being half-equine, might be shown as such). And women were not the primary viewers of such images: if anything, it was the prevalence of pederasty, and the respectability of homosexual attachments, which encouraged the display of what were homoerotically considered fine young bodies. But we can nevertheless say that for statues such as the *kouroi*, and the gravestones we shall look at presently, nudity should be considered a costume. The figures we see here are unlikely to have been portraits in the proper sense: the costume of nudity is worn by men aspiring to be something (or someone) on a higher level. Greek men did not normally walk around with no clothes on, so if

80 A *kouros* torso, from Miletos, *c.* 480–470 BC, showing the development of the treatment of musculature.

figures are glimpsed naked (or nude) in the context of what appears to be a 'realistic' scene, then the chances are that the scene has been elevated from the realistic to the supernatural. Such is the case with the Parthenon frieze: its cavalcade of naked or semi-naked riders is enough to rule out the idea that it represents a normal Panathenaic procession (Athenian cavalry may have gone naked on some occasions, but not in a sacred event such as this).

Some call this nudity, then, 'ideal'; others, 'heroic'. It is both, and may even be called 'aristocratic' too. For a general characterization, these may be unsatisfactory terms, but if we now turn to some examples of overt heroization, it becomes clear why we must hold on to the concept of 'heroic nudity'. Simply by a process of association, we shall find that most men considered as heroes are shown naked: nudity, therefore, becomes a costume that may be donned by anyone who thinks he should be counted among their number.

The Tyrannicides

The statue-group of the Tyrannicides (*ill. 81*) furnishes us with a fine example of the heroic image. This is despite a number of historical ambiguities surrounding the two Athenians, Harmodius and Aristogeiton, figured in the group; and also despite the fact that we are left only with a copy of a copy of the original statue (see below). Still, we are given some measure of the gap between the image-making and the actuality of events. For whatever else happened, Harmodius and Aristogeiton were heroized very shortly after their own deaths in 514 BC.

The background to the deaths of these two is the tyranny of the Peisistratids at Athens. Peisistratos we have already encountered as the tyrant who may have presented himself as a second Herakles. He was succeeded by two sons, Hippias and Hipparchus. Their names imply that they were good with horses; it is not clear how well they could deal with people (moderately, according to Thucydides), but at least one of them, Hippias, goes down in Athenian records as a rogue (we shall encounter him, too, as an old man attempting to assist the Persians to seize Athens in 490 BC: see Chapter 6). At the Panathenaic Festival of 514 BC, Harmodius and Aristogeiton assassinated Hipparchus. It seems that they had originally intended to kill the elder brother, Hippias, but found Hipparchus an easier target. In any case, they both nursed grudges against Hipparchus: Aristogeiton because Hipparchus was repeatedly making overtures to his boyfriend Harmodius; Harmodius because Hipparchus had lately insulted his sister. In the tumult of the attack, Harmodius was himself killed; and though Aristogeiton escaped, he was later tortured to death by Hippias.

So much for the event. Should it be labelled as 'tyrannicide'? Not strictly, if we follow Thucydides, whose account of what happened (VI. 54–9) is perhaps not as honest as it at first seems (the introduction of Harmodius' sister is suspiciously archetypal), but credibly stresses that the original motive for the killing came from a love affair (*erotike lype*). That is, Harmodius and Aristogeiton seem not to have conceived their plot from political motives; if it chanced to develop that way, that was almost accidental.

Nor, strictly speaking, did they effectively rid Athens of tyranny: things got worse before they got better. Hippias remained in power another four years, growing ever more malevolent towards his subjects, until a coalition of the powerful family exiled by Peisistratos, the Alkmaionids, and the Spartan army, succeeded in driving Hippias out. It was probably then – in 510 BC, or the following year – that the original statue of Harmodius and Aristogeiton was raised in the Athenian Agora. What it looked like, we cannot be sure, for it was abducted in 480 BC when the Persians occupied Athens, and although there is a story that it was returned to Athens by Alexander the Great or some other Hellenistic king, the version of which we possess a Roman copy is a replacement, entrusted to the sculptors Kritios and Nesiotes, and apparently raised in 477 BC. Quite possibly this more or less replicates the original, ascribed to the sculptor Antenor. Both groups were in bronze, and both enjoyed the unusual distinction of being placed in the heart of Athenian civic life. There is subsequent evidence of special laws prohibiting the erection of any other statues in their vicinity. This group was a very cherished image, no doubt the more so because by fixing the birth of democracy upon these supposed tyrannicides, Athenians might conveniently erase in vulgar consciousness the role of the Spartan army in expelling the last Peisistratid. And its resonance may be registered throughout the iconographic record of Classical Athens, on vases, coins and other monuments. The striking gesture of Harmodius ('the Harmodius blow') may be consciously or subconsciously mimicked by other Athenian heroes in art, such as Theseus. In short, the group became a talismanic icon for the Athenian democracy. As a symbol of a political faith, it was not only the focus of subsequent admiration by the allies of Athens, but seems to have been copied by them: a fourth-century BC inscription from Chios enjoins the clerks of the market-place to keep the local tyrannicide statue spotless, adorned with garlands, and shining (*lampros*).

Harmodius and Aristogeiton were cult figures. Were their images in any sense portraits, as some sources suggest? Superficially, they present the ideal pederastic couple: Aristogeiton bearded, and protective; Harmodius, as Thucydides describes him, 'in the full bloom of youth', an object of desire both to the man he is killing and the man protecting him. Both are

81 The Tyrannicides: a Roman copy of a bronze Greek original of *c.* 477 BC, itself a copy of the first version, kidnapped by the Persians.

naked – or rather, since they would not have been participating in a religious procession without their clothes on, they are given the costume of nudity. And we must call this heroic nudity, for in every technical sense Harmodius and Aristogeiton, very soon after their deaths, were worshipped as heroes or demi-gods. At their cenotaph in the Kerameikos, annual offerings (*enagismata*) were made by the city's war-minister or *polemarch*, perhaps cognitively treating the pair like those fallen in battle. In this sense, it is important to recognize that the cult of Harmodius and Aristogeiton focused not so much on the fact that they ended the tyranny, but that the tyranny ended them.

Both Herodotus and Thucydides felt some need to deflate the heroization of Harmodius and Aristogeiton. This is hardly surprising, when we consider how mawkishly the pair were celebrated in Athenian drinking-songs, or *skolia*, sung at symposia. These credited the tyrannicides as the founders of political equality of rights (*isonomia*) in Athens, and certainly exaggerated the political purity of their intentions. But the *skolia* also reveal much about the mentality of heroization. Here is one such, addressed in particular to young Harmodius:

> Harmodius, most beloved! Surely you are not at all dead,
> but they say that you are on the Isles of the Blessed,
> the same place where swift-footed Achilles is,
> and they say that worthy Diomedes, son of Tydeus, is there too.

(*Skolion* 894P: see D.L. Page, *Poetae Melici Graeci*, Oxford 1962)

Rowdy and drunken the contexts of such choruses may have been: but the vigorous denial of death in this salutation of Harmodius is highly significant in the heroizing process, and demands further demonstration.

Heroes beyond the grave

In 399 BC Socrates was condemned to death. His valedictory words to the court, as recorded in Plato's *Apology*, contain inspirational self-comforting reasoning. Death, declares Socrates, presents two options to us. Either it is a complete cessation of consciousness, in which case it will come like a deep and dreamless sleep – perfectly blissful oblivion. Or else it is as many eschatologies and poets predict – a migration to another place, a nether world of spirits where there is a vast accumulative club of all who have gone before. This, too, says Socrates, must be regarded as a pleasant prospect. 'What would you not give, gentlemen, to be able to question the leader of that great host against Troy, or Odysseus, or Sisyphus, or the thousands of other men and women one could mention, to talk and mix and argue with whom would be unimaginable happiness?'.

The Socratic gloss on self-extinction is attractive, even though the way in which Kleobis and Biton settle down forever in death's 'holy sleep' (*hieros hypnos*) might imply that it need not be a choice: seemingly one could become an active member of the eternal community of the dead, *and* enjoy uninterrupted slumber too. But we must not press our Greek literary and philosophical sources for too much consistency in this matter. What concerns us here is how far such sources contribute to our understanding of funerary iconography.

Both the sympotic salutation to Harmodius and the farewell speech from Socrates offer a particular prospect to the dead: that is, of mingling in the nether world with the acknowledged heroes of old. This single aspect of Greek beliefs about the afterlife goes a very long way towards making sense of the images we find on grave-markers or *stelai*. We have already seen how the *kouroi* could serve as such grave-markers, and represent a man who died in old age as being in the physical splendour of his youth. The youthful form may anticipate a rejuvenation beyond the grave; it may leave behind a *mnema* of how he was in his prime – but most importantly, it puts him in the ranks of the great and good. At one sanctuary in Boeotia, Mount Ptoion, some 120 *kouroi* were found. Though they are not grave-markers, these must have seemed like an immortalized host, the flower of Boeotian manhood, bound one day to join Achilles and Agamemnon and all the recreations of Elysium. And from another Boeotian site, Tanagra, comes the double memorial raised by one Amphalkes for Dermys and Kittylos, *c.* 600 BC (*ill. 82*). This is from a cemetery and we suspect that Dermys and Kittylos were the sons, possibly twins, of Amphalkes. They, too, are stripped bare, with their knees nicely flexed: model boys, heroized in readiness for the place they are due to remain. There is no epitaph here, but the sort of epitaph that might be inscribed on the base of a *kouros* is exemplified by one recorded from late sixth-century BC Athens: 'Look on the memorial [*mnema*] of Kleoitis, the son of Menesaichmos, and pity him for dying, with such beauty [*hos kalos*]'.

Other inscriptions assist iconography to define not only the beauty, but also perhaps some special skill of the deceased. From Athens again, in the mid-sixth century BC, we find the following: 'Anyone with any sense, Xenokles, will know when he looks at your marker [*sema*] that it belongs to a spearman'.

The *stele* of the runner wearing a helmet (*ill. 83*), despite appearances, probably does not show the subject dead or unconscious. His pose is better read as one of triumph: crossing the finish gloriously. The monument reassures those who knew the deceased (and informs those who did not) that he has gone to a Hades where his fleet-footedness will be appreciated; whatever victory of his we may remember from the Games, we are to imagine him now matching Homer's nimble heroes.

Of course, grave monuments were expensive, and from Athens at least there is some evidence for intermittent legislation to curb excessive spending on funerary protocol. But the *polis* was obliged to honour those who died defending it: as Sally Humphreys has observed, 'it was the state funerals for war dead which first brought the honours of heroic burial within the range of every Athenian citizen', and families with cavalry connections were particularly fond of displaying their status. So we notice, on the lower part of a *stele* shaft, of *c.* 525 BC, showing now just the feet of a figure with a spear (*ill. 84*), a secondary figure on horseback, carrying two spears and a sword: this will be the squire of the dead warrior, marking him out as a cavalryman (*hippeus*) who could afford to keep not only horse but also

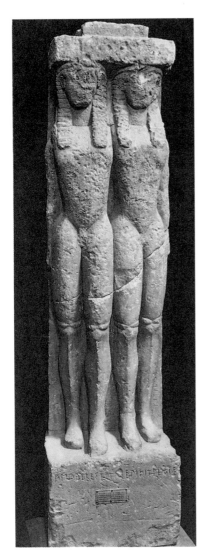

82 *(above)* Dermys and Kittylos: an early sixth-century BC limestone grave marker from Boeotia.

83 *(above right)* A helmeted runner on a late sixth-century BC Athenian stele.

84 *(right)* A horseman, possibly the squire of the dead person, whose feet are visible above, is shown on this fragment of an Attic stele; c. 525 BC.

squire. And a well-known relief from the Athenian Kerameikos cemetery over a century later develops this allusion into overt heroization (*ill. 85*). This is the relief commemorating Dexileos, who died, aged twenty, at Nemea in 394 BC, in the first battle of the Corinthian War. It is not actually a grave-marker: as a casualty of war, Dexileos was placed in the state burial ground (*Demosion Sema*) of Athens. But this relief adorns his family's own burial precinct (*peribolos*) in the Kerameikos. The accompanying inscription defines Dexileos as one of 'the five knights' who fell in this battle. Since a separate monument to the casualties specifies eleven cavalry dead, it is proposed that Dexileos belonged to a special shock force within the cavalry – an elite within an elite, of which his father was duly proud.

85 The stele of Dexileos; early fourth century BC.

The image of Dexileos does not show his death, but rather the sort of death he was prepared to deal out to the enemies of Athens. Astride his rearing horse, he strikes his lance down into the chest of a collapsing opponent (bridles and lance were evidently separate bronze fittings). To show Dexileos clothed not only gives the sculptor the opportunity of creating movement with a flying cloak, but also adds credibility to the triumph. The nudity of the victim – frozen in a diagonal combat posture that would be much exploited by the sculptors of the friezes of the Mausoleum – then heroizes by association the exploits of young Dexileos. And the archaeological circumstances of the cenotaph suggest that it may have functioned as the focal point of a proper hero-shrine, or *heroon*. Excavation at the precinct showed that offerings had been made here in the hero-cult manner: among the small jugs dedicated was one featuring, perhaps symbolically, the sketched figures of the Tyrannicides.

The Dexileos memorial has in common with many others the fact that it was erected by parents for a deceased child. The same holds for another well-known relief, the so-called Ilissos *stele* (*ill. 86*), in which the sentiments of the living are made apparent. The dead youth gazes out at us, relaxed in his heroic nudity, while he in turn is regarded by an old man, probably his father, in appropriately pensive mood. A dog miserably sniffs the ground where once his master trod; and perched on a step is the hunched figure of a boy, perhaps a slave or valet, who looks to have wept himself into a state of exhaustion.

Greek tombs were places of worship – places where a fellowship (*koinonia*) was established and maintained between the living and the dead. Many grave-markers show the motif of a handshake (*dexiosis*) between the deceased and the living, symbolic of a bond that does not cease with death. We may readily sympathize with the terrible grief of parents who have had to bury their own children; we should also realize that there was a strong social obligation, and some legal requirement, for children to honour their parents beyond the grave. This called for regular visits to the grave and the enactment of certain rituals. Gravestones would be decorated with wreaths and ribbons. Food would be brought to feed the dead: honey cakes, or perhaps some favourite dish which the deceased was imagined still to relish (there is a record of one tomb receiving plates of fried fish). Sacrifices were also conducted, which would release 'blood for the shades' (warm blood is what even the heroes crave, when in Book Eleven of the *Odyssey* Homer conducts us to Hades); there might then be a meal for the participants, unless the sacrifice was an all-consuming holocaust. On some grave-reliefs such pieties are recorded: we see the extended family group, processing to the grave, with their intended objects of sacrifice (*ill. 87*).

Since the difference between tomb-cult and hero-cult is only one of

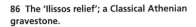

86 The 'Ilissos relief'; a Classical Athenian
gravestone.

87 Fragment of fourth-century BC relief showing
a family taking offerings to sacrifice at a tomb.

88 A sixth-century BC funerary relief from
Chrysapha, Lakonia.

degree, it is fair to speak of ancestral veneration as a sort of heroization, even when heroization is couched in quaintly familiar terms (inscriptions speak of a child being remembered by his nickname of 'Chatterbox', or a wife commended because she loved her husband more than her clothes and her jewelry). A relief from Chrysapha in Lakonia illustrates best this process of posthumous aggrandizement (*ill. 88*). The enthroned figures here are so dominating that have been taken as Pluto and Persephone, the presiding deities of the underworld. But they are more likely to be the hero-ized ancestors of the diminutive figures seen dutifully bringing tribute – a hen and an egg from the boy, a pomegranate and a flower from the girl. A serpent, the standard symbol of the underworld, rises conspicuously behind the throne. It is not clear whether the Dionysiac *kantharos* extended by one of the enthroned giants indicates a state of bliss or is a vessel demanding to be filled by the living. But the message is clear enough. Those who have died may have disappeared and been buried below; but conceptually they are greater than ever, and accordingly not below but above the living. They are members of a society requiring respect. They are heroes; they are 'the powerful dead'.

So we should acknowledge, generally, the pervasive influence in ancient Greece of an 'archaeology of ancestors'. It is clear from innumerable liter-ary sources that the chronological distance established between the living and their deceased heroes tended to be telescoped into a matter of a few generations. In the case of the Tyrannicides, heroization actually hap-pened within a decade; in the case of those who fell at Marathon (as we shall see in Chapter 6), it occurred virtually overnight. Though the events described by Homer may have been broadly associated with what we moderns call 'the Mycenaean period' (roughly 1400–1100 BC), the Greeks of the eighth century BC onwards were not concerned to establish some annalistic chronicle of exactly when the Trojan war took place. The heroic 'fame' and 'glory' (to which the Greek concepts *kleos* and *kudos* more or less correspond) acquired by Homer's heroes were actively beneficial to those who considered themselves inheritors or successors of the world of Agamemnon and Odysseus; and, more importantly, these were heroic attributes to which any athlete or infantryman could aspire. Women were not entirely excluded from this brave old world: a good citizen wife could become a heroine in the mould of the patient Penelope, who busied herself during the protracted absence of Odysseus by dutiful patience at the loom, diligently repelling all suitors. And the sculptural contribution to this heroic and heroizing culture is highly important. It sets the physical tone for the practice of emulation and aspiration. It embodies those standards of appearance and self-presentation which both show the heroes as larger than life and yet at the same time make them attainable.

6

FROM MARATHON TO THE PARTHENON

[The Greeks] knew that the decisive events of history are not momentary coin-cidences, mere collisions – as of two planets in space; they instinctively felt that what made them significant was the moral context in which the accident occurred. Hence a mere happening was not a subject for serious art: it was . . . the business of an artist to immobilize in a symbolic form a whole complex of passions and actions. In plastic art this can only be achieved by resorting to allegory.

Roger Hinks, *Myth and Allegory in Ancient Art* (London 1939), 66

Marathon: 'the run to the rescue'

'The battle of Marathon, as an event in English history, is more important than the battle of Hastings.' Thus claimed John Stuart Mill, writing in the mid-nineteenth century. This statement may sound hyperbolic, if not ridiculous: what is it to the English that the Persians failed to conquer Attica in 490 BC, when Iron Age Britons were camped in their rude hill-forts, utterly ignorant of democracy, mathematics, literature and marble statues?

Mill's implied logic is that if the Greeks had failed at Marathon, the following might have happened: a Persian annexation of Greece and subsequent subordination of the Greek colonies in the West; the end of democracy, and all that is entailed by the phrase 'Greek culture'; capped, perhaps, by the extension of Persian rule to northern Europe – in which case, the Iron Age Britons would have become simply another subject people, bound to deliver tithes to the King of the Medes and the Persians.

Such *what if . . .?* exercises are essentially futile, and this one is more improbable than most: for even if the Persians had been victorious at Marathon, they would still have had the Spartans to face; and in any case, our knowledge of Persian war aims is scanty. But J.S. Mill is not alone in retrospectively raising the stakes at Marathon. This was a battle the Athenians regarded as their finest military achievement and most crucial act of self-preservation. Since so much of Classical sculpture comes from post-Marathon Athens, and we know that the battle increased in its perceived significance throughout the fifth century (and well into the fourth) we shall here have to recall its legendary, florid and grim details, in order to comprehend their durable resonance in Greek art – and Greek historical consciousness.

According to the histories available to us, the Athenians started with the considerable advantage of being underdogs. In Herodotus, the Athenians see themselves as few (*oligoi*), and are perceived as ridiculously few by their enemy. The Persians had a large force, reportedly travelling on a fleet of six hundred ships, and comprising, by one estimate, some ninety thousand men. This force had already passed imperiously through the Cyclades, and destroyed the state of Eretria. It was led by Datis, a Mede, and Artaphernes, a Persian royal, on behalf of King Darius; and, with an eye to the seizure of Athens, it carried a quisling: Hippias, the exiled Peisistratid, who was counting on his residual Athenian supporters to send a signal for the advance on Athens, where presumably, despite his age (he was about eighty, and according to Herodotus lost one of his teeth immediately on landing in Attica) he would be installed as a Persian satrap or client-king. In readiness for that signal, the Persians disembarked in the bay of Marathon, only a short journey across from Eretria, and about 26 miles (42 km) northeast of Athens.

When Eretria fell, Athens communicated the news to Sparta by a celebrated runner, Philippides, with a plea for assistance. The Spartans, however, had a major, annual religious festival in progress and, obedient to its ritual demands, they delayed their mobilization. The Athenians, on the other hand, decided to move quickly towards Marathon, rather than barricade themselves in the city and await the Persian advance. They marched up to the bay and were joined by a detachment from Boeotian Plataea, making a total force of perhaps ten thousand men. Ten Athenian *strategoi* led the expedition, along with an official, the *polemarch*, aptly named Kallimachos ('Mr Fights-Well'). Athens would eventually celebrate this rapid deployment within a festival of Artemis, as the *Boedromion*: 'the dash to battle', or 'run to the rescue'. It was sufficiently swift to contain the Persian force within the plain of Marathon bay. For what happened next, extracts from Herodotus will explain:

> Among the Athenian commanders opinion was divided: some were against risking a battle, on the ground that the Athenian force was too small to stand a chance of success; others – and amongst them Miltiades – urged it. It seemed for a time as if the more faint-hearted policy would be adopted – and so it would have been but for the action of Miltiades. In addition to the ten commanders, there was another person entitled to vote, namely the *polemarch* ['War Minister' in the Athenian constitution] . . . Kallimachos of Aphidne. To

Kallimachos, therefore, Miltiades turned. 'It is now in your hands, Kallimachos,' he said, 'either to enslave Athens, or to make her free and leave behind you for all future generations a memory more glorious than ever Harmodius and Aristogeiton left. Never in the course of our long history have we Athenians been in such peril as now. If we submit to the Persian invader, Hippias will be restored to power in Athens – and there is little doubt what misery must then ensue; but if we fight and win, then this city of ours may well grow to pre-eminence amongst all the cities of Greece. . .'

(Herodotus VI. 109ff., trans. de Selincourt)

So Miltiades, about whom we shall have more to say presently, held sway. Herodotus points out, perhaps with one eye on Miltiades' troubled political career both before and after Marathon, that there was a daily rota among the ten generals as to who should have supreme command, and emphasizes that Miltiades waited dutifully until his turn before launching the attack. That democratic piety recorded, Herodotus is not very enlightening about how the battle itself was conducted, beyond saying that the fighting lasted 'a long time' (though not more than a day). The Persians were apparently at first mystified by the Greek tactics – an infantry charge, at the double, with no archers or cavalry involved – and then alarmed at how soon they were hemmed in on the Marathon plain, with no room to deploy their speciality troops, the mounted archers. Herodotus, who uses the verb *boethein* (to trot, to hasten) several times in his account of Marathon, implies that Miltiades was successful by virtue of quick decisions and rapid execution of orders: he had what would much later be known as 'the Nelson touch' – the gift of gambling successfully on the power of surprise.

For the Greeks, armed with jabbing spears and swords, fighting the Persians at close quarters was, as Herodotus notes, a big psychological victory: their collective phobia of strangely dressed, non-phalanx fighting *barbaroi* was overcome. And it seems as though it was eventually a rout. Part of the Marathon plain was a swamp, and many Persians were cut down as they were driven towards it. There was also, in fine Homeric fashion, a battle at the ships along the shore, as the Persians sought a seaborne retreat. The casualty figures recorded by Herodotus, in a sense, relieve him of the onus of a detailed description of the day's fighting. The Persian dead amounted to 6400; the Athenian dead, a mere 192.

The figures for the Plataeans are not known, nor is it recorded how many slaves died on the Greek side. But anyone faced with those statistics alone is bound to be impressed, amazed, or downright sceptical about what the Athenians achieved at Marathon. Military historians face a similar disparity for the battle of Agincourt, in France, in 1415, where something like 25 English deaths are reckoned, compared with 5000 French, and conclude that in extraordinary tactical situations, such victories (or disasters) can happen.

We are told that Kallimachos, the *polemarch*, had ordered that for every Persian slain, a kid goat was to be sacrificed to Artemis. If his instructions were carried out (Kallimachos was one of the fallen), a precise count of Persian bodies must have taken place. A later source – Xenophon – tells us that since 6400 kid goats were not then available, a custom had grown up of annually sacrificing 500 goats instead on every 'Marathon Day' – the sixth day of the *Boedromion* festival. And as we shall see, the name of every Athenian who died was inscribed on their collective battlefield grave. So although we may not go as far as one historian (Nicholas Hammond) in claiming that 'the salient facts in Herodotus' narrative are completely unimpeachable', we may have to accept that the basis of the Marathon paradigm (for such it would become, as the fifth century progressed) was indeed a remarkable victory.

The ingredients for a mythical enhancement of the victory were there from the start. The Greek forces, prior to engaging the Persians, camped by an ancient shrine of Herakles, whom, according to their own claim, the Marathonians were the first in Attica to worship. One practical reason for the Athenians' hurry to meet the Persians may have been to prevent the Persians spoiling their September crops. Not surprisingly, then, we learn that a previously unheard-of hero, called Echetlaeus ('of the ploughshare'), was witnessed weighing into the thick of the battle, cutting a swathe through the Persians with his plough. Others claimed visions of Theseus, founder of Attica and the Athenian community, fighting on the Greek side. Marathon was a highly suggestive place, where remains from the Bronze Age were still visible. When Pausanias visited it in the second century AD, he records how ghostly he found it. 'Every night', he wrote, 'you can hear the noise of horses whinnying, and the clash of fighting'; and the locals, he noted, still worship the Greek dead, 'deeming them heroes' (*heroas onomazontes*: I. 32.4).

If Marathon was ripe for transformation into myth-history so, too, was it generously loaded with potential ideological and political significance. The return of Hippias the tyrant, in league with would-be barbarian despots, made Marathon a painfully close reminder of democracy's youth in Athens. Miltiades, in the speech Herodotus attributes to him (or retrospectively writes for him), explicitly both likens the prospect of the battle to the anti-tyrannical action of Harmodius and Aristogeiton, and links the survival of Athenian freedom, democratic *eleutheria*, to a successful engagement. Marathon was the first serious test of the young democracy, and Herodotus makes Miltiades thoroughly aware that a retreat from the fight would bring not only Persian rule over Athens, but an internally divided, politically distraught Athens at that.

'For their singular and extraordinary valour, those slain at Marathon were interred on the spot.' Thucydides (II. 34.5) alerts us to a highly unusual deposition of the 192 Athenian dead. Normally, they would have been brought back and given 'state honours' with a procession, and burial in the Demosion Sema suburb of Athens. Instead, it appears that a tumulus was raised over their bodies, which were cremated; the ashes were quenched with libations poured from old-fashioned flasks (black-figured *lekythoi*, to be precise, of which some thirty have been recovered from the site), and trenches were provided around the tumulus for offerings and homage. Inscribed pillars, or *stelai*, were also erected by the mound, declaring the identity of the dead according to their Athenian tribes.

Those archaeologically unfamiliar with Athenian burials of this period may see nothing odd in this manner of burial. In fact, it is very unusual: the exceptional choice of burying war dead at the site of battle is trumped by burying them, effectively, according to the protocols normally reserved, in the Greek imagination, for epic heroes. More than mildly archaizing, the burial of the Marathon dead was performed in a manner that immediately promoted them to heroic status: they were sent off as if they were a Patroklos or a Hector.

When Pausanias visited Marathon, he recorded four visible monuments. There was, principally, the grave raised on the plain for the Athenian dead; then another mound for the casualties among the Plataeans and slaves; a private memorial to Miltiades; and a simple trophy of white marble. As we have seen, Pausanias was fully aware of the extent of commemoration enjoyed by the heroes of Marathon some seven hundred years after their action, and it is thanks to Pausanias alone that we learn about the plough-hero Echetlaeus, who sounds very like a mythical metaphor for the battle as a struggle to save the very soil of Attica from barbarians. At Marathon, in the second century AD, the years, indeed the centuries, had not condemned the dead of the original battle. Far from it. But the point about the exceptional nature of the burial of those who fell at Marathon is that it was perceived as an extraordinary action as soon as it was over. And that perception of Marathon as an exceptional example of Greek heroism was to haunt or inspire Athenian artists throughout the fifth century.

Marathon magnified

> The bravery of these men will seem forever an imperishable glory
> To whomsoever the gods allot tough struggles for the common good:
> For these, on foot and on the swift-sailing ships,
> Rescued all Greece from the prospect of slavery.

So runs one of the two epigrams once etched on the base of a monument to Marathon set up in the Athenian Agora. This monument may have been created immediately after the victory, in which case its reference to fighting 'on the swift-sailing ships' may specifically allude to the second stage of the battle, when the Greeks routed the Persians on board their own ships; or it may belong to a later memorial, erected some time after the Persian sack of Athens in 480 BC – in which case the victory at Marathon has absorbed the subsequent naval defeat of the Persians at Salamis. If that is the case, it is typical of the civic spell cast by Marathon: as a piece of paradigmatic history, Marathon had the power both to absorb and to obliterate subsequent events. And in that epigram, we have one of the key commonplaces about the battle: that it saved Greece from enslavement (literally, 'slavery's day': *doulion hemar*).

The second epigram on the same monument reads:

> These men had hearts of adamant inside them, when they set up
> Their line of battle by the gates, opposing a myriad host;
> They thwarted the army of Persians, who had sought
> By force to waste their well-known city by the sea.

Whether the Persians in 490 BC had actually wanted to waste (literally 'burn down') the city of Athens is hardly clear from the Herodotean narrative, where it is implied that the aim was the restoration of a pro-Persian or 'Medizing' Peisistratid tyranny. The monument to which these epigrams pertained was very probably damaged in 480 BC when the Persians under Xerxes returned and occupied Athens; its replacement after this event gives the epigrams extra retrospective piquancy, and in fact we cannot be sure whether both epigrams were inscribed on the original monument. But what archaeologists, historians and art historians must come to terms with is the patent magnification of Marathon, at least in Athens, at the expense of all subsequent Greek victories over the Persians. Students of the intermittent clashes between Greece and Persia during the fifth century will discover what appear to be more telling engagements than Marathon: the naval battle off Salamis in 480 BC, when Themistokles captained a Greek force to victory over a combined Persian-Phoenician fleet; the combined Greek action at Plataea in 479 BC, which was reckoned to have entailed very high casualty figures among the Persians; the Athenian-led pursuit of the Persians to their Asian garrisons, such as Eion, guarding the River Strymon in Thrace, where Kimon, the son of Miltiades, prevailed, *c.* 476 BC; and Kimon's further success at the mouth of the Pamphylian River Eurymedon *c.* 467 BC. These were, it seems, the encounters which repelled the Persians from Europe, if Europe is considered as the Greeks themselves conceived it, that is the Greek mainland and the landmass lying west of Greece. So why did Marathon so dominate the commemorative record of the Persian wars?

It may be that particular political circumstances in Athens connived to elevate Marathon. Some historians believe that Salamis, being a naval victory, had less *kudos* attached to it than an infantry action; that sailors did not constitute the 'senior service' in Athens, and that the commander at Salamis, Themistokles, became a vassal of the Persians, and was accordingly maligned by his political opponents – including Kimon. Yet Kimon himself would become conspicuous for his skill as an admiral, and an Athenian affection for Salamis might easily be attested not only from its account in Herodotus, but also in the patriotic dramatization the battle received from one of its combatants, the poet Aeschylus (his *Persae* was produced in 472 BC, with a young Perikles serving as the play's chorus-leader).

Other scholars have drawn upon the Athenian orators to show that Marathon, unlike the battle of Plataea, was a predominantly Athenian triumph. Indeed, Athenian orators of the fourth century BC would present Marathon as an exclusively Athenian victory. As Nicole Loraux argues, it thus became a peculiarly simple paradigm of old-fashioned Athenian virtue, the testament of sound education (*archaia paideia*) – and a reach-me-down touchstone for any hack speechmaker. 'A compulsory topos of national history, Marathon provides the orator in search of grandiloquence with a purple passage and inexhaustible lessons in virtue for generations of young Athenians.' The Athenian rhetorical catch-phrase, *oligoi pros pollous*, though it means 'few against many' rather than 'few on behalf of many', can easily be likened to Churchill's epitome of the Battle of Britain – 'Never in the field of human conduct was so much owed by so many to so few'. Marathon, for many generations of Athenians, would go down the millennia (to extend Churchillian echoes) as the city's 'finest hour'.

Proof of the extent of this sentiment in the fifth century itself comes from a number of literary sources, but perhaps none more telling than Aristophanes, whose half-satirical, half-sincere references to the glorification of Marathon are enough to indicate its excess. He also alerts us to the existence of *hoi Marathonomachai* – 'Old Contemptibles' of the battle itself, still allegedly doddering around in the 420s BC, and apparently prone to remind young bloods of what bliss it was to have fought at the dawn of the Athenian empire. Such veterans, argues Hammond, would also have been present around 446 BC when Herodotus is supposed to have delivered his *Histories* to an Athenian audience. Hammond's logic, that the presence of Marathon veterans at the Herodotean recitation means that the Herodotean account of the battle must be 'unimpeachable', is highly arguable, but need not concern us here. What we can establish instead is a sequence of monuments commemorating Marathon that will powerfully complement this literary record – and illuminate, eventually, the iconography of the Parthenon itself.

What follows is not a definitive account – not everyone is convinced of what Pausanias records about Marathonian memorials, and some of the monuments he notes as Marathon-inspired, for example the Temple of Artemis Eukleia at Athens (I. 14.5), have simply not been traced. But there is nevertheless a substantial archaeological witness to Marathon's legacy.

The Athenian Treasury at Delphi. It is a measure of the confidence that some Classical archaeologists have in their own dating systems that they are prepared to challenge Pausanias when he states (X. 11.5) that the Athenian Treasury at Delphi was put up with the spoils seized after Marathon. In purely stylistic terms, the architecture and sculptural decoration of this bijou building are plausibly pre-490 BC, though by hardly more than a decade. Those reluctant to accept Pausanias hypothesize that he gained his idea of a Marathonian memorial from an inscription which runs along a base below the south-facing wall of the Treasury, and which can be reconstructed as: *Athenaioi toi Apolloni apo Medon akrothinia tes Marathoni maches*: 'The Athenians [dedicate] to Apollo spoils from the Medes of the battle at Marathon'. This, they say, was a subsequent dedication, and does not relate to the entire Treasury. And yet Pausanias is unequivocal about his attribution: moreover, rather than quoting the inscription, he mentions the Median general at Marathon, Datis, as if he fully understood the historical implications of this commemorative building.

A solution to the dating difficulties may be to regard the Athenian Treasury as a turn of the century project which was 'usurped' by Marathon: that is to say, the victory became a retrospective *raison d'être* for the Treasury, very soon after its erection. If so, the choice of subjects for the metopal decoration of the Treasury was uncannily apt. On the north side were select deeds of Herakles – and it should be remembered that the Athenians and their Plataean allies gathered at the shrine of Herakles at Marathon before the engagement (and that later mythology alleged the participation of Herakles himself in the battle). On the east side was a scene of Greeks versus Amazons; Amazons who had, mythically, invaded and been repulsed from Attica like the Persians and also dressed like them (trouser-suits), and fought like them (bows and arrows, on horseback), and came from the Orient too. On the south side – which was the most conspicuous, since it faced the Sacred Way, and would have been noticed by all pilgrims toiling up to the main Temple of Apollo – were deeds of Theseus, including his forays against the Amazons, and one of his exploits in Attica: wrestling with the monstrous bull of Marathon (*ill. 89*). If these metopes were carved before 490 BC, they were done with great iconographic foresight. It was under these scenes of Theseus – also believed to have come to the aid of the Greeks at Marathon – that the Persian spoils (*akrothinia*) would be displayed.

This makes sense as a symbolic ensemble. It has to be pointed out, however, that the inscribed base was much altered in antiquity, and some have wondered whether this was not in fact the base of the monument that Pausanias saw just inside the entrance to Delphi, with statues of Apollo, Athena, Miltiades and others upon it, which in a subsequent re-ordering of the sanctuary was shifted up to the Athenian Treasury. We shall address that monument shortly (below), but, whatever the truth of the matter, we are still left with the fact that Pausanias thought the Treasury a Marathonian monument.

Delphi was certainly an effective site for broadcasting triumph to other Greek states. The sanctuary could almost be termed a gigantic pan-Hellenic war memorial. At another Athenian contribution to the sanctuary, the Athenian Stoa, pride of place went to the display of lengths of cable cut from the pontoon bridge Xerxes built across the Hellespont. Even if it was not originally conceived as such, it was entirely appropriate that the Athenian Treasury should have been presented at Delphi as a thank-offering for the Marathon victory.

The Stoa Poikile. Erected in the northwest corner of the Athenian Agora, the Stoa Poikile ('Painted Colonnade') was, for hundreds of years, one of the great rendezvous-points of Athens. Frequented not only by philosophers (hence 'Stoics'), its public location heightened the importance and influence of the paintings commissioned to decorate its walls. Though we

89 Theseus and the Marathonian Bull on an early fifth-century BC metope from the Athenian Treasury at Delphi.

cannot be sure what they looked like, nor even who painted them, their subjects – described by Pausanias and others – are crucial knowledge for anyone seeking to understand the iconography of Classical art. One mural depicted a battle between Spartans and Athenians at a Peloponnesian site called Oenoe, a battle which remains otherwise undocumented, though commemorative inscriptions at Delphi refer to it. Another mural, by the painter Mikon, depicted a battle between Greeks and Amazons, perhaps placing this mythological encounter at Marathon. A third mural, by Polygnotus, depicted the Greek seizure of Troy; and the fourth, perhaps a joint enterprise between several painters, showed Marathon.

The Marathon painting was undoubtedly considered the most important of this quartet. Pausanias says that it portrayed the main engagement of the Athenian–Plataean troops with the enemy, the flight of the Persians into marshy ground, and further action at the Persian ships. In addition to a portrait of Miltiades, other figures within the scene were recognizable: one Kynegeiros, who had his hand lopped off as he grabbed a Persian prow; Kallimachos, the *polemarch*, who, though pierced by multiple arrows, refused to collapse; an Athenian struck blind in the heat of the action; a loyal dog who charged into battle with his master. The plough-hero Echetlaeus, mentioned elsewhere by Pausanias, was apparently depicted; also Theseus, 'seeming to rise out of the earth' – a timely epiphany or *anodos* by Attica's proprietary hero (cf. Plutarch, *Life of Theseus*, 35).

The Stoa Poikile may have been put up by Kimon's brother-in-law, Peisianax, and Kimonian touches are manifest: distinction for his father, Miltiades, and assistance from Theseus, whose bones Kimon claimed to have found on the island of Skyros in the course of one of his eastward campaigns. But more importantly, we see (as the Classical Athenians saw) where Marathon stood as an event: on a par with the mythical struggles against Amazons and Trojans, and as a battle which not only defined Greeks against barbarians, but also Athenians against Spartans – hence perhaps the inclusion of the battle of Oenoe in this programme of paintings. Even if we do not know much about it, Oenoe at least reinforces the conspicuous failure of the Spartans to join the action at Marathon. Some scholars, worried by our paucity of information about the battle of Oenoe, suggest that Pausanias got it wrong, and the painting showed Athenian and Plataean forces meeting up at another Oenoe, very close to Marathon. But it seems unlikely that Pausanias should have seriously misinterpreted such a well-known piece of Athenian propaganda (and even more unlikely that the role of the Plataeans should have been made so conspicuous at Athens).

Athena Promachos. Pausanias (I. 28.2) records that this large bronze statue was made by Pheidias, funded by booty collected from the Persians at

Marathon. The fragmentary public accounts that survive for the statue do not clarify whether this involved melting down captured Persian weapons and armour and turning them into the statue, but it seems likely that it occupied a very central position on the Akropolis, perhaps close to where other Persian spoils (*aristeia*, 'best things', as they were proudly called) were displayed. The basic image is known from coins – Athena helmeted, with spear and shield; and the accounts imply exterior ornamentation in silver. 'Promachos' – literally 'the frontline fighter' – is a post-Classical designation: even after the creation of the colossal Athena Parthenos, Athenians seem usually to have referred to the Promachos as 'the big one' (*ten megalen*). It is estimated to have stood about 9 m (30 ft) high: sailors approaching Athens from Cape Sounion, claims Pausanias, could glimpse the shining helmet crest and the tip of Athena's spear. In time, evidently, and despite the monumentalization all around (the massive Periklean gateways, or Propylaea, must have diminished the general visibility of the statue), Athena Promachos became a landmark of good luck or *tyche*.

If the Promachos was indeed *techne Pheidiou* as Pausanias relates, then it was probably not erected until some twenty or thirty years after Marathon. The accounts relating to the statue, although fragmentary, record that it occupied at least eight years of work, at a public cost of 500,000 drachmas, and epigraphers put the date of the statue at around 465–455 BC. Was much booty seized at Marathon – and more importantly, did it survive the Persian occupation of Athens? That we cannot tell. Historical accounts of the battle of Plataea in 479 BC say that Greek forces there gathered large quantities of precious vessels and ceremonial weapons, some of which (for example the golden dagger of the Persian general Mardonius) were eventually displayed within the Parthenon. But perhaps it is misguided to question whether the Promachos was made from spoils taken at Marathon or spoils taken at Plataea. The important point to register is that this talismanic statue of Athena was considered as a thank-offering for Marathon: Marathon, in the Athenian imagination, overshadowed Plataea.

A lesser image of the goddess, carved around 470 BC, may be mentioned here (*ill. 90*). Recent scholarship prefers not to commit the epithet 'Mourning' to this relief of a barefoot Athena, leaning gravely on her spear by some *stele* or marker-stone (*horos*), but the old interpretation, that Athena is here grieving for Athenian casualties, makes perfectly good sense. The Marathonian dead were listed on just such *stelai*.

The trophy at Marathon. There is no certitude as to the whereabouts or nature of the monument in honour of Miltiades which Pausanias says he saw at Marathon; but of the 'white marble trophy' mentioned by him there are traces built into a medieval tower on the site. This seems to have been

90 'Mourning Athena'; a relief of c. 470 BC.

a single, large column, about 10 m (33 ft) high, capped by an Ionic capital and a statue (probably a Nike figure) with some emblematic trophy. It is thought that it originally stood near the marshy area at Marathon, where the Persians suffered their heaviest losses. Dating the column is a problem: Vanderpool's estimate is the mid-fifth century BC.

The Marathon monument at Delphi. From Pausanias' description of this monument, we learn that Miltiades was truly heroized as the inspirational *strategos* of Marathon: he stood next to Apollo and Athena, in an ensemble that comprised thirteen figures. Of the remaining ten, seven of those named match the Eponymous Heroes of Attica, and perhaps reflect the tribal order of battle at Marathon: Erechtheus, Kekrops, Pandion, Leos, Antiochos, Aigeus and Akamas. Pausanias then lists three further names: Kodros, Theseus and Philaios (or Neleus, in some manuscripts). The usual representatives of the tribes Hippothontis, Aiantis and Oineis seem to be missing. In that respect, these three intruders are perplexing. Herodotus

91 Statue B of the Riace Bronzes, found in the sea off southern Italy; c. 450 BC.

(VI. 35) says that Miltiades was descended from one Philaios, so perhaps one Eponymous Hero has been dislodged on that account. It has been surmised that Ajax's omission may be part of Marathon's magnification at the expense of Salamis. Ajax was the cult hero of Salamis, and in the Herodotean account of the battle of Salamis was invoked by the Greeks before their successful action. Such would also be a reason for inserting Theseus, who magically appeared at Marathon. About Kodros, a legendary early king of Athens, we can say little with respect to Marathon, though mythology involves him with the Delphic Oracle. But since we know that the monument was tampered with by Hellenistic monarchs, and Pausanias is not always accurate in his transcriptions of names and identities, it is probably foolish to get obsessed by precisely who stood in the group, and why. What is most conspicuous is the inclusion of Miltiades.

92 Detail of Riace Statue B, which once wore a tipped-back helmet.

If, as is generally accepted, the Marathon monument was dedicated from Athenian public funds under the sponsorship of Kimon around 450 BC (that is, between Kimon's return from ostracism and his fatal expedition to Cyprus), it is perhaps not surprising to find Miltiades so elevated at Delphi (and another reason for Theseus muscling in on the Eponymous Heroes). Overweening of the Kimonids it may have been, but the lapse of time between the death of Miltiades and this monument, the precedent of his individual heroization in the Stoa Poikile, and perhaps the distance of Delphi from Athens, would have diminished the chances of denunciation by other Athenian factions. And the inclusion of a heroized *strategos* at this monument has opened the way for a persuasive argument that the Riace Bronzes are two survivors of the group of thirteen figures that Pausanias saw at Delphi.

That the group should have suffered wholesale or piecemeal theft by Roman collectors is perfectly plausible; nor is there anything implausible about the eventual recovery of the bronzes from south Italian waters in 1972, though one theory would prefer them to be original Greek work from Sicily, perhaps representing a pair of colonial founding fathers (*oikistai*) from some city such as Gela or Akragas. But what favours the Delphi connection is the statue we know simply as 'Statue B' (*ills 91* and 92), who patently once wore a helmet, tipped back in the style that posthumous portraits of Athenian generals, such as the well-known bust of Perikles (*ill. 93*), usually adopt. Most scholars believe that the Riace figures are from an ensemble of similar bronzes – that is, a 'set' of statues relating, with minor variations, to a single type or model – and are stylistically datable to the mid-fifth century BC. The options for an attested provenance, then, are limited to three. The first is the group of Greek ('Achaean') heroes that stood by the Temple of Zeus at Olympia, waiting to see who would fight against Hector: Pausanias (V. 25.8) says that ten figures comprised the group. Riace 'Statue A' might well accord with the imagined iconography

93 Bust of Perikles: a copy, from Hadrian's Villa at Tivoli, of an original of perhaps 425 BC.

of these figures, as an Agamemnon or an Odysseus; it is harder to see why any of the Homeric heroes should have been portrayed like an Athenian general. The second is the line of the Eponymous Heroes erected in the Athenian Agora; but from what we understand of their iconography, these were not bellicose figures and were more likely to have been draped and contemplative. The third option is the Marathon monument at Delphi. And here, obviously, is a place for 'Statue B': bearded, as later images of Miltiades were – and, more convincingly, directly evoking his role at Marathon with the tipped-back helmet. (It would have been neat to have found the actual helmet of Miltiades at Delphi, but this seems to have survived as a trophy from Olympia.)

The case for placing the Riace Bronzes at Delphi cannot be fully proved, though it remains the most attractive provenance available. Whether or not the bronzes belong, however, is not essential to the present argument. All that needs to be registered here is that the Athenians, forty years on from Marathon, chose to commemorate the battle very conspicuously at Delphi (no pilgrim to Delphi could miss the group, immediately on the left-hand side of the main entrance to the sanctuary); and, if only thanks to Kimon's shrewd filial piety, they were prepared to acknowledge Miltiades, the prime mover of Marathon, as one of the immortals. The nostalgic heroization of Miltiades would not be without parallel elsewhere in Greece: in the 440s BC the Spartans would stage fresh funeral rites for their hero-general Leonidas, who in 480 BC had staged the suicidal gallantry of holding back the Persians at Thermopylae.

Readers who accept this much will shortly be required to accept even more: the hypothesis that the Parthenon frieze, conceived a decade after the Delphi monument, and under the political sponsorship of Perikles, enemy of Kimon, also contained an element of Marathon commemoration. But before we approach that proposal, let us take stock of the wider circumstantial politics of Athens and Persia in the mid-fifth century BC.

Kimon's campaigns against the Persians were based on an alliance which we know as the Delian League. The facts of its establishment are not clear: it is called 'Delian' because the island sanctuary of Delos was originally chosen as the treasury for the funds pooled by all those Greek city-states (mostly in Ionia) who needed to protect themselves against Persian aggression. Later (probably in 454 BC) the funds were transferred to Athens: a recognition that effectively the allies relied upon the largely Athenian navy for their protection. Tribute continued to be collected by Athens, in fact, even after peace had been negotiated with the Persians. This is the agreement known as the 'Peace of Kallias', apparently arranged in 448 BC, not long after Kimon's death in 450 BC, during his campaign to 'liberate' Cyprus from the Persians.

Even in antiquity the terms of the treaty accredited to Kallias (brother-in-law of Kimon) were challenged, but that need not concern us. Back in Athens, Perikles was ascendant, and he almost immediately began that massive programme of public spending which we call the Parthenon (though it includes the monumental entrance to the Akropolis, the Propylaea, and elides into other temples: the Erechtheum, and the Nike Bastion). Even today we can still capture something of the spectacular nature of this project (*ill. 94*). It may be that Kimon himself had started a 'hundred-footer' (*Hekatompedon*) temple on the Akropolis: Rhys Carpenter once argued optimistically that this was why the metopes of the Parthenon look, in stylistic terms, out of kilter with the rest of the sculptural project – because they were meant for a 'Kimonian' Parthenon, whose architect was dismissed when Perikles replaced Kimon. The initiative, however, may have been entirely Periklean; and the sources suggest that it depended very much on the use or abuse of Delian League funds, which might be deemed 'available' for non-military use once peace had been negotiated with the Persians. But the settlement of peace did not betoken an end to the definition of the Persians as, generically, 'the enemy'. Triumphalism was bound to permeate public works, and it is entirely credible that one of the less-discussed Periklean buildings, the Odeion – a huge, multi-pillared auditorium erected on the south slope of the Akropolis – featured a conical roof based on the shape of Xerxes' tent (as Pausanias reports: I. 20.5), and that masts and spars of Persian ships captured at Salamis were incorporated into the roof structures.

94 General view of the Athenian Akropolis, from the northwest.

The cynical will reckon the Periklean building programme to have been a political ploy: the classic means of gaining public support, and to provide both high levels of employment and the morale-boost of brave new monuments (as Thucydides noted in the preamble to his account of the Peloponnesian War, the Periklean monumentality of Athens made the city seem far more powerful than it actually was). But two factors are worth considering in any discussion of the ideology of the Parthenon. The first is admittedly tenuous, depending again on a mistrusted historical record. This, if we are to believe it, stated that before the battle of Plataea in 479 BC the Greeks made a joint declaration (the 'Oath of Plataea') whereby they promised to fight together, punish any Greek city that took the Persian side, and – this is the important clause – 'not to rebuild any of the temples that have been burnt and destroyed by the barbarians, but let them be left as a memorial to those who come after of the sacrilege of the barbarians' (Lycurgus, *Against Leocrates*, 81).

The logic of this is comparable to the deliberate non-renovation of parts of Coventry cathedral in England, left in a bombed-out state as a memorial of World War II. While we may suspect the historical existence of the Oath of Plataea, it is an archaeological fact that on the Athenian Akropolis, at least, very little development took place in the two decades after the Persian occupations and desecrations of the sanctuary. A marble temple whose construction had been started shortly after Marathon, then burned by the Persians while in mid-construction, may have been left as a series of charred half-columns. What statuary the Persians wrecked was piously interred. Single dedications, such as the Athena Promachos, were allowed but no co-ordinated attempt to replace the ruined Archaic temples was made until 447 BC. A motive of belated reparation is thus understandable, and an obvious focus for the sentiment of revenge for Persian crimes was, of course, the never-forgotten triumph of Marathon.

The second factor concerns ethnic rivalry and self-definition. The monumentalization of the Akropolis did not happen in a worldwide vacuum. Even the Spartans, notoriously reluctant to spend money on beautifying their city, erected a colonnade to commemorate their part in repelling the Persians. But more importantly, the Persians themselves – traditionally a nomadic people, without a significant history of monumental settlements – were creating their own centres of empire, most notably a grand complex at Persepolis (near Shiraz, in modern Iran). Persepolis lies not far from Pasargadae, the family home and burial place of what we know as the Achaemenid dynasty. And it is Darius I, whose reign (522–486 BC) included Marathon, who should be credited with the initial development of this ceremonial centre at Persepolis. Work on the complex continued more intensively under Xerxes (486–465 BC), and his son Artaxerxes (465–424 BC): it was a vast project, laid out on a terraced eminence, whose

95 The Persian king slaying a lion: fifth-century BC relief on a door-jamb at Persepolis (*in situ*).

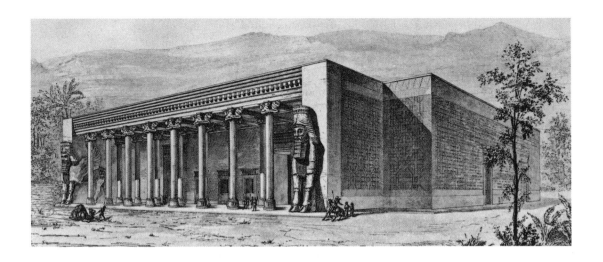

monumentality survived its sack by Alexander in 330 BC, and later raids by European archaeologists.

According to a surviving decree of Darius from Susa, and confirmed by masons' marks at Pasargadae, Greeks were involved in the various sixth- and fifth-century BC building projects of the Persians. More specifically, they were Ionians. At Persepolis, they were conscripted or enslaved in gangs to assist in not only the sculptural decoration, but also the fortification and architecture of the site. It is claimed that there are stylistic traces of Greek workmanship, though the evidence of this will probably be lost on most observers, whose main impression is of an iconography, and a schematism to that iconography, entirely Oriental. When one realizes that a serious analysis of the two thousand or so figures carved at Persepolis has been conducted on mathematical grounds, the extent to which Persian and Greek concepts of decoration diverged seems enormous. The reaction of one Western viewer to this repetitious, unengaging imagery (already quoted in Chapter 2 of this book: 'all the same, and the same again, and yet again') might discourage any notion that the Parthenon was launched as a rival enterprise to Persepolis. And yet that notion deserves to be taken very seriously: as A. W. Lawrence noted, it is 'conceivable that some particular sculptor may have carved figures in the friezes of both Persepolis and the Parthenon'.

Putting aside the issue of Greek craftsmen at Persepolis, we may imagine the reactions to this complex of a visiting Athenian delegation at about the time of the Peace of Kallias. Perhaps, like a Spartan embassy to Susa recorded by Herodotus (VII. 136), they may have refused to obey the protocols of *proskynesis* – abasing themselves at the feet of the king. But all around they would have seen symbols of the king's irresistible power. Quite

96 Reconstruction of the Apadana, the great audience chamber at Persepolis.

apart from the legions of archers at his disposal, he himself was a slayer of lions and gryphons (*ill. 95*). The vast throne upon which he sat was symbolically supported by his subject nations; and once inside the Apadana, Xerxes' great reception hall (*ill. 96*), visitors were intimidated by a continuous frieze which showed ('again and again') client kingdoms bringing tribute to this very place. Figures move almost invariably in a linear direction; intriguingly, the rare occasions when they are shown turning round to interact with each other are judged to be touches by Greek sculptors at Persepolis.

The cognitive associations created at Persepolis between Oriental despotism, symbols and sculptural style can hardly have been wasted on Athenians who grew up with their own associations of figurative naturalism, democracy and Hellenic identity. It has been argued that the Parthenon frieze attempts in several respects of both style and design to mirror or challenge the reliefs at Persepolis, in particular those of the Apadana. And yet more difference than similitude is apparent. Though the Parthenon frieze is 'Orientalizing' in terms of its unrelieved processional solemnity, its designer has tried his utmost to display all the self-defining elements of the Greek Revolution: the Polykleitan nude or semi-nude musculatures, the figures turning to front, side and back with equal facility, the 'minor incidents' (restless horses, chatting deities) of the depicted ceremony – all these proclaim to the (imaginary) visitor from Persia, and to the actual visitors from allied Greek cities: this is *our* world view.

What better focus of commemoration for such a statement than the battle of Marathon?

Myth-history and the Parthenon

The Parthenon was a work of art. That statement is dragged reluctantly from an author who largely denies the production of art for art's sake in ancient Greece, but it is difficult for anyone to describe the Parthenon purely in terms of its cult functions, and hence tempting to treat its decoration as functionally redundant. Where was the altar of this temple? What festivals were celebrated here? Why did another temple, the Erechtheum, have to be built to house *the* cult statue of the Akropolis – the small olden image of Athena Polias – and was the luxurious assemblage of the Athena Parthenos no more than a treasury dressed up as a goddess? Can the Parthenon be termed 'a temple' at all?

The columns of the Parthenon were specially designed to accommodate a viewer from a certain distance: by a process known as *entasis*, the columns were carved wider in the centre so that they would not look (according to a natural optical distortion) concave. In fact, the architects

of the Parthenon built in a host of 'refinements' to make the temple appear beautifully symmetrical. But otherwise the Parthenon was a work of art not specially considerate of those wanting to see it: the frieze particularly so. On the exterior wall of the inner temple chamber, boxed in and almost 12 m (40 ft) above the floor (*ill. 97*), no one could comfortably secure a proper view of even sections of it, let alone the whole (as is now deceptively easy, given the eye-level, all-round display of the frieze at the British Museum). 'Artistic *hubris*' is how one response to this inaccessibility goes; according to another, we should desist from seeking coherent scholarly accounts of the meaning of the frieze, if its iconography were based on getting no more than lofty glimpses.

Works of art, however, are not necessarily bound to care whether anyone sees them or not: as Paul Veyne has pointed out, the logic of monuments such as Trajan's Column may be precisely based on their 'visual non-visibility'. Just as the sculptors of the figures on the Parthenon pediments took care to finish those rear parts of their statues that no ground-based viewer would ever be able to see, so the creators of the frieze worked according to the specifications of the 'ideal spectator' who would espouse the same perspective, and comprehend the artistic intentions.

No ancient writer has told us what iconographic programme informed the Parthenon's decoration. With regard to the metopes, the first of the Parthenon sculptures to be executed (in the mid-440s BC), this is not perhaps a great problem. They may be read as plainly invested with a mythical symbolism that exalted Greek or Athenian order over those who would challenge it. On the east side there were excerpts from an old favourite, the Gods versus the Giants. The Giants courted their own primordial destruction by a challenge of extreme self-esteem or *hubris* –

97 A cavalcade on the Parthenon frieze, west side, slabs VIII–XVI, *in situ*. The frieze is almost 12 m (40 ft) above the ground and so would have been scarcely visible to visitors to the temple.

the same sort of *hubris* that Xerxes would manifest when he launched his invasion via the Hellespont, threatening the very elements of the earth (the story of Xerxes' fury when a storm broke up his bridge, and how he had his minions whip the waves in vain revenge, was archetypal of the Greek characterization of their Oriental enemy). On the west side were scenes from the combat against the Amazons. Here the enemy was again Asiatic, and more specifically anticipated the Persians: fighting on horseback, with bows and arrows, and seeking (as we have noted in the description of the paintings at the Stoa) to seize Attica – and even (as the shield of the Athena Parthenos would show) storm the Akropolis itself.

The south metopes featured a Centauromachy. According to Xenophon's *Cyropaedia* (IV. 3.17–22), admittedly more a work of imagination than history, the Persians admired the Centaurs, stemming from pride in their own horsemanship, and thought it amusing that the Greeks should regard them as terrifying as Centaurs. It requires little effort to understand how the Centaurs' mythical violation of the wedding of the Lapith prince Pirithoos became a fifth-century BC metaphor for the barbaric intrusion of the Persians upon Greek territory.

The north side metopes are badly preserved, but seem to have shown episodes from the Ilioupersis ('Troy Taken'). Depending on which version

98 Tribute-bringers, on a relief from the Throne Hall of Xerxes at Persepolis.

of it one consults, that epic contained episodes which cast little credit on the Greek victors: unfortunately, whatever nuances the Parthenon displayed are largely lost to us. It is hardly necessary to elaborate on the possible metaphorical force of the Ilioupersis in the context of an Athenian monument celebrating triumph over an Eastern enemy, but it is worth pointing out that its pairing with the Amazonomachy was already established in the Stoa Poikile; alongside, of course, the battle of Marathon.

Approaching the Parthenon from the Propylaea, the monumental Akropolis gateways also commissioned by Perikles, the most obvious element of sculptural decoration was the temple's west pediment. Perhaps because it was so obvious, no ancient writer ever thought to describe it properly. It appears to show Athena contesting the possession of Attica with Poseidon. From what survives of the pediment, and various echoes of it, it seems likely that what most ancient viewers would chiefly have registered was the central group of this arrangement – Athena versus Poseidon. The mythographers tell us that both deities produced the tokens of their claim to Attica on the Akropolis itself: in Athena's case, an olive tree, and in Poseidon's, a salt spring. Given the choice, it is not difficult to see why Athena won the contest. But our ancient sources cannot agree quite how it was adjudicated, and the west pediment does little to clarify the situation.

As for the opposite, east, pediment, we are no better informed by ancient commentators. The central sculptures evidently showed the Birth of Athena. Hers is a bizarre genesis, not easily represented in stone: she must appear, in all her glory, from the head of Zeus, thanks to an axe-blow of Hephaistos (and Zeus must appear unharmed by all this). Deities witnessing the act should register astonishment and delight, and the cosmic forces acclaim it, too. To the Athenian viewer, the central importance here was the arrival of Athena, the city's protectress. Specific identities of the circumstantial figures, still subject to scholarly debate, were presumably once fixed; but they may have been obscured or forgotten within a couple of decades. As with the west pediment, certain figures here have been more or less plausibly given half a dozen different identities by modern scholars but nearly all are tentative, and again we remain unsure how far the original programme was patent to those gazing up at it in ancient times. One may question, indeed, whether the executive sculptors of this work, and those who paid them for it, knew exactly what programme they were supposed to be following. The building accounts that relate to the frieze of the Erechtheum, quoted at greater length elsewhere in this book (see Chapter 7), are disturbingly anonymous in this respect: figures singled out for piece-by-piece payment are identified by posture, not name (thus 'the man leaning on a staff', or 'the chariot, the youth, and the horses being harnessed' – such phrases could so easily describe figures from the Parthenon frieze too).

Familiarity with 'the Elgin marbles' as works of art, then, is no guarantee of our knowing what they are and it is quite wrong of the British Museum guidebooks to suggest (as they do) that a history of meticulous museum tutelage has ensured a proper understanding of the Parthenon sculptures. It is evident from the manifold variants in the Classical and post-Classical mythography of the Athena versus Poseidon episode that the Parthenon pediments were curiously ineffective at canonizing that story. And yet on a basic level of comprehension, we can see as clearly as any ancient viewer what the Parthenon was about: very simply, the glorification of Athens, Athena and everything Athenian.

The limited success of scholars in clarifying the iconographic components of the pedimental ensembles does not augur well for a detailed explanation of what was the least accessible part of the Parthenon's decoration: the frieze. Again, no ancient writer comes to our aid, though that is not to say that the frieze went ignored in antiquity (its resonance is surely felt, for example, in the Ara Pacis of Augustus in Rome). As we have noted, some element of rivalry with the Apadana at Persepolis is plausible in both the general concept and the detailed execution of the frieze, perhaps creating a heightened sense among Athenian viewers of their own democratic identity. Where the Apadana reliefs show client states trailing along with

tribute for the Great King (*ill. 98*), the Parthenon frieze shows the unmistakable tokens of religious ritual being performed: here the portage of *hydriai* (water) (*ill. 99*), elsewhere also *spondai* (libations), *skaphai* (trays of cakes) and other items of sacrificial paraphernalia. From what basic understanding we have of the Parthenon's programme, this should be a religious ritual with an Atheno-centric (or Athena-centric) focus. What might that focus be?

The first recorded response to the Parthenon frieze comes from the fifteenth-century traveller Cyriac of Ancona, who judged it to represent 'Athenian victories in the time of Perikles'. This suggestion has found few supporters: historically it is difficult to attach much military success to the name of Perikles. If indeed a victory is being celebrated, it must be one from the past. But most scholars (since at least the end of the eighteenth century) have preferred to see here no victory celebration as such, but some representation or evocation of the festival special to Athens, the Panathenaia, celebrated on the date assigned as Athena's birthday. This was honoured annually, but every four years there was a grander version, the 'Great Panathenaia', which involved replacing the peplos dress on the statue of Athena Polias by a new one woven by the ladies of Athens. Since a central section of the east side of the frieze appears to show the exchange of just such a garment (*ill. 100*), it is true to say that, if any interpretation of the frieze can be called 'standard', then the Panathenaic festival reading is just such.

100 Parthenon frieze, east side, slab V. Usually regarded as the presentation of a new peplos to Athena at the Panathenaic festival, a new interpretation sees it as Erechtheus about to sacrifice one of his daughters.

We know more about the Panathenaia as a festival than most other occasions in the busy Athenian religious calendar, but this knowledge does not invariably assist the full explanation of what we see happening in the frieze. In no sense can it be treated as a 'realistic' depiction of a particular year's festival: the presence of twelve Olympian deities is enough to scotch any notion of a documentary enterprise, and in any case, the decorum of Greek temple decoration generally rules out the direct depiction of contemporary events. Might the frieze then show us an early, paradigmatic celebration of the Panathenaia – possibly the very first festival? Perhaps: some consonance would then be achieved with the pediments, at least. However, as with the pediments, we will then find ourselves blundering about in all the obscurities of Athenian myth and aetiology, and possibly no better off in our grasp of artistic intentions than the ancient viewers were.

A much more attractive interpretation – though it takes us into the same area of essential obscurities – has been made by Joan Connelly. She minimizes the Panathenaiac element, and draws attention instead to the story of King Erechtheus as recounted in a play by Euripides, probably performed at Athens in the 420s BC. The play is only partially preserved, but its tragic core is known. Erechtheus, in order to ensure Athenian victory over a Thracian force poised to invade Attica, was bound by the Delphic Oracle to sacrifice one of his daughters. The central scene of the east frieze thereby becomes a rather grisly vignette of sacrificial preparations. For the sake of his city, Erechtheus will cut the throat of his own daughter. His wife Praxithea, and other daughters (there are three or four in the mythology) assist at the scene. As for the cloth here, it is not a peplos at all, but the wrapping in which the sacrificial victim will be conducted to the altar.

It was suggested a century ago (by A. Furtwängler) that the tussle between Athena and Poseidon on the Parthenon's west pediment symbolized two competing myth-historical and cultic claims on the Akropolis, those of Kekrops and his family (for Athena), and those of Erechtheus and his daughters (for Poseidon). A reading of the Parthenon frieze that aligns it within the mythical proto-history of Athens has much to recommend it, especially when one considers that Erechtheus was shortly to have his own temple on the Akropolis. But worries about this interpretation remain. Athenians in the fifth century BC probably knew as much about Erechtheus as the British know about King Lear. To see his personal vicissitudes unfold on the stage was one thing; to have them carved on a monument designed to commemorate triumph over the Persians was another. True, the extent to which King Erechtheus was prepared to go to save his country from invasion may be regarded as exemplary. But human sacrifice was not a feature of Greek religion. On the contrary, the Greeks regarded it as barbarian (hence the myth of Herakles exploding against the Egyptian pharaoh Busiris who was preparing to sacrifice him); and no Greek temple either

before or after the Parthenon shows anything like this. And what of the rest of the frieze? Obviously, sacrificial attendants can be accounted for, and the Olympians too; Connelly is prepared to see the frieze as an explanation of the myth-heroic origins of the Panathenaia. But in quantitative terms, the most striking feature of the Parthenon frieze is its display of young men with horses, and to explain them as the celebratory mustering of King Erechtheus' forces after their success in battle with the Thracians at Eleusis is not quite convincing. Where, for a start, are their weapons? If they are celebrating victory in a sanctuary, why has the virgin sacrifice to ensure victory not yet taken place?

Objections against and points in favour of various individual readings of the Parthenon frieze can be exchanged endlessly. We return to the original theme of this chapter with those young horsemen (*ill. 101*). Cantering along in a state of semi-nudity may have been an actual privilege of the Athenian cavalry, but hardly in the associated context of a religious ritual. Why is the frieze so dominated by them – as it undoubtedly is, and was?

From what we know of the Panathenaia, the cavalry did not take part in the procession involved in the ritual to replace Athena's peplos. Foot-soldiers did, and fully armed too – but not cavalry. So the horsemen hardly square with a conventional Panathenaia. They exhibit some differentiation of dress, perhaps sufficient (as some have suggested) to indicate their membership of the ten Athenian tribes. But what they exhibit more than anything else is an ethos of heroization. To glimpse just one of these figures (*ill. 102*) is to be left in little doubt how to read it as a piece of fifth-century BC sculpture: Polykleitan torso, flying cloak and features of athletic, self-

102 A heroic figure from the Parthenon frieze.

conscious seriousness. These may be ideal *epheboi*, the best examples of young Athenian manhood, dedicating themselves to both Athena and her *polis*. But temple decorum requires that they should not be portraits of the living. Instead, they must evoke a generation that is to come – or a generation that has already been.

It must be stressed again: no interpretation of the Parthenon frieze which attempts to be specific is free from problems. Conversely, each specific interpretation has something in its favour. And the one so far only anticipated, but not discussed, is as follows: that if you count the number of heroized figures on the frieze, their total comes out at a very significant number – 192.

This is, of course, the number enshrined in Herodotus as those who fell at Marathon. As a tally of 'heroized' figures (subject to some dispute, admittedly) it was first noticed by W.-H. Schuchhardt in 1930. John Boardman then incorporated it into his argument that the frieze 'shows the fighters of Marathon celebrating the prime festival of their goddess, on the temple dedicated to her as a thanksgiving for her aid at Marathon and afterwards, and in a manner which indicates the heroic status of those who fell there'. This is not the place to rehearse the substance and detail of Boardman's interpretation, which readers may explore for themselves (see Further Reading). But with regard to what has already been said about the burial of the Marathonian dead – in a consciously archaizing, even Homeric style – we cannot be surprised to find them presented here with horses and chariots. Yes, those who fought at Marathon fought on foot. But those who died in that battle were conceived as joining the same nether-world as Ajax, Achilles and Agamemnon. Just as large grave-marking vases from eighth-century BC Attic cemeteries show the heroized dead with 'Mycenaean' shields and fleets of chariots, so the Parthenon frieze shows the glory-clad Marathonians as riders and chariot-owners. Everything we know about the Greek historical consciousness of the fifth century BC points to a blurring of boundaries between myth and history. There is also discernible a tendency for the 'factoids' of history to become the stuff of both myth and religion, and the communion (*koinonia*) of living and dead maintained by the imaginative 'visibility' of heroic ancestors.

We must admit that the circumstantial pressure upon the Parthenon-designers to make some allusion to the heroes of Marathon was extremely strong. Of course, once in place, the frieze offered no chance to viewers, especially not the dim-sighted old *Marathonomachai*, to count out the glorious 192. But the conception of an ultimate Marathon memorial may once have been there (see *ill. 105*) for the perfect viewer. In fact, given the lineage of Marathon commemorations already established, we should rather be amazed by its absence.

Coda: the Erechtheum Caryatids and the Temple of Athena Nike

'Architects should inform themselves about history.' So writes Vitruvius, in the opening pages of his *De Architectura* (I. 5). If they do, then inquisitive members of the public may be quickly satisfied. Suppose, continues Vitruvius, that someone asks why an architect has replaced columns with 'marble statues of long-robed women, which are called caryatids'. It is the cue for a display of historical erudition. Caryatids, according to Vitruvius, are thus called because during the Persian wars, the Laconian city of Caryae was one of those Greek states which sided with the Persians. After defeating the Persians, the Greek allies turned on Caryae. The menfolk they killed; the women were put into slavery, however 'high-born' they were. And the architects of the time symbolized their shame with 'Caryatids': stone figures of the heavy-laden women, whose punishment would thus be broadcast to posterity.

103 The caryatid porch of the Erechtheum, on the Akropolis, Athens.

The notion that serving as a column represents a form of punishment is not controversial. Figures of Giants or Atlantes, when they serve to hold up a building, may readily be explained as Giants defeated by the gods in the primal Gigantomachy. Yet this explanation of the Caryatids has encountered general scepticism. Scholars suspicious of the Vitruvian idea of history will point out that the Erechtheum (*ill. 103*) is not in fact the first building to use female figures as columns: the late sixth-century BC building at Delphi which we know as the Siphnian Treasury also has them, and as anthropomorphic basin-stands (*perirrhanteria*) 'Caryatids' have a long Archaic tradition. But this does not exclude the possibility that they acquired a fresh significance of humiliation in the fifth century. And why should Vitruvius be making up his explanation? He goes on to say that the Spartans, when they laid out their 'Persian Stoa', similarly set up supports in Persian garb (*statuas Persicas sustinentes*) as architectural emblems of victory. If he is right, and the construction of the Erechtheum begins in 421 BC, then we are bound to extend our survey of post-Persian wars commemoration thus far. At the time that the Erechtheum was being built, Athens had agreed a truce, or even peace, with Sparta: and to dwell on old successes had become a form of refuge from the present, which offered precious little to celebrate.

The same may be said for the little Ionic temple perched on a bastion of the Akropolis, which we know as the Temple of Athena Nike. Again, it is reckoned to have been built and decorated in the late 420s BC; and again, despite the lapse of time, one is impelled to explain its decoration in terms of retrospective commemoration. Being Ionic, the temple carried a frieze above the architrave on all four sides. Though it has survived poorly, this is the tentative consensus on what the frieze represents: on the east side, a gathering of gods, with Athena probably central; on the south side, Greeks fighting Orientals – some (e.g. Evelyn Harrison) go so far as to call this the battle of Marathon; and on the west and north sides, battles which appear to show Greeks against Greeks – according to one suggestion, scenes from the battle of Megara in 458 BC, when the Athenians indecisively took on Corinth, or perhaps more contemporaneously, evocations of the Peloponnesian War itself (*ill. 104*).

The structurally unusual feature of the Nike temple is its decorated parapet or balustrade. The reliefs from this part of the building seem equally unusual: Athena, in the company of assorted *Nikai,* or female victory figures, is vigorously conducting bovine sacrifice, and arranging piles of armour as trophies. Though there appears some inclination on the part of the sculptors to dwell on the femininity of Athena and her companions (the erotic possibilities of deep-cut and wayward drapery are fully explored, as one figure, for instance, stoops to adjust her sandal), there is in fact no ladylike delicacy at this sacrifice. The bulls are wrestled to the

ground: at least one is shown having its throat slit. But there is no sign of any altar. So where is this supposed to be happening? Quite possibly on the battlefield itself. The presence of the bulls has favoured suggestions that some connection with Theseus may be implied here, but he is nowhere to be seen. A more cogent solution is that the victory being celebrated here is (or rather was) a cosmically-ordained triumph. Athena herself may be imagined on the battlefield, helping to set up trophies, plunging herself into the protocols of post-battle thanksgiving.

Which battlefield might qualify for such honours? At the time of this temple's construction, there is really only one candidate. Over half a century on, there is still no forgetting. Its exhortatory power will have been felt by all those who gazed on the Nike bastion (and it was hard to miss). The source of that power was Marathon.

104 Detail of the south side of the frieze of the temple of Athena Nike, on the Akropolis, Athens, showing Greeks versus Persians.

7

IN SEARCH OF PHEIDIAS

Here, as P. Vidal-Naquet has pointed out, is one of the most profound contra-dictions of Greek civilization. Greece, particularly in the fifth and fourth cen-turies, was a 'civilization of the craftsman'; but its ideology, that of the ruling class (as expressed, for example, in the works of Plato), denies the importance and the effective role of the craftsman. He is condemned to the shadows: to be none other than 'the secret hero of Greek history'.

Translated from F. Frontisi-Ducroix, *Dédale* (Paris 1975), 25

Pheidias lost

Opus LX of Sir Lawrence Alma-Tadema is not a great painting, but it is (albeit not quite in the sense it was intended to be) an instructive one. *Pheidias and the Parthenon Frieze* (*ill. 105*) aims to recreate, in almost doc-umentary fashion, the first 'private viewing' of the Parthenon frieze: Pheidias, scroll in hand, stands somewhat bashfully by his handiwork; sundry prominent Athenians, including Perikles with Aspasia, and Socrates with young Alcibiades, perambulate the scaffolding to inspect the details – as well they might, since for all its bright paintwork (boldly imag-ined by Alma-Tadema), the frieze will be very difficult for anyone to see properly once the scaffolding is down.

This was one of the first of Alma-Tadema's pseudo-photographic recon-structions of Classical subjects, and in relative terms one of his most con-vincing (reveries of languid nymphs thence dominate his work). It is instructive for us not, however, because it reminds us of polychromy in Greek sculpture, but rather insofar as it reflects a powerful and durable art-historical image. This is the image of Pheidias the immortal sculptor; Pheidias the *divino artista*, the masterhand, the unparalleled virtuoso; Pheidias the epitome of creative energy in that nursery of genius, Periklean Athens. Typical of the enthusiasm buzzing for this Pheidias after the arrival of the Elgin marbles in London is an anonymous sonnet on the sculptures which ends by apostrophizing their creator thus:

105 *Pheidias and the Parthenon Frieze*, by L. Alma-Tadema (1868).

> Phidias! thou hast immortalized thy name
> In these thy handy-works, and they will tell
> Loud as ten thousand thunderings thy fame
> Wherever truth and beauty deign to dwell.

(From *The Gentleman's Magazine*, January 1818, 65: the suspected author is Benjamin Haydon, friend of the poet, John Keats.)

This enthusiasm entered the streams of serious art-appreciation. A little after Alma-Tadema's painting, in 1871, John Ruskin would hold up a portion of the Parthenon frieze and eulogize 'the noble hand' which wrought it. Indeed, he claimed that the great artistry of Pheidias was directly betrayed by the work: 'you may recognize the decision of his thought, and the glow of his temper, *no less in the workmanship than the design*' (my italics).

Alas, the truth is this: not a single work survives which can be attributed with real certitude to one artist called Pheidias. The Riace Bronzes may be by him; and there is a sense in which Alma-Tadema could rightly show one man standing to take the credit for the Parthenon frieze: some*one* – say Pheidias, the man with the scroll in his hands – may have sketched its design, even if forty other sculptors actually carved it. But we need to think very carefully about what it means to attribute Greek sculptures to individual artists. Attribution is a game in which we have so far refused to participate: this chapter should help to explain why.

Before we address modern critical theories about authorship and their relevance to Classical art history, it is worth taking stock of the 'Pheidias' who confronts us here. Since it is generally admitted that his work is known to us perhaps entirely through copies, our figurative evidence for 'Pheidias' is largely secondhand. The limits of copy-studies (*Kopienforschungen*) were, in fact, drastically exposed by the discovery of the Riace Bronzes: at a conference organized in 1983, over a decade after the discovery itself, scholars who had devoted most of their lives to the study of Greek sculpture variously attributed the Riace Bronzes to Pheidias, Onatas, Myron and Alkamenes – and some experts remain unconvinced that the statues were made in the fifth century BC at all. (Such dissonance of opinion should be a caution to anyone using handbooks of Greek sculpture that are organized according to names of supposed sculptors.)

To compound the inadequacies of copy-studies, and hardly to compensate for them, there is the 'Pheidias' of antique literature. This is extensive, and much of it consists simply of secondary sources feeding off each other. But it is worth sampling in a stratified way – that is, working towards those sources which are least likely to carry commonplaces (*topoi*) or inventions. We may find, at the end of our literary excavations, some semblance of an artist.

What follows, then, is a sample of Pheidian sources:

Plotinus. This philosopher, writing in the third century AD, is usually described as a Neoplatonist. What he has to say about Pheidias, however, has little in common with Plato's own view of artistic 'imitation' (*mimesis*), as stated in *Republic* (10.597b). Here is Plotinus, focusing (like many others) on Pheidias' contribution to the Seven Wonders of the Ancient World, the colossal cult statue of Zeus at Olympia: 'Pheidias did not make his Zeus from any model perceived by the senses, but understood what Zeus would look like if he wanted to make himself visible [*phanenai*]' (Plotinus, *Ennead* V. 8.1).

This is a classic statement of divine artistic insight, which puts Pheidias on the same level as those poets and dramatists whose imaginations gave them windows on to the heavenly. Pheidias has an inspiration (*enthousiasmos*) direct from Zeus; in his mind's eye, Pheidias can see not simply the appearance, but the very essence of Zeus. An earlier statement of this, though with less refined metaphysics, comes from Cicero in the late first century BC: Pheidias, argues Cicero (in *Orator* 2. 8–9), did not replicate a model when he made the Zeus, but an image of perfected beauty in his own mind (*in mente insidebat species pulchritudinis eximia*) which directed him (*manum dirigebat*). And a subsequent rhetorician, Quintilian, allows Pheidias to be better at representing gods than humans – to the extent that his Zeus, by its beauty, augments the awesomeness of Zeus the godhead and enhances received religion (*adiecisse aliquid etiam receptae religioni videtur*: Quintilian XII. 10.9).

Dio Chrysostom. More rhetoric here, from the 'golden-mouthed' Dio's *Olympic Discourse* of AD 97. Dio stages an imaginary defence by Pheidias of his Olympian Zeus, against those who are sceptical that gods can be rendered in human form. It runs like this: we need (says Pheidias) closer contact with the gods than simply gazing at the skies; it is part of Greek nature to conceive of gods in mortal guise (from Homer onwards); this statue is not trying to deceive anyone that Zeus is a man; Zeus is many-faceted – the best a sculptor can do is seek to reflect some of those mortal-conceived epithets for Zeus, such as 'Father' (*Pater*), 'King' (*Basileus*), and so on; no sculptor will ever capture the thunder and lightning wielded by Zeus; and, finally, Zeus will not be displeased at this attempt at his representation – for Zeus himself is the supreme technician (*megasthenes aristo-techna pater*).

Artificial as it is, this piece by Dio indicates an important part of the definition of the 'genius' of Pheidias: the artist's supposed access to supernatural knowledge – his extraordinary plane of existence, a superiority of vision that permits him to relay back to lesser mortals a hint of how Zeus appears.

Pliny. Not quite in chronological sequence (he was writing in the mid-first century AD), but inserted here for evidence of the Roman art-historical niche for Pheidias; Pliny (*Natural History* XXXIV. 54) wrote of the sculptor that he was 'rightly judged to be the first who opened the path for the art of chryselephantine sculpture and explored its possibilities' (*primusque artem toreuticen aperuisse atque demonstrasse merito iudicatur*). Pliny's recourse to the Greek word *toreutike*, sometimes strictly translated as the art of metal-chasing, must be understood as the working of gold and ivory. Elsewhere (*Natural History* XXXVI.15), Pliny allows that Pheidias 'also worked in marble'. He gives Pheidias a *floruit* of 448 BC, without explaining why but perhaps linking his fortunes with the political ascendancy of Perikles.

Plutarch. Plutarch's *Life of Perikles* is our most informative source for what little we know about the life and milieu of Pheidias, but we can only surmise whence Plutarch, writing in the late first and early second centuries AD, derived his tales (here probably Euphorus, an Attic historian active in the fourth century BC). Pheidias is introduced in this biography as the specific 'contractor' (*ergolabos*) of the Athena Parthenos statue, and as overall designer and surveyor (*episkopos*) of the Parthenon project. By 'the Parthenon project' is apparently entailed all the monumentalization of the Akropolis at the instigation of Perikles. Plutarch says that many great craftsmen (*technitai*) were involved – but he assigns a special role to Pheidias, 'on account of his friendship with Perikles' (*dia philian Perikleous*). This then also explains, for Plutarch, the sculptor's downfall, for the political opponents of Perikles sought to use Pheidias as a means of discrediting Perikles. They first encouraged a stooge from the sculptor's own workshop, called Menon, to accuse Pheidias formally (at the Assembly, or *ekklesia*) of peculation – reducing the gold content in the gold assigned to gild the cult statue of Athena Parthenos, and keeping some back himself – a charge which Pheidias, apparently, was able to disprove; then they brought a new charge against him, one of impiety (*blasphemia*), on the grounds that he had represented both himself and his sponsor Perikles on the shield of the Athena Parthenos statue, participating in an Amazonomachy (Perikles brandishing a spear, Pheidias – a nice self-image, if he ever made it – balding, but still capable of lifting a boulder). This charge stuck, and Pheidias died in prison: a sorry end which Plutarch caps by suggesting that he may have been poisoned too.

Well, Plutarch values entertainment in history, and has no doubt polished whatever sources he had at his disposal. One has to admit, though, that the charge of 'misrendering accounts' (*paralogizesthai*) is inherently plausible. We know from subsequent inscriptions related to the Parthenos statue that it was regularly inspected to weigh and inventory the amount of gold on it, and discrepancies seem to have beset this exercise: for instance, the gold crown (*stephanos*) on the Nike carried by Athena, when assessed in 428/427 BC, weighed both 50 and 70 drachms, implying either disagreement or skullduggery (or both). The statue – popularly referred to as 'the golden one' (*to chrysoun agalma*) – may have stood intact at least until the early third century BC, when she was stripped of her gold; but other gold fittings and monies which were technically 'Athena's property' were at intervals 'borrowed' from her in times of civic need, and it is easy to imagine financial scandals generated from the first conception of the statue.

As we shall see, there is some archaeological evidence to be added into any putative biography of Pheidias, but we should end with the two earliest (and thus most reliable) mentions of the sculptor in Greek literature.

Plato. Scholastic detectives might regard the following as an implicit corroboration of Plutarch's story of embezzlement: Plato, in *Meno* 91d, has Socrates measure the wealth of a philosopher (Protagoras) by reference to Pheidias – Protagoras, claims Socrates, made more from his teachings (*sophias*) than Pheidias, 'who made such conspicuously fine works of art' (*kala erga*), and ten other sculptors put together. A further mention of Pheidias (in *Protagoras* 311c) would suggest that 'the Pheidias legend' started early: Plato is not given to name-dropping of artists, and only Pheidias and Polykleitos are ever mentioned in his many works – implying that those sculptors were household names at least by the early fourth century BC (when Plato was writing).

Aristophanes. A comedian may not be deemed a decent source, but even a satirical mention of our elusive genius is valuable when it comes within a decade of his presumed death. In 421 BC Aristophanes presented his play *Peace* (*Eirene*) at Athens, and in lines 605–18 of that play, a protest against the Peloponnesian War (the war between Athens and Sparta which had begun in 431 BC, and was destined to grind on another twenty years yet), Pheidias is nominated as the man who started the whole conflict off with his 'misdemeanours' (*praxas kakos*). These crimes are not specified, but they implicitly embarrass Perikles, who resorts to a war-mongering edict as a means of diverting public attention from his embarrassment.

The citation of Pheidias as a cause of the flight of Peace from Attica is made in the play by Hermes, and it is greeted with astonishment by the rustics whom the god is addressing: good heavens, they respond – we'd never thought of that! And most historians of the Peloponnesian War, finding no corroboration of the story at all in Thucydides, dismiss it as 'pure invention' (thus G.E.M. de Ste Croix). As well it might be; but again, we have to concede that Pheidias was at least a name to conjure with on the Athenian stage – and that Plutarch's narrative of anti-Periklean plotting may have some substance to it.

How should we summarize all this? Prior to Plutarch, Diodorus Siculus gives another account of the legal arraigning of Pheidias, on the grounds of the 'theft of sacred materials' or 'temple-robbery' (*hierosylia*): again Pheidias seems to be used as a scapegoat by the enemies of Perikles, but both Diodorus and Plutarch are probably telescoping events in their image of a politically beleaguered Perikles (they say that charges were brought not only against Pheidias as Perikles' friend, but also against Aspasia, Perikles' mistress, and Anaxagoras, his old mentor). True, as one of the guardians or 'assessors' (*epistatai*) of the Parthenos statue, Perikles would be vulnerable to any charge of embezzlement successfully brought against its sculptor; but there again, Perikles was only one of several assessors – five, to be precise, were appointed annually – and therefore he cannot have borne sole responsibility. We are bound to allow that something went amiss in the litigious world of Athenian democracy – something that involved Pheidias in his capacity as maestro of the cult statue for the Parthenon. The question remains: when?

An ancient annotator of Aristophanes (commenting on *Peace*, lines 605ff.) alerts us to one further historian whom we have not so far mentioned, called Philochorus. In one of his (now lost) accounts of Athenian history, written during the third century BC, Philochorus fixed a date for both the dedication of the Parthenos statue and the accusal of Pheidias at 438/437 BC (a date, unfortunately, which cannot be regarded as entirely secure: one reading of the Parthenon accounts would move the completion of the Parthenos to 435/434 BC). And Pheidias, according to Philochorus, was not imprisoned at Athens but fled to Elis (i.e. Olympia) instead, where he made the Olympian Zeus before being again charged with peculation and ending his days in Elean custody.

One might be inclined to despair of establishing the truth amidst all these reported comings and goings of Pheidias, but here is a case where archaeology comes to the rescue. In 1958 the German excavators of Olympia turned their attention to the remains of the building identified as formerly the workshop of Pheidias (Pausanias saw it before a small Byzantine church was raised on its site: Pausanias V. 15.1). We shall say more about the finds from the workshop shortly, in connection with evidence for the making of chryselephantine statues; for now, it is enough to register the almost miraculous recovery of a drinking-cup whose base was inscribed ΦΕΙΔΙΟ ΕΙΜΙ – 'I belong to Pheidias'; and the dating of this and associated painted pottery to the 430s BC.

Readers with a sharp eye for chronology may have already guessed where all this is leading. As noted in Chapter 6, the Parthenon was dedicated in 432 BC: that is, with its metopes, frieze and pedimental sculptures finished off. The usual sequence of the carving of the component sculptures of the Parthenon consists of metopes first, then frieze and cult statue, then pediments. Quite apart from any stylistic indications, there are account records surviving from the Parthenon which chronicle some of these stages (following Alison Burford's resumé – Phase I, 447–444 BC: foundations; Phase II, 444–437 BC: columns, doors, metopes, frieze, cult statue; Phase III, 437–432 BC: pedimental sculptures).

But if we accept that the archaeological evidence from Olympia confirms the account that Philochorus gives of the vicissitudes of Pheidias, then the consequence is clear. Pheidias was at Olympia when the last stages of the sculptural decoration of the Parthenon were being executed; therefore, *Pheidias was not directly involved in the carving of the figures of the Parthenon pediments.* And here is another bold statement worth italicizing: *no ancient source attributes the pedimental sculptures of the Parthenon to Pheidias.*

Indeed, the origin of the attribution of the integral sculptures of the Parthenon to Pheidias is obscure, though as early as the mid-fifteenth century we find our traveller to Athens, Cyriac of Ancona, ascribing the entire Parthenon to his name. Pausanias, so thorough in his description of Olympia, is frustratingly laconic about the Akropolis in general, and the Parthenon in particular. Though he spares a valuable sentence about the subject-matter of the pediments, he says nothing about Pheidias. The only possible hint in antiquity that Pheidias should be credited with the Parthenon pediments is Plutarch's characterization of the role of the sculptor as *episkopos* or overseer. Though Plutarch does not specify what the brief of such an *episkopos* was, we can readily imagine that it included the provision of models (*paradeigmata*) for other sculptors to work from; and most specialist scholars, while admitting that an attribution of 'the Parthenon sculptures' to one 'Pheidias' is impossible, argue for a general homogeneity of style that bespeaks a guiding hand, or a finishing touch.

This homogeneity of style is arguable: the metopes in particular look not only uneven, but so much earlier than the rest of the decoration that there is some speculation that they might have been prepared for a 'pre-Periklean' Parthenon; and different 'hands' are fairly easy to distinguish on the frieze, when one has the advantage of seeing it clearly and at eye-level in the British Museum. The pediments demanded fifty figures, all over life-size. If we read the accounts rightly, to get those fifty figures from quarried blocks into polished and painted forms *in situ* within the pediments took only six years. This means a carving staff of literally hundreds: who was their *episkopos*, if Pheidias was then at Olympia?

The search for Pheidias is plagued with questions that are unanswerable. No convincing account of his career is possible. So what shall we do with him?

Rationalizing genius

As we have seen, the reputation of Pheidias is moderately well attested by sources not completely distant from his own life and times: Plato at least implies that there was once a sought-after and talked-about sculptor called Pheidias. Plato does not call Pheidias a genius, for the good reason that there is no word in Greek directly equating to 'genius' (that is to say, 'genius' as we have been using the word: as distinct from 'talent' – a difference established in Italian by 1600, and in English it is a late eighteenth-century, Romantic-leaning distinction). But that is not to say that the Greeks did not recognize something akin to our own notion of genius. They knew about inspiration (*enthousiasmos*); and they knew about possession, divine or creative; or rather, divine *and* creative, since great art was the result of heavenly afflatus, the breeze of creativity blowing through select human channels, which might seem to others like a kind of madness (*mania*). When Plato and other Greek thinkers talk about this sort of inspiration, they invariably call upon literary or poetic examples. It was left to Hellenistic art historians to extend the terminology to painting and sculpture. Thence Pliny and other Roman writers capitalized on the anecdotal possibilities of this, creating character vignettes of the artistic genius – solitary, single-minded, socially marginal, greedy, competitive, vain; and in due time Renaissance biographers such as Condivi and Vasari used these same ancient tokens or symptoms of genius to define the 'divine' artists such as Giotto and Michelangelo. So it is fair to say that the Greeks began a Western tradition in this respect: it may even begin when Homer smote his lyre and called upon the blessed Muses to assist his song.

Those who like their art history to be peppered with genius may invent for themselves some epic of agony and ecstasy for Pheidias in the fifth century BC. As we have seen, the starting materials are there: grand projects, vile enemies, court cases, gaol, suspected poison. (Plutarch also mentions pretty women, too.) Here, we shall attempt to rationalize the evidence. We shall find that while this analysis does not give us the graphic details of the death of Pheidias, it actually saves him from a worse theoretical fate, alluded to in the Introduction to this book – 'la mort de l'auteur'.

The Greeks themselves came up with one strategy for rationalizing genius. Medical researchers in the Aristotelian tradition (from the fourth century BC onwards) argued that outstanding individuals tended to have melancholic temperaments, due to an excess of black bile in their systems. If this bile became too over-heated in their bodies, or got too close to the powers of reasoning (which lay, as far as Greek physiologists knew, in the thorax – where the voice came from), then the results could be explosive, ecstatic or epileptic. Hence the link between manic behaviour and artistic inspiration: all explicable according to the doctrine of the bodily humours.

We may prefer a different strategy. This is one which historians of the Renaissance increasingly favour: that is, to trace the opportunities offered by art for upward mobility and to frame genius, perhaps rather cynically, in terms of entrepreneurial initiative. As we saw in Chapter 2, the social status of artists in Greece was banausic: theirs was manual work, bordering on the slavish, and thus disparaged as ignoble by a citizenry disposed to spending its days occupied in politics, athletics or military training. In the seventh century BC, the poet Hesiod went so far as to dismiss artists as beggars (ptochoi: the Greek is onomatopoeic of a spat-out disparagement). Yet displays of exceptional techne were evidently rewarded. Perhaps democracy did have something to do with it; certainly artists proliferated in the economics of the polis. The inscriptions on Archaic statue bases from Athens, at any rate, attest to a patent degree of self-satisfaction among smiths and potters, who dedicate reliefs and statues as tithes of their earnings, or else donate conspicuous examples of their handiwork. Sculptors, too, are not reluctant to sign themselves. And by the end of the fifth century we have records such as that on the base of the Nike of Paionios at Olympia (see *ill. 51*). This tells us not only what fund paid for the statue and its occasion (the Messenian victory over the Spartans at Sphacteria in 425 BC is cited) but just as importantly, it boasts the fact that Paionios of Mende made the Nike and also 'won the competition' to make the *akroteria* or rooftop-figures of the nearby Temple of Zeus. Such epigraphic evidence goes a long way towards substantiating the otherwise suspicious anecdotes that survive about contests between leading sculptors at various sites regarding various subjects – such as the tale of the statues of Amazons submitted for view at Ephesus by Pheidias, Polykleitos, Kresilas and others (Pliny, *Natural History* XXXIV. 53).

One fourth-century sculptor, Praxiteles, is officially listed as being among the three hundred richest men in Athens. Plato, as we have noted, implies that Pheidias became wealthy, though not as wealthy as some Sophists he could name. Let us try to measure this in cash terms. The Parthenon accounts do not mention individual craftsmen at all, but it seems Pheidias would not have needed to earn very much (in absolute terms) to put himself ahead (relatively) of most jobbing stonemasons or sculptors. The accounts record that in one year the wages bill for work on the pedimental sculptures totalled 16,392 drachmas. Assuming a work-force of twenty sculptors, working three hundred days in the year, this gives them a daily pay of only two or three drachmas each; to put that into context, Plato tells us (*Cratylus* 384b) that a Sophist might charge fifty drachmas to give a single lecture.

Could a *banausos* like Pheidias aspire to mix with philosophers? Perhaps. To judge from the recorded iconography of the base of the Parthenos statue, it was programmatic in a literary way, following, and possibly even reinterpreting, poetic legends of the Birth of Pandora. The Olympian Zeus was said to be an 'Homeric' characterization by Pheidias. Such literary ramifications of conspicuous public statuary may seem too elementary to be termed 'academic', but it is possible that Pheidias thus projected himself as a member of what has been called, in Renaissance Italy, 'the creative elite'. Likewise, when Polykleitos drew up the sculptor's handbook which we know as the *Canon*, he may have provided us with further evidence for the social advancement of artists. If Plato banned entrance to his Academy to all those 'ignorant of geometry', then Polykleitos and his followers were not excluded.

The making of chryselephantine statues obviously put sculptors in contact with, if not in charge of, vast budgets. Forty-four talents of gold – over a thousand kilos – are reckoned to have been invested in the Parthenos statue, not to mention other precious materials (see below). According to Plutarch, political protests were raised about the cost of the entire temple, and Perikles only repelled them by threatening to pay for it himself, and then have it named after him too (presumably a tremendous bluff, but it seems to have worked). But the inscribed Parthenon accounts tend to reduce the whole project to logistics, obscuring by their democratic bureaucracy the lead roles some might want to assign to Perikles or Pheidias as the 'men of vision' here. So our rationalization of genius must rely on a comparative model.

The model is Michelangelo. Like Pheidias, his aura of genius is enough to confound any sensible account of how his works were accomplished.

But like Pheidias, too, Michelangelo lived in a society which allowed upward mobility to those who worked with their hands, so long as that work was highly skilled. A recent study of Michelangelo's involvement in the making of the Florentine church of San Lorenzo is subtitled *The Genius as Entrepreneur*: a subtitle which some might almost regard as a contradiction in terms (certainly Vasari, who defended Michelangelo stoutly against charges of avariciousness, and preferred his sculptors to be like Donatello – earning lots of money but so bent on his work that he tipped it into a basket and let people help themselves). But it is clear from the documentation associated with San Lorenzo that Michelangelo's role in the project was as much 'managerial' as artistic. That is, he was personally responsible for hiring and supervising a staff of two to three hundred workers; he selected all the materials for the job, negotiated their prices, and organized their transport; he designed carts, cranes and scaffolding, as well as drawing templates for even the smallest architectural mouldings; and, of course, he was both the architect commissioned for the San Lorenzo façade, and sculptor of the tombs of the Medici Chapel inside. In short, he was his own foreman, and his own clerk of works. Simply considering the range of responsibilities undertaken by a man in his late forties is enough to make one feel vicariously exhausted. The documentary evidence for Michelangelo's activity, in fact, is every bit as intimidating as the legends of his 'superhuman genius'. But it is a way of rationalizing genius: and it probably makes sense to think of Pheidias in these terms.

The documentation that survives for San Lorenzo, showing how Michelangelo supervised his many collaborators and subordinates – as many as three hundred, at full strength – cannot be matched by the Parthenon inscriptions. But it is instructive to look at the somewhat fuller records that we possess from a later temple on the Akropolis, the Erechtheum, which would house the little Athena Polias statue. Among the inscribed accounts for the year 408/407 BC, we find details of an annual 'sculpture bill' (*kephalaion agalmatopoiko*) which totalled 3315 drachmas. Here is an excerpt from the cash reconciliation columns:

To Phyromachos, for the youth beside the breast plate	60
To Praxias, for the horse and the man beside it	120
To Antiphanes, for the chariot, the youth, and the horses being harnessed	240
To Phyromachos, for the man leading the horse	60
To Mynnion, for the horse, the man striking it, and the *stele*	127
To Sokles, for the man holding the bridle	60
To Phyromachos, for the man leaning on the staff	60
To Iasos, for the woman with the little girl leaning against her	80

No ancient source tells us who, if anyone, was overall designer of the frieze of the Erechtheum. On these inscribed tablets we simply see how individual sculptors have been paid, according to piece-work. It seems the accountants went around the frieze figure by figure, and allocated payment accordingly. One man, Phyromachos, seems to have been busier than the others; but it looks very much as though each sculptor worked on the frieze as it was convenient to the progress of the work – that there was no division of sections of the relief. And the going rate for each figure carved was sixty drachmas: not much, if (as a rough guess) to carve a marble relief figure can hardly have taken much less than six weeks (modern sculptors would need six months). To cut the fluting of a column on the same temple was worth a hundred drachmas, by comparison; and to make a wax model for an architectural detail, such as an acanthus, only eight drachmas. No 'genius' figure can be plucked from the Erechtheum: indeed, one would be very wary here of distinguishing 'sculptors' from 'stonemasons'. So even with our Michelangelo model, we might, given the added circumstantial evidence suggesting that Pheidias himself was absent from the pedimental stages of the Parthenon, want to put aside our search for the presiding genius and imagine instead a more collective artistic enterprise – a 'commonwealth' of skilled sculptors, brought together for an unusually ambitious project, and sharing an unusually clear notion of what it was they were all trying to do.

Such an approach to the Parthenon and its sculptures would not be new. Long ago, Percy Gardner wrote: 'the Parthenon is less the work of individuals than the highest artistic bloom of a city and a period. Every worker on it seems to have partaken of a common inspiration, which worked rather in the unconscious than in the conscious strata of his mind.' Plutarch would have agreed: arguing that Perikles undertook the embellishment of the Akropolis as a means of bringing full employment to Athens, he explains the economic ripples created by that project:

> The raw materials were stone, bronze, ivory, gold, ebony, cypress-wood: to fashion and work them were the craftsmen – carpenters, moulders, coppersmiths, stone-workers, goldsmiths, ivory-workers, painters, pattern-weavers, and workers in relief. Then there were the men engaged in transport and carriage – merchants, sailors, helmsmen by sea, cartwrights by land, and men who kept yokes of beasts, and drovers; rope-makers, flax-workers, shoemakers, roadmakers, and miners. And each craft, like a general with his own army, had its own crowd of hired workmen and individual craftsmen organized like an instrument and body for the service to be performed; so, in short, the various needs to be met created and spread prosperity through every age and condition.
>
> (Plutarch, *Life of Perikles* 12)

And elsewhere, with an anecdote that relates to the shifting of stone up to the Akropolis – some 22,000 tons of marble were moved from the

Pentelikon quarry to Athens – Plutarch cannot resist extending his vision of collective enterprise:

> When Perikles was building the Hekatompedon [Parthenon] on the Akropolis, stones were naturally brought up by numerous teams of draught animals every day. And there was one mule who had assisted gallantly in the work, but had been put out to grass because of old age: this mule used to go down to the Kerameikos every day, and meet the other donkeys carrying stones, and he would trot along with them, as if to encourage and cheer them on. The people of Athens, admiring the mule's spirit, gave orders for it to be looked after at public expense, and voted it free meals, like an athlete receiving a pension.
>
> (Plutarch, *Moralia* 970; cf. *Life of Cato*, 5).

Such was the level of collective participation behind the Parthenon that even donkeys, animals not known for their co-operative disposition, were keen to see the temple finished. And indeed, to judge from the building accounts, Plutarch is right to say that it was achieved 'with miraculous speed'. For fifty large pedimental figures to be made and installed in six years argues a tremendous consonance of art, logistics and sheer hard work.

So it does. But do we want to follow Plutarch in allowing the Parthenon as a project to be the work of one master-designer, or resort to a committee? Ultimately, neither option can be proven. It is rash to go chasing the 'works of Pheidias' via Roman copies, and equally rash to extrapolate from any part of the surviving Parthenon sculptures the details of 'Pheidian style'. But it is also unwarranted to deny that Pheidias ever existed. To the literary testimonia already surveyed, we may add three further items that summarize the ancient Greek status of this sculptor. In Xenophon's *Memorabilia* (I. 4.3), written in the early fourth century BC, a character interrogated by Socrates gives a short list of men he admires for their wisdom. Along with Homer and Sophocles, he cites Polykleitos, the painter Zeuxis – and Pheidias. Later in the fourth century, Aristotle is also addressing the question of what constitutes wisdom (*sophia*); and he notes that there is a popular, colloquial understanding of 'the wise' which measures it by 'precision' (*akribeia*), or rather reserves it for 'the most precise' (*akribestate*). Artists, says Aristotle – *technitai, demiourgoi* – are credited with this sort of wisdom: 'thus we speak of Pheidias as a wise sculptor [*lithourgos sophos*], and of Polykleitos as a wise bronzesmith [*andriantopoios sophos*]' (*Nicomachean Ethics* 1141a10). Finally, in a speech dated to around 354 BC, the stylish orator Isocrates, opening his *Antidosis* with the notice that some of his detractors liken his speech-making to common pleading in the courts, scornfully rebuts them by saying: 'one might as well call Pheidias, who made our statue of Athena [Parthenos], a mere doll-manufacturer [*koroplathos*]'. Isocrates plainly wants to draw the distinction between the artist and the artisan: and Pheidias is the measure of the difference.

So Pheidias is not chimerical. But it is clear from all our ancient sources that what raised the esteem of Pheidias – what promoted him, as it were, into the ranks of the creative elite – were his two celebrated large-scale chryselephantine cult statues, the Athena Parthenos and the Zeus at Olympia. Not a fragment of either work survives; in our mind's eye, therefore, if we want to glimpse the 'genius of Pheidias', we shall have to reconstruct them.

Pheidias found

The Athena Parthenos statue has, in fact, twice been reconstructed for modern edification. One reconstruction belongs to the larger project of replicating the entire Parthenon in an unlikely second home at Nashville, Tennessee. The other is in the Royal Ontario Museum at Toronto: a model at one-tenth of the original scale, which makes Athena look indeed rather doll-like, though in detail it is probably accurate enough (*ill. 106*). A number of ancient souvenir copies (*ills 107* and *108*) have survived, some of them of very shoddy quality: the best is the 'Varvakeion' statue in Athens (*ill. 107*), carved from marble and standing just over 1 m (3¼ ft) high. A larger marble version, undoubtedly a 'free' version, which once stood in the Library at Pergamum, probably best captures the dignity of the Parthenos, and the Pergamene location is significant: two centuries after the Parthenos was dedicated on the Akropolis, Pergamum was rising as 'the Athens of the East', and the kings of Pergamum were making their own sculptural dedications on the Akropolis (see Chapter 9).

The historian Philochorus relates that 44 talents of precious material were invested in the drapery of the Parthenos. The ancient Greek talent is equivalent to around 26 kg (over 50 lb); if by 'precious material' we assume gold, the total weight of gold on the statue was 1144 kg – worth something like £9 million, or $15 million, at current rates. This sheer quantity of gold, and the allegations of its occasional theft or 'borrowing' from the statue, have encouraged some scholars to think of the Parthenos not so much as a work of art as a glorified treasury – or a rather overstated way of keeping public funds under public scrutiny. But this concept is wrong on two counts. First, it should be noted that the simple olive-wood statue of Athena Polias, which the Parthenos supplanted (or complemented) as the main cult image of Athena on the Akropolis, was, as early as the sixth century BC, embellished with a *kosmos* of gold trappings. The prehistoric Polias image may have had an essentially aniconic core, but its exterior was bright and golden (perhaps including a mask for a face). So

although it was on a small scale, the principle of associating precious metal with the divinity of Athena was already established.

As for the colossal scale of the Parthenos, we have some evidence that huge size was cognitively associated with divinity. In the Homeric Hymn to Aphrodite, for example, Aphrodite first manifests herself as a young submissive virgin to the shepherd Anchises, who delightedly makes love to her; she then wakes him from his post-coital sleep as Aphrodite the goddess, so large that her head 'touches the well-hewn roof' of his house, terrifying the small mortal man. Much later, we find in the rhetorician Aelius Aristeides (second century AD) a 'Sacred Tale' relating to a vision of the Athena Parthenos, in which the statue ('the Athena of Pheidias', as Aelius calls it), appears 'in all her beauty and magnitude' (*kai to kallos kai to megathos*: *Sacred Tales* II.41). The phrase is immediately repeated, like some prophylactic formula; and the conjunction of beauty with size to

106 A reconstructed model of the Athena Parthenos – the chryselephantine sculpture in the Parthenon by Pheidias – in the Royal Ontario Museum, Toronto.

delineate Athena incarnate is unlikely to be a novel concept belonging to Aelius. So one is inclined to allow a genuinely religious motive for the commission of such a huge statue.

The paradoxes of Athena the female patron of a city dominated by men; of Athena Parthenos ('the Virgin') and yet the Mother of Men (a chorus of old men in Euripides' *Heracleidae*, lines 770–72, hails Athena not only as 'Queen', *potnia*, but also as 'Mother, Mistress and Protectress' – *mater, despoina, phylax*), cannot themselves be resolved here, though the Parthenos statue embodies them. As they gazed on her, Athenians saw a figure at once comforting and threatening. Athena's warrior status was implied by her helmet, from whose visor sprang winged horses, like the *protomai* of old-fashioned tripods; the spear resting against her left shoulder; and by the Nike figure, flourishing a wreath, in her extended hand: victory assured. In the myth-history of Athens, and specifically of the

107 The 'Lenormant' statuette: a second- or third-century AD version of the Athena Parthenos.

108 The 'Varvakeion' statuette: a second-century AD model of the Athena Parthenos.

Akropolis, Athena – whom most Athenians would simply refer to as 'the goddess', *he theos* – was protective beyond the normal bounds of maternal instinct. She had her shawl with its aegis, the apotropaic gorgoneion; and her shield, propped up by the 'home-guarding snake' (*oikouros ophis*): thus she harboured the city, its mythical founders and all its manhood past and present. At the same time, she sponsored the model behaviour of the citizen woman. Not quite so overtly as Archaic versions of the Athena 'Palladium' statue, which brandished a javelin in one hand, and a distaff and spindle in the other; but by her title-claim to chastity, and the voluminous style of her dress, the 'sensible' Doric peplos, the Parthenos embodied the testing ideal which Athenian men created for their women – to be sexually pure, rear children and keep the citizenry well fed and well clothed.

Pheidias, as ancient commentators noted, explored every available space for extra figurative decoration. Just as an orator turned his speech around a series of topics or paragraph-headings, said Pliny, so Pheidias used each 'junction' of the Parthenos to build up its thematic swell (*Natural History* XXXVI.18). Hence the Gigantomachy on the inside of the shield. Athena's part in the cosmic defeat of the Giants was an almost obligatory part of her iconography, and every year the peplos woven for the little old Athena Polias statue carried some sort of Gigantomachy. Here Pheidias chose to show the Giants storming Mount Olympus itself. Then, on the shield's exterior, an Amazonomachy – a clever pairing of themes, since the Amazons, like the Giants, were shown assailing an eminence, obviously implying a shared sort of impiety. Here, frissons of recent myth-history were evoked by the resemblance of Amazons to Persians, and the object of Amazon attack being the Akropolis; and further frissons were generated, apparently, by the sculptor showing himself and his friend Perikles among the heroic Greeks repelling the Amazon–Persians.

On the sandals of the statue were scenes of Lapiths fighting Centaurs, and the allegorical force of that story must by then have been widely appreciated by contemporary viewers. But what are we to make of the most innovative scenes on the Parthenos – the reliefs along the base, which evidently featured the birth of Pandora, in the company of twenty Olympians? The myth of Pandora, at least as related by Hesiod in the seventh century BC (partly in his *Theogony*, and more fully in *Works and Days*, 42–105), seems at first sight inappropriate; Hesiod is after all obsessed with the *pithos* of Pandora, brimming with evils, and presents her creation as a curse on the male gender. Of all the gifts bestowed on Pandora, the 'all-endowed', Hesiod dwells with most relish on the 'bitchy character' (*kuneos noos*) given to her by Hermes. But this disenchanted Hesiodic reading may have softened by the fifth century. Pandora may be deemed pertinent to this statue because she is a *parthenos* too, who will be dressed by Athena. Some scholars imagine that the multiple act of divine endowment, the focus of the Pheidian relief, served as a metaphor for all the divine blessings conferred on the city of Athens; and one recent reading of the Parthenon frieze would argue that it too features a reference to the Pandora story. But perhaps we may see, despite our austere suspicion of the sculptor-as-genius, an overweening input from the sculptor here. Pandora was fashioned by Hephaistos, for the delight of mankind: she walked, she talked, she was laden with grace (*charis*). Pheidias had made an Athena popularly viewed as animate; perhaps, following the dictum of an anonymous Archaic poet, he believed that 'a beautiful woman can conquer iron and fire'. To liken his own work to that of Hephaistos might have been an irresistible temptation.

The other acknowledged achievement of Pheidias, the Olympic Zeus, was seen by Pausanias in AD 174. It was fortunate still to remain at Olympia, since the emperor Caligula, around AD 40, is said to have attempted to abduct it to Rome (and only desisted, so it is said, when lightning struck the ship intended to transport the statue, and workmen sent to dismantle him heard the Zeus emit a terrible laugh). Pausanias describes a figure made of gold and ivory, seated on an ebony throne, wearing a mantle and an olive wreath; in the right hand was a Nike; in the left, a sceptre topped by an eagle. He also states (V. 11.1–9): 'I know that the height and breadth of the Olympic Zeus have been measured and recorded but even the records fall short of the impression made by the external appearance [*doxa*] of the statue.' A series of coins minted between AD 98 and 198 vaguely substantiates this description, and permits a reconstruction of the statue, which became one of the Seven Wonders of the Ancient World (*ill. 109*).

According to the first-century geographer Strabo, the Olympic Zeus was an essentially Homeric creation; he reminds us (VIII. 3.30) of *Iliad* I. 528 – 'The son of Kronos spoke, nodding his dark brows; ambrosial locks streamed forward from the great god's immortal head, and all Olympus quaked'. Yet Strabo registers a worry about the scale of the statue, just fitting the temple cella as a seated image: 'If Zeus arose he would unroof the temple'. But perhaps only the most convinced devotees of animated statues admitted that worry.

In itself, perhaps, the statue boasted not absolutely massive dimensions: on a pedestal just over 1 m (3¼ ft) high, it reached just short of the temple ceiling (about 14 m, or 45 ft high). But its size was magnified by a distinctive setting: in a shallow pool, made of dark limestone, containing olive oil. This basin had practical purposes – the olive oil kept the ivory parts of the statue moist, and also reflected light up on to the statue, functioning as a great mirror. This strategy echoed a similar recourse with the Parthenos, though there the pool is said to have held water, not oil. At Olympia, keeping the chryselephantine parts of the Zeus in good fettle was a dedicated job: we are told by Pausanias about some hereditary retainers, the *phaidruntai* ('shiners'), who improbably claimed that they were *apogonoi Pheidiou*, descendants of Pheidias himself.

Like the Parthenos, the Olympic Zeus must have taken the best part of a decade to make. But unlike the Parthenos, we know precisely where the Zeus was assembled. As noted above, before it was knocked down to make way for a small Christian basilica, the workshop or *ergasterion* of Pheidias was visible at Olympia. Pausanias saw it (V. 15.1), and in 1958 it was brought to light by the German excavators at Olympia. Mention has already been made of the quaintest attestation of a Pheidian presence here, the little black-glazed mug inscribed 'I belong to Pheidias'; but perhaps what is most important about the workshop is that its dimensions closely match the dimensions of the cella of the Temple of Zeus, so that the statue could be fully assembled and 'tried' before its transference there. As such, this was a near-monumental workshop. It had painted terracotta antefixes on its roof, and the fact that it was left standing long after the work was completed implies a residual reverence for the place where the Zeus was made. As the excavators have demonstrated, ample traces of the fabrication of a chryselephantine statue were found in and around the workshop – traces of ivory and obsidian; of gold-chasing tools, woodworking, terracotta kilns and metal-working furnaces – but a number of moulds and matrices recovered among this debris must, by virtue of their scale, belong to a statue (or statues) other than the Zeus. So Pheidias and his associates must have carried out other commissions here, or perhaps the studio continued in use for some time after the 430s.

Scraps of workshop debris, and a little black mug, may seem unworthy testimonia with which to close an account of Pheidias. Let us remember instead the impact his work had on those who actually saw it. Perhaps the most significant echo of the capacity of this sculptor to capture a divine essence in his work comes from the Roman historian Livy. The context is the military campaign in Greece and Macedonia of L. Aemilius Paullus, who in 167 BC, having opened up the way for a full Roman annexation of Greece with his victory at the battle of Pydna, decided to educate himself with a tour of Greek sites and sanctuaries. Livy prefaces his account of the general's grand tour (XLV. 27–8) with the sniffy observation that the glories of Greek art and architecture were 'greater by reputation than by visual acquaintance'. But Olympia was one site that did not disappoint expectations. *Iovem velut praesentem intuens motus animo est*: the general's 'soul was stirred, as he gazed upon what seemed Jove's very incarnation'.

That was surely the response which Pheidias would have wanted.

109 A reconstruction drawing of the Olympic Zeus, a colossal chryselephantine sculpture by Pheidias.

8

REVEALING APHRODITE

Far from being merely an entertainment for males, the nude, as a genre, is one of many cultural phenomena that teaches women to see themselves through male eyes and in terms of dominating male interests. While it sanctions and reinforces in men the identification of virility with domination, it holds up to women self-images in which even sexual self-expression is prohibited.

Carol Duncan, *The Aesthetics of Power* (Cambridge 1993), 113

I would rather see her lovely walk and the shining sparkle of her face than the chariots of the Lydians and armed infantry fighting.

Sappho of Lesbos (*Greek Lyric* I, 67)

The stirrings of pornography

In a strictly etymological sense, the Greeks endowed the world with pornography: *porne*, prostitute or whore; *graphein*, to depict. The Greeks were not the first culture to depict their women erotically naked, nor did the first female nudes in Greek art properly belong to an erotic ambience: statuettes of 'fertility goddesses' or *kourotrophoi* can be invoked as fore-runners. But the appropriation of the female nude as an *objet d'art* by male artists and male voyeurs undoubtedly derives from the realms and institutions the Greeks associated with *porneia* or 'bodily desire'.

'Prostitution' is perhaps a misleading term here, since the functions of the Greek courtesan entailed rather more than the straightforward exchange of sex for cash. Bearing in mind the circumstances of the respectable Greek wife – not only confined to mostly domestic duties, but also largely uneducated – we should recognize that Greek prostitutes offered their minds as well as their bodies. Commercial promiscuity was based on more than a range of skilful sexual manoeuvres: these were unusual women who knew how to drink wine, play music, dance dances and quote Homer. Such women were called *hetairai*, which means simply 'female companions'.

(opposite)

110 Aphrodite of Knidos; a cast of a Roman copy of the Greek original.

They appear where we should expect to find them: on the decorated drinking vessels produced for symposia. The symposium was essentially a drinking party, and primarily for men. But it admitted women who could match men in their drinking and conversation, and go beyond that in musical and sensual entertainment. On vases used for liquid refreshment at these parties we often see the *hetairai* partaking themselves, and usually they are naked save for a garland or two. The whiff of ambitious sex is never very far away from their bodies, whether according to male fantasy or indeed because symposia were regularly orgiastic. For now, however, we may content ourselves with a class of quieter images. These are the glimpses of *hetairai* when the women are not actually on show: the *hetairai* at their toilette.

Sometimes such images are splashed over the exterior surface of a vase – groups of girls at a pool, washing and drying themselves. More often, though, they are on the insides of drinking cups: small tondo depictions that the drinker (usually male) would come across as he drained his wine. If the wine was dark, as it generally was, then the image may be reckoned to have a sort of surprise element to it. One such scene is shown in *ill. 111*, painted in Athens during the early to mid-fifth century BC. On this and other vases similar to it, the girl is shown next to a wash-stand and basin. She may be hanging up her boots, or carrying her clothes and towel in a bundle. Such figures tend to look boyish, for reasons that we shall encounter shortly, but they are definitely female, and the vase illustrated includes the inscription *kale* – 'lovely girl!' – beside its subject.

111 A naked female figure in the interior of an early fifth-century BC Athenian drinking-cup by Onesimos.

The element of voyeurism here is undeniable. It is the artistic prehistory of what has been characterized as 'the male gaze'. This, as John Berger has pointed out, is an essentially European artistic tradition, mythologized in the Judgment of Paris, and later sustained by centuries of oil painting, in which the woman is always set up to be surveyed by male viewers – and now knows that she is being surveyed. The pretence of invaded privacy is part of the game: a peeping-tom may lurk unseen, but is still representative of the male gaze.

The voyeuristic element is also important in determining the difference between the naked and the nude (discussed earlier). These *hetairai* are not naked ladies, but nudes: women whose naive nakedness has been transformed into a focus of artistic appreciation; women who have therefore become nudes in the long art-historical procession of nudes. It is a loss of innocence, and a loss of innocence that the Greeks themselves must have registered.

The images from vase-painting are significant for sculpture in several ways. In the first place, the favourite moment for catching the *hetaira* naked (or nude) is when she is washing. The statues of Aphrodite, as we shall see, also prefer this *bagneuse* moment, with one key difference. Whereas the vase-painter is simply training a telescope on a woman unaware that she is being watched, Aphrodite will be shown to respond to the male gaze – gathering up her dress, or shielding her breasts or genitals. As gestures go, these are hopelessly counterproductive, serving only to direct the viewer's attention in certain directions. But such is the development of the artistic nude: once there is the notion that certain parts of the female body are 'pudenda', parts that ought not to be seen, then interest in seeing them burgeons.

Secondly, the vases convey some titillating intentions. The source of titillation is not only the sight of the naked female body (there is evidence to suggest that Athenian men rarely saw their wives completely naked, and that Athenian wives wore wraps even during sexual intercourse with their husbands); it is also the surprise of seeing it as one tips one's wine-cup dry. This yields the frisson of unexpected pleasure – and it conjures up a number of powerful taboos. In the first book of Herodotus (I. 7–13), for example, there is the story of Gyges and Candaules. Candaules, King of Lydia, was so proud of his wife's body that he insisted that his best friend Gyges should have a surreptitious glimpse of it in her boudoir. The queen notices Gyges, however, and presents him with an ultimatum: either face execution himself, or kill the king and marry her. Whatever the relative associations of this story (e.g. David and Uriah, in the Second Book of Samuel) and literary reworkings (by André Gide and others), its anthropological force remains: the male gaze could be transgressive. Herodotus comments on nakedness being shameful (*aischros*) to the Lydians, but he expected his Greek audience to share a sense of transgression. Later on (V. 92) he will describe as an outrage the occasion when the Corinthian tyrant Periander invites women to a sanctuary of Hera and then humiliates them by stripping them of their clothes. But perhaps what lodged most firmly in the Greek male mind was the myth of Actaeon: the hunter whose chase took him, quite by chance, to the pool where Artemis was bathing. Actaeon could not help espying the goddess naked, but that pleasure hardly mitigated his punishment: his own dogs tore him apart. (An Archaic metope from Selinus Temple E vigorously depicts this story.)

Attestations in Greek culture of the purity of clothes (for women) and the danger of nakedness (for women) could be multiplied, but we have enough to serve as a preface to the revealing of Aphrodite. And although the vases do not specifically depict the goddess, they are a reminder that the patroness of *hetairai* might be known as Aphrodite Hetaira (as she was worshipped at Athens) or Aphrodite Porne (as at Ephesus and Abydos in Asia Minor). And ultimately it was the cult of Aphrodite, with a strong admixture of Oriental elements and syncretisms, which opened the way for Greek sculptors to create the basis for the Western fetish that is the female nude.

Aphrodite's genesis; Aphrodite's cult

All Greek deities carried a bundle of sobriquets with them, but Aphrodite carried more than most. She was Ambologera: Postponer of Old Age. She was Epistrophia: the Heart-twister. She was Psithyros: the Whispering One. She was Parakyptousa: the Side-glancer. She was Peitho: Persuasion. Above all she was Charidotes: the Joy-giver. Some of her early temple images presented her as armed, reminding us of Aphrodite's dalliance with Ares; but in general her cult was a shameless salutation of life below the navel. And it was from below the navel, but in a bizarre manner, that she was born.

In Hesiod's mythical Greek cosmology, Gaia, Mother Earth, was coupled with Uranus, who was Heaven in name but a brute by nature. Gaia bore the many unruly sons of Uranus, but eventually tired of his deceits and visitations. She made a flint sickle and enlisted the help of her youngest son, Cronos, in punishing Uranus. The punishment was drastic. Cronos lopped off his father's genitals, which tumbled into the sea. A divine foam arose where they fell and out of that foam (*aphros*) came Aphrodite. Some said she came ashore on the island of Kythera; others that she was 'Kyprogene', Cyprus-born. The southwest coast of Cyprus has a number of foamy beaches which claim this aetiology; and at Cypriot Paphos a large meteoric baetyl-stone was worshipped, presumably as one of the lost parts of Uranus.

Specialists are bound, however, to discount the link between *aphros* and Aphrodite. The name is more likely a Hellenization of the Near Eastern deity Ashtoreth or Astarte, a Mother-Goddess figure whom the Phoenicians in particular made known to the Greeks. The Cypriot genesis of Aphrodite may reflect no more than the Phoenician colonization of Kition (Larnaka) in the mid-ninth century BC. At certain cult sites around the Mediterranean, in due time, Phoenician Astarte and Greek Aphrodite shared cult centres: at Eryx, in Sicily, for example, as well as on Kythera. Phoenician merchants probably encouraged the development of the Aphrodite cult at Corinth; they were certainly involved in the promotion of Astarte at the Graeco-Etruscan port of Pyrgi in Etruria. It hardly comes as a surprise to learn that the cult of Aphrodite thrived at sites visited by sailors, nor that the temples of the goddess were designed to accommodate the sex-hungry. Aphrodite's vicars at her Corinthian temple, up on the eminence of Acrocorinth, were reckoned in the early Roman empire to number a thousand or so. These women were *hierodouloi*, 'priestesses', insofar as they officiated on behalf of Aphrodite. But since the goddess herself was synonymous with making love – *aphrodisia*, the act; *aphro-disiazein*, the action – her priestesses necessarily acted, under sacred guise, as *hetairai*.

Precisely when this aspect of Aphrodite's cult began to be practised in Greece is not clear. Herodotus (I. 199) speaks rather distastefully of sacred prostitution as a Babylonian phenomenon, noting that it is also present on Cyprus. Later, an inscription from Athens dated to 333 BC records permission given to men of Kition (i.e. Phoenicians) to establish a temple to Aphrodite in the Piraeus. As we shall see, the most celebrated Greek statue of Aphrodite was in a temple whose *temenos* was used by Aphrodite's followers (*Aphrodisiazontes*) to practical effect, and it is tempting to connect the overtly erotic development of Aphrodite's image with the overtly erotic nature of her cult. We might also note that Near Eastern images of Astarte (in Babylon known as Ishtar) created obvious precedents for naked depictions of Aphrodite, although L.R. Farnell, who fully acknowledged the Semitic cult origins of Aphrodite, allowed that 'the idea of representing the goddess of beauty and love as naked may have occurred quite naturally and spontaneously to the Greek artists of the fourth century'. But before we address the issue of Aphrodite's nudity, there is one important element of the Aphrodite mythology and the Aphrodite cult worth highlighting.

Structuralist analysis of Aphrodite's attributes and modes of worship finds an antithesis to Aphrodite, not far from the goddess herself. This is Demeter, governess of fertility and renewal – partly in terms of human procreation, but predominantly in agriculture. As Marcel Detienne has shown, we can set up a series of oppositions between Aphrodite and Demeter: the one worshipped by courtesans, the other by wives and virgins; the cult occasions of the one marked by feasting and licence, of the other by fasting and abstinence; the one bathed in perfumes, the other in seriousness. Aphrodite has her cherished boy, Adonis – eternally young, eternally to be petted and cosseted; Demeter, in much more matronly fashion, has Persephone, rescued from sexual abduction to bring flowers to the earth.

In the language of images these polarities could hardly be made plainer. The best-known statue of Demeter is to be found in the British Museum and was one of E.M. Forster's favourite pieces: awesomely demure – with her deeply drilled, multiple-layered drapery, and soft benign features, she is as solid a package of maternity as one could ever imagine (*ill. 112*). This Demeter was made in the mid- to late fourth century BC, and was originally housed in a sanctuary at Knidos. Not far away, within easy walking distance, stood Aphrodite. She was not enthroned, but caught as she bathed; not swathed in folds, but completely undressed. The contrast between the two goddesses, as they were presented at Knidos, must have been striking. Pausanias says that there were several temples of Aphrodite here, but one in particular warrants our attention. This was the one which became notorious precisely because of its statue: the statue which, in Kenneth Clark's phrase, sustained a 'sensual tremor' for five hundred years, and arguably laid the basis for the female nude in subsequent Western art.

Knidos: the shock of the nude?

At some point in the early to mid-fourth century BC – 360, or thereabouts – the people of Knidos, an old Greek colony in the region of Caria, in Asia Minor, decided to build themselves a new city. The site they chose was a headland plus adjacent island (which they connected to the mainland, thus creating a useful double harbour). It was a grand project: the city was not only laid out along the orthogonal protocols established over a century earlier by Hippodamos of Miletus, but it was also terraced up a fairly steep hillside. Quite why the Knidians elected to leave their former centre – further down the peninsula, near modern Datça – is not known. But what matters here is the fact that a new city was created and was a promising sponsor for something new in sculpture.

The opportunity seems to have arisen just at the right moment. This is the story as related by the Elder Pliny in the first century AD; it appears in the context of his discussion of the artistic career of Praxiteles:

> The greatest work of this sculptor, indeed one of the greatest sculptures in the whole world, is his Venus, which many people have sailed to Knidos to see. Praxiteles in fact made two statues which he put up for sale together. One of them was draped, and because it was draped was preferred by the people of Kos, who had first choice of the statues (which were offered at the same price). They thought this the decent thing to do. But the statue they refused was taken instead by the people of Knidos, and it was this statue which became renowned. Later King Nicomedes [of Kos] tried to buy it from the Knidians, promising to discharge their enormous state debt. But the Knidians resolutely held on to their statue, and rightly so: for it was this work of Praxiteles which made Knidos famous. The shrine in which it stands is openly constructed in order to allow the statue of the goddess to be viewed from every angle, and they say that the goddess encouraged this herself. And indeed the statue is equally marvellous whichever way you look at it.
>
> (*Natural History* XXXVI.4.20–1)

Pliny's claim that Praxiteles' statue put the new Knidos on the map is confirmed by numerous Knidian coin issues (mostly Roman) showing a nude Aphrodite by a vase. Further confirmation of the statue's celebrity had to wait until 1969, when an unorthodox yet aptly named archaeologist, Iris Love, began excavating at Knidos. Her excavations have never been fully published, but they were at least halfway successful as regards the Knidian Aphrodite. That is, the statue itself was not found; but its temple was.

112 Demeter of Knidos; mid-fourth century BC.

Being marble, the statue had a better chance of survival than a bronze. It was probably removed from Knidos at the time Constantine installed his capital at Byzantium. Bishops of the Early Church reserved especial venom for the cult of Aphrodite, and they may eventually have had the Knidian

113 A reconstruction of the temple of Aphrodite at Knidos, with the famous cult statue in the centre.

statue destroyed; or else it ended up in Ottoman lime-kilns. It is now gone, and we get only an approximate idea of the statue from two types of copies (or rather, adaptations) – one showing the goddess bathing *al fresco*, the other seemingly an interior scene, with a huge water carrier involved. These approximations are so stodgy and sexless that they can only be something of a disappointment (*ill. 110*). Instead we may contemplate an imagined reconstruction of the Knidian temple (*ill. 113*) and review the archaeological context in the light of a literary account which is basically convincing as a description, though of dubious authorship.

This is a dialogue titled *Erotes* ('Loves', or 'Affairs of the Heart') and attached, with scholarly misgivings, to the work of a Greek satirist and essayist called Lucian, who was writing in the second century AD. The actual authorship is not important to us here; it provides us with a vignette of what it was like to visit the Knidian temple in Roman times. As Pliny says, many people made the journey simply to see the statue (*quam ut viderent multi navigaverunt Cnidum*). Lucian sails there – he calls it 'Aphrodite's city' (*polis Aphrodites*) – in the company of two friends. One is Corinthian, and avowedly heterosexual; the other is Athenian, and of homosexual orientation.

Once disembarked, the three men wander through the porticoes of the terraced city. The remains of a stoa have indeed been uncovered at Knidos, and its colonnades would be the first features of the city to strike the visitor landing at the commercial harbour. Lucian and his friends then progress upwards. Thanks to the steep terracing, the temple of Aphrodite must have been clearly visible. What the 1969 excavations brought to light was a circular Doric temple at the western end of the uppermost terrace. A simple but unusual structure, it has no separate *naos* (inner-sanctum) for the cult image. Eighteen columns are raised on a stepped base or socle and there is an inner perimeter wall which may have been low enough for visitors to peer over, or perhaps could be entered via a door. A statue-base was found *in situ* in the centre of the enclosed area. Two inscriptions were recovered from elsewhere in the city, both incomplete, but one clearly refers to both Praxiteles and Aphrodite, and the other perhaps defines Aphrodite as *gymne* (naked). There is little doubt that this is the temple which housed the statue, and the temple which Lucian visited (what clinches the identification is the exact resemblance of both design and circumference to the copy of the Knidian temple created by Hadrian at his villa at Tivoli).

Remains of altars and little treasuries have been found in this vicinity, but no paving of the temple's *temenos* (sacred precinct) has been identified as contemporary with its original state, which helps us to make sense of what Lucian proceeds to relate. For Lucian and his friends, once within the precincts of the temple, found themselves in a fragrant and luxuriant orchard, a garden dominated by myrtle-trees and entangled with ivy and vines. In this bower they note 'happy couches' (*hilarai klisiai*), where devotees of the goddess could practise her arts (*ta Aphrodisia* could equate to cuddles and sex). Then they see the statue: a figure who is completely 'revealed' (*akalyptos*), save for a modest gesture to conceal her erogenous zones. Lucian's heterosexual companion shrieks with delight, and immediately plants kisses on the lips of the statue.

The trio then make their way around the rotonda for a back view of Aphrodite. Here it is the turn of the Athenian to get excited. As Lucian comments, he appreciates 'those parts of the goddess which would befit a boy': her flanks (*lagones*) are what the homosexual admires, likening her from this aspect to Ganymede, the twinkling acolyte of Zeus. But the beauty of the image brings tears to the eyes of them all.

It is at this juncture that Lucian notes a blot on the glorious backside of Aphrodite. Could it possibly be a defect in the marble, he wonders? The answer is at hand, from an attendant priestess. She tells the visitors about an unfortunate lad who fell hopelessly in love with the cult image, and one night contrived to have himself covertly locked inside the temple. The stain on the statue was no less than a relic of the boy's attempt to consummate his passion. When discovered, in his shame, he hurled himself over a cliff (there is indeed a precipitous drop into the sea just by the temple).

A number of ancient writers relate this tale. Lucian's, despite its dubious date and authorship, is the best version, and nicely conjures up the heady ambience of the sanctuary in which such a passion could be fostered. Those who frequented this and other cult places of Aphrodite were perfumed *Aphrodisiazontes*. No wonder at Knidos there was little space immediately close to the temple for conducting sacrifices: the garden, with its happily ensconced couples, was where the practical worship took place. On a lower terrace below the temple the Knidians built a large altar, with rows of seats above it, where the duller protocols of animal sacrifice to Aphrodite could be observed.

As Michel Foucault has analysed it, Lucian's setting of his dialogue at Knidos is deliberately ambiguous. The story of the youth who left his mark on Aphrodite's behind anticipates the debate between heterosexual and homosexual modes: for the boy took the statue as he would take another boy (*paidikos*), from the rear. Aphrodite virtually becomes hermaphroditic in this incarnation. So on that account is would be misleading to characterize this statue as some ancient equivalent of the modern pin-up girl. But it is still a matter of the male gaze, of course; and the aggregation of ancient sources leaves us in little doubt that the statue at Knidos evoked erotic responses from those who went to see it – and that such responses were not only indulged but perhaps even encouraged by the temple staff.

Why did the statue acquire such notoriety? The answer that it was the first nude Aphrodite is simple, but not wholly satisfactory. A metaphor used by Euripides in the fifth century BC should alert us: in his *Hecuba*, describing the brutal sacrifice at an altar of Polyxena, he relates how the young girl bared her breasts, which were 'as lovely as a statue's' (*hos agalmatos kallista*: lines 558–60). So which statues did Euripides have in mind? The fact that sculpted female nudes from the fifth century have not survived does not mean that none existed. In fact it looks very much as though there was an undraped Aphrodite on the Parthenon: in the seventeenth-century drawing of the west pediment by Jacques Carrey a figure (now lost) of a woman, apparently naked, has been plausibly identified as Aphrodite (*ill. 114*). She would be rising from the lap of Thalassa, the Sea; her presence at the central event, Poseidon contesting Attica with Athena, is quite to be expected. It is true that relief sculptures of the fifth century showing the birth of Aphrodite retain her drapery – but even then one is inclined to allow Greek sculptors the same sensual insight as modern image-makers, who are well aware that wet or wind-blown drapery can be just as effective as nudity, if not more so, in accentuating erotic appeal (the figures from the parapet of the Nike Temple in Athens are good examples of this; also the Nike of Paionios at Olympia, see *ill. 51*).

There were cult centres of Aphrodite in Athens from which no cult images survive: a temple to Aphrodite and Eros on the North Slope of the Acropolis, for example, and a 'Garden' temple mentioned by Pausanias (I. 19.2: *Aphrodite en kepois*), probably by the River Ilissos, with a late fifth-century cult statue attributed to Alkamenes. This latter temple looks to afford at least a precedent for 'visiting' the goddess in perfumed surroundings, though the appearance of the cult statue is not known to us. We should, however, be wary of defining Aphrodite's nudity in itself as shocking; indeed, of making too much of a taboo on female nakedness in the fifth century. While it does seem to be the case that the citizen-women of Athens (and other Greek states, with the exception of Sparta) maintained decorous veils around their bodies, this does not mean that their husbands were unaccustomed to the sight of a naked female body. There were the *hetairai*, as we have seen; and the comedian Aristophanes more than once has naked women on his stage (or male actors 'dressed-up' as such).

Pliny is the only source for the notion that the Knidian Aphrodite, produced in the mid-fourth century BC by Praxiteles, was scandalously unclad. Being Roman, Pliny was sensitive to the issue of nudity. He may have foisted his own prudishness on to the tale of a statue's refusal by Kos and acceptance by Knidos. A rather more likely objection that Greeks in the fourth century might have harboured was that Praxiteles made no secret of using his own *hetaira* as the model for Aphrodite. This lady, called Phryne, gathered an impressive reputation around her: the most memorable of several stories relating to her sex appeal is the one about her appearance in an Athenian court, when she convinced the jury of her innocence simply by revealing to them her breasts. Considering the many clichéd epigrams which were penned to the Knidian Aphrodite, along the lines of Aphrodite saying to the sculptor, 'Just when did you see me naked, Praxiteles?' (see Vol. V of the Loeb *Greek Anthology*, 159–70), one can imagine a certain risk of impropriety in presenting a living courtesan as a cult figure. But even that may be too much: as one who had happily viewed Aphrodite, Praxiteles could allow himself to join mythical predecessors, including Paris and Anchises. The goddess also allowed herself to be vicariously approached through her many priestesses; and it was a straight consequence of anthropomorphic religion that encouraged young men to kiss and copulate with statues of the goddess of love.

Perhaps what stood in the rotonda at Knidos was simply a very fine and very suggestive work of art. To judge from later 'editions' of it – the best, though incomplete, is probably the one recovered from Hadrian's Villa,

114 A drawing of part of the west pediment of the Parthenon, attributed to Jacques Carrey, *c.* 1674. It includes a naked female figure, now lost, probably Aphrodite.

now in the museum at Tivoli – its naturalism was not its source of enchantment. One conspicuous feature is the absence of pubic hair. Greek sculptors were not averse to showing male pubic hair, and the *hetairai* painted on fifth-century vases seem to display it. Possibly Phryne shaved or depilated herself. If she did, then she perhaps should be held ultimately responsible for that unfortunate honeymoon experience of John Ruskin – apocryphal or not – when a man thoroughly versed in Western art was horrified to discover that women possess hairy genitals (and is said never to have admitted his wife to his bed again). Such may be the extent of the influence of this nude at Knidos, that all subsequent nudes were given smooth pubic triangles. We shall never be able to appreciate how fine in other respects the statue was. But it is clear that its resonance was stylistically, and socially, deeply felt around the Mediterranean.

Aphrodite at large

Aphrodite at Knidos was worshipped as Aphrodite Euploia – Aphrodite of 'fair sailing', or 'blessed navigation'. The increase of sea-borne trade in the Hellenistic Mediterranean naturally fostered the spread and expansion of Aphrodite's cult. Before we look at the variations of the cult image generated after the fourth century, we might note that the round temple itself became a celebrated design. Hadrian's act of architectural homage was only the latest of many previous ones. For instance, one of the Hellenistic rulers of Egypt, Ptolemy Philopater (222–205 BC), replicated the temple

on board one of his ships, close to his own cabin, complete with marble cult statue. Similar temples were erected to rival that of Knidos – at nearby Caunos, for example; and on Kos an alternative attraction was created by a painting of Aphrodite Anadyomene – Aphrodite rising from the waves – by Apelles. Knowledge of this from literary sources doubtless inspired Botticelli's well-known versions of the same subject, now in Florence and Berlin. Apelles is said to have served as court painter to Alexander the Great; the stories allege that his model too was Phryne, sketched as Aphrodite when she walked into the sea near Eleusis with her hair down. (She would appear to have aged elegantly.)

The eroticism of the Knidian Aphrodite was most overtly trumped by the cult and cult images of Aphrodite Kallipygos – Aphrodite of the Beautiful Buttocks (sometimes also Aphrodite Kalligloutos). A number of statues and reliefs attest a figure who, as if in the course of a dance, lifts up her skirts to reveal her bottom – and glances over her shoulder to check its beauty for herself. We are told, unreliably, that a cult to Aphrodite Kallipygos grew up at Syracuse after two peasant sisters began bickering as to which of them possessed the fairer behind, and eventually asked a passer-by to adjudicate (the passer-by not only fell violently in love with one of girls, but despatched his younger brother along to inspect the other: double nuptials ensued); and we are told that *hetairai* might stage, among themselves, bottom competitions (*philoneikia hyper tes pyges*), though

115 The 'Venus de Milo'. Though the statue was found on Melos it was made elsewhere and probably dates from the second century BC.

116 'Crouching Aphrodite'. On her back is a small hand, all that now remains of Eros.

admittedly, the source for this is a late writer called Alciphron, who composed imaginary letters. The bottom competition is described, perhaps with an input of male fantasy, in the fourteenth of his *Epistolai Hetairikai*, or 'Letters of Courtesans'. What is significant about the account is not so much what determines a lovely bottom (there is talk of buttocks 'quivering like jelly', and marvellous rippling motions, and so on), but that Aphrodite is invoked as patroness, and this is explicitly Aphrodite's world. That the goddess herself should be represented gazing down at her own divine *kallipygia* adds an extra dimension to the sensual depiction of Aphrodite. There is no coyness here. She is not trying to conceal herself at all.

One can understand that the Knidian Aphrodite was a hard act to follow. What more of Aphrodite was there to see? So Hellenistic statues of Aphrodite played about with her image, titillating the viewer by showing the slippage of drapes from her body, and adding a tinge of transgression by placing the half-naked goddess in a pseudo-domestic context – pulling thread from a loom, for example. It is not certain what situation the Venus de Milo (*ill. 115*) was originally set in – reaching out to entice her lover Ares? Threading a needle, or holding a plaque or a mirror? Or, as some have supposed, personifying Lust in a group whose other constituents were Virtue (with all her clothes on) and the young Herakles (being invited by the two ladies to follow their respective ways)? What is sure is that the statue is not Classical, but Hellenistic (probably mid-second century BC); and not made on Melos, but in Asia Minor (probably Tralles).

On Cyprus, Aphrodite's alleged birthplace, the goddess became assimilated with the Egyptian Isis: at Soloi, Aphrodite and Isis shared not only the same temple but also the same cult image. At Locri Epizephyri in Magna Graecia, Aphrodite and Persephone were worshipped almost as one. In Asia Minor, syncretisms of Aphrodite and Cybele were popular. The cultic association of Aphrodite and Eros flourished in many places, providing sculptors with plentiful opportunities for playful groups, of which the Louvre's 'Crouching Aphrodite' is a well-known survivor, though of Eros nothing remains save a toddler's paw (*ill. 116*). This grouping allowed sculptors again to tease Aphrodite into a semi-domestic role – in this case, being maternal to the impish Eros. And Aphrodite half-returns to her Near Eastern roots with the creation of her eponymous city along the Maeander, Aphrodisias. Once a Babylonian cult centre for Ishtar-Astarte, the site was renamed by the Greeks in the sixth century BC, and then handsomely endowed by the Romans from the first century BC onwards – largely because Aphrodite was not only the mother of Aeneas, Rome's ultimate founder, but also claimed as divine mother by the Julio-Claudian dynasty, and hence all Roman emperors.

How important her sculptural image remained may be assessed from the manifold literary references to it. The Knidian Aphrodite is not always specified, but seems likely to be in the mind's eye of any writer wanting to make a shorthand description of female pulchritude, especially in writing intended to titillate (*logos erotikos*). A nice instance of this comes in the romance *Chaireas and Callirhoe*, attributed to Chariton, and thought to belong to some time between 100 BC and AD 150. Callirhoe is introduced to us as 'a maiden of amazing beauty, the ornament [*agalma*] of all Sicily'; and in Book Two of the story, we are given a lingering vignette of this beauty at her bath, through the eyes of female companions:

> When she undressed, they were awestruck.... Her skin gleamed white, sparkling just like some shining substance [*marmarygei* – implying marble]; her flesh was so soft that you were afraid even the touch of a finger would cause a bad wound.
>
> (*Chaireas and Callirhoe*, II. 2.2, trans Reardon)

Like Pygmalion's statue coming to life, there is the fantasy of an object gleaming and unblemished as carved marble, yet also wondrously soft to the touch. The image of Aphrodite *baigneuse* has become a quick and easy literary means of evoking the fantasy of ideal – but attainable – beauty.

We may conclude with a Roman image, from the Flavian period (*c*. AD 80). Roman matrons, like Greek citizen-wives, did not customarily display their bodies in public. But such was the power and ubiquity of Aphrodite's nude image in the Roman world that a number of Roman women, some with direct Imperial connections, had themselves portrayed in the mode of *Venus pudica* – essentially the Knidian Aphrodite, with her hands shielding breasts and genitals. They kept their own 'veristic' portrait features, and there is nothing Classically Greek about their beehive hair-dos. One lady, called Ulpia Epigone, went so far as to have herself commemorated for eternity as a semi-divine semi-nude (*ill. 117*). She may be imagining herself as a sleeping Ariadne here, and is firmly clutching the lower half of her modesty. But the exposed breasts are thanks to Aphrodite – or rather, thanks to that sculptural tradition from the Late Classical period onwards which took artistic delight in revealing Aphrodite.

117 The Roman matron Ulpia Epigone shown on her funerary relief; *c*. AD 80.

9

THE PATRONAGE OF KINGS

The king was . . . a political actor, power among powers as well as sign among signs. It was the king's cult that created him, raised him from lord to icon; for, without the dramas of the theatre state, the image of composed divinity could not even take form.

Clifford Geertz, Negara (Princeton 1980), 131.

The rise of 'Hellenistic' sculpture

The lengths to which architects will go to get a commission have never, perhaps, outstripped the exploit of Dinocrates the Macedonian, who, 'confident in his own ideas and skill', tried to present himself to the attention of Alexander the Great. Having attempted the usual formalities of gaining access, and been frustrated by a shield of regal bureaucracy, Dinocrates capitalized on his own powerful physique: he anointed himself with oil, placed a wreath of leaves on his head and a lion's skin on his shoulder, and, brandishing a club, walked prominently in front of a law tribunal where Alexander was giving judgment. Semi-naked, dressed as a second Herakles, he could hardly fail to be noticed. Alexander duly beckoned him over, and asked who he was. 'I am Dinocrates, a Macedonian architect: I come with ideas and plans worthy of your majesty. Look, I have shaped Mount Athos itself into the statue of a man, whose left hand cradles the ramparts of a substantial city; in his right he holds a bowl, to catch all the waters of the rivers running down from the mountain.'

Alexander was delighted (*delectatus*) with this proposal: perhaps he realized immediately that the statue could be made in his likeness. But a practical objection strikes him: how will the city's corn supply be provided? There is no satisfactory answer to this problem, so the Mount Athos project is stalled. Dinocrates is taken into royal service, however, and eventually entrusted with the layout of Alexander's eponymous city in the Nile Delta.

Vitruvius, who tells this story (*De Architectura* II. 1–4), is also trying to curry favour from a patron – the emperor Augustus – to whom he adopts a grovelling tone throughout his book (and here craves the emperor's pardon that he, Vitruvius, cannot depend on a Heraklean stature for such attention-seeking stunts). One wonders if Vitruvius was aware that Alexander himself claimed descent from Herakles and was shown with Heraklean features in some of his portraits. But in any case, the nature of the project suggested by Dinocrates is a useful index of what it takes to please a holder of absolute power. Vanity, megalomania, gross paternalism, all these are satisfied by the Mount Athos design. That anyone could contemplate carving a mountain into a portrait will not seem so extraordinary to twentieth-century readers acquainted with Mount Rushmore in South Dakota, where a number of distinguished Americans have been drilled and blasted into the rockface to commemorate their achievements. One would still dismiss the Dinocrates story as a fiction, were it not for all the other evidence supporting the megalomaniac tendencies of Alexander, and some of his fellow monarchs. In the Classical Greek democracies, self-advertisement was discouraged, or even penalized (by the device of ostracism, whereby citizens voted for the temporary expulsion of anyone who seemed to be getting too powerful). The autocrats who came to dominate the Greek world (and beyond) towards the end of the fourth century BC observed no such decorum.

The Mount Athos project was never begun, but that did not deter later attempts at extravagantly massive sculptural projects. Alexander is said to have retained a court sculptor, Lysippos. Lysippos constructed some colossal statues, including one of Herakles and one of Zeus for the Greek colony of Tarentum, but in turn was trumped by his own pupil, called Chares. This Chares it was who raised the Colossus of Rhodes, early in the third century BC: a hollow-cast bronze reckoned to have stood some 40 m or 120 ft high (about the same size as the Statue of Liberty in New York harbour). Its dimensions are best understood by the ancient estimate that 'few men can get their arms around the statue's thumb'. It was a doomed project: sixty years after it was raised, the Colossus was rocked by an earthquake and collapsed at the knees. For several centuries it lay where it had fallen, its cavernous hollow limbs providing a picturesque tourist experience. Even in its ruined state it was reckoned as one of the Seven Wonders of the Ancient World, until Saracens finally removed it. Reconstructions of the original must remain largely fantastic (*ill. 118*): they may more or less get the gesture of the raised arm right, but the statue is unlikely to have straddled the harbour of Rhodes. What is significant about the statue, however, is its genealogy. Some might imagine that it was indebted to Classical Greek precedents, among others, the colossal statues by Pheidias of Athena Parthenos and Zeus at Olympia (see Chapter 7). But both the size and the subject of the statue are more plausibly attributed to Egyptian influence. The Rhodians commissioned it after surviving a protracted siege

118 An imaginary reconstruction of the Colossus of Rhodes (1830).

mounted by Demetrios Poliorketes ('Besieger of cities': a flamboyant Macedonian monarch about whom we shall have more to say presently). The allies of Rhodes were the Ptolemies of Egypt, and Egyptians were no strangers to vast statues. Nor were the Egyptians unaccustomed to images of the sun-god, whom the Greeks termed Helios. So when Chares proposed to 'give the world a second sun to match the first', this was a patently Egyptianizing enterprise. The choice of medium, bronze, was Greek; and for all we can tell, the style of the image may have been Greek. But the cross-fertilization of Greek style and Greek medium with non-Greek subject and non-Greek scale is typical of what happens in the period we know of as 'Hellenistic'.

In standard accounts of Greek art, 'Hellenistic' is a term borrowed from historians to describe a chronological period whose parameters are generally fixed as the death of Alexander in 323 BC and the battle of Actium in 31 BC (when Octavian, later Augustus, saw off the combined challenge of his fellow Roman, Antony, and the Egyptian queen, Cleopatra). It is an entirely artificial denomination, apparently taken from the use by German scholars of the word *Hellenismos* to denote this period. This in turn comes from a non-Classical Greek usage of the same term in the Greek New Testament, where it refers to communities which may be Jewish, but in language belong to the Greek-speaking world (*koine*). Slightly earlier, it is used in a narrative which Protestant Bibles place among the Apocrypha – Maccabees (II. 4.13) – to describe culpable 'Hellenizing' in Judaea.

So it looks as though the idea of 'Hellenistic' as opposed to 'Hellenic' was not recognized until the first century AD; and we can safely say that the concept of a Hellenistic period is entirely modern. A dictionary definition of 'Hellenistic' as 'following Greek modes of thought or life' remains reasonable, and in fact most of the sculptures mentioned in this chapter were made by Greeks proper. As we shall see, Classical styles and Classical symbols survive in this strictly non-Classical world. But much of the interest of Hellenistic art lies not so much in its Greek as in its barbarian elements. In Athens, furious oratory was directed at the prospect of surrendering democracy to kingship: and a situation in which Athenian artists danced to the tunes called by a monarch must have been almost unimaginable to the makers of the Parthenon (although at the Persian capital Susa, at the end of the sixth century BC, Darius the Great boasted of having employed sculptors from Ionia). But patronage was there, none the less, and often generous patronage: it is only the lack of modern aesthetic sympathy with Hellenistic sculpture that makes its achievements seem less than they really were.

Whether (following most scholars) *Hellenismos* begins with Alexander the Great (356–323 BC) or (following a minority) with his father Philip II, who became ruler of Macedon in 359 BC, the end of 'Classical Greece' and the beginning of 'the Hellenistic world' is a phenomenon traditionally explained in Macedonian terms. The issue of how far the Macedonian kings considered themselves Greek is difficult, and a tender point of modern nationalistic politics in Greece and the Balkans. Traditional histories will assert that the Macedonians effectively 'conquered' Greece. The battle of Chaeronea, in 338 BC, when Philip II of Macedon and his eighteen-year old son Alexander crushed a combined Athenian and Theban army, is usually given as a fixed point of Greek 'enslavement' to the Macedonians. At the same time, Philip endowed Olympia with a family statue-group that suggested a Macedonian at-homeness in the pan-Hellenic world; and Alexander's personal tutor was none other than Aristotle. Undoubtedly, the cultural ambitions of the Macedonian dynasts in the fourth century BC were directed towards Greece, and the phenomenon of Alexander makes Hellenistic art easy to explain. But if 'Hellenistic' implies Greek artists working on non-Greek commissions, we shall have to begin our account of Hellenistic sculpture not in Macedonia but Asia Minor, and at a slightly earlier date than is usually allocated for the 'Hellenistic' category. Certain coastal kingdoms in Asia Minor – Lycia and Caria are the two examples we shall address, though others would also be relevant – maintained, throughout the wars between Greeks and Persians, a sort of independence (if not political, then at least cultural); and inevitably served as buffer zones, in terms of the meeting of Greek and Asiatic minds. Alexander himself would sweep through them in the 330s BC, technically incorporating them into the Macedonian empire, but long before he arrived, these kingdoms had offered work to Greek sculptors.

The results of such commissions may sometimes seem hybrid or 'grotesque'. At Sidon, a Phoenician city on the Levantine coast (Lebanese Saida), we find a series of royal sarcophagi from the fifth century BC onwards which must have been inspired by the anthropoid coffins first designed in Egypt. Yet this Egyptian concept was soon adapted by Greek sculptors, as seen in the use of marble and the Hellenizing features of the face (*ill. 119*). Further stylistic evidence of Greek sculptors at work is to be found in the statuary from the sanctuary of the Phoenician deity

119 An anthropoid sarcophagus from Sidon, with Hellenizing features applied to an Egyptian form; fourth century BC.

Eschmun at Sidon, even when the votive inscriptions accompanying these statues reveal a largely local clientele. Technically, perhaps, this sculpture ought to be called Graeco-Phoenician, or even Graeco-Egypto-Phoenician in the case of the royal sarcophagi – but an extension of the term 'Hellenistic' seems warranted here. And if not here, then most certainly for the most conspicuous act of royal patronage before Alexander: the Mausoleum at Halicarnassus.

The Mausoleum and its antecedents

Modern Bodrum is a town more plagued than dignified by its tourists, and few of them are concerned whether much of ancient Halicarnassus is to be seen. The site of the Mausoleum, which once dominated the capital of Caria, presents a satisfying example of ruined royal arrogance: from the scattered column-drums that now remain one would hardly guess that this structure once stood some 50 m (165 ft) high.

The Mausoleum is named after its ancient occupant, Mausolus, satrap of Caria. To describe the office 'satrap' as 'governor on behalf of the Persians' is normal enough, but this definition should not be taken to imply that Mausolus was a Persian puppet. He was born of a local Carian dynasty, the Hekatomnids. (Hekatomnos preceded Mausolus as satrap, and may have initiated some of the 'proto-Hellenistic' policies with which Mausolus is credited.) His wife, Artemisia, shared the same name as a formidable fifth-century BC queen who had assisted (with distinction) the Persian king, Xerxes, at the battle of Salamis. But although Caria as a province extends some way inland, its seaboard was its main route to prosperity; and Mausolus, whose rule began around 377 BC, seems to have determined that the cultural orientation of his country should face westwards to Greece, rather than eastwards to Persia. He founded his new capital at Halicarnassus, hitherto a modest settlement, which he made into a fortified port by encircling an orthogonal grid of streets with city walls 7 km (4 miles) long (it was to be a populous community, a *polis myriandros*). He also built a palace for himself at the harbour entrance and planned his own enormous tomb so that it would be in full view of all those who sailed by Halicarnassus.

Some ancient writers, fascinated by the energy or piety of his wife, ascribe the tomb to Artemisia, who is said to have organized an epic send-off or *agon* for Mausolus after his death in 353 BC. But Artemisia only survived her husband by two years, scarcely time enough to complete such a complex project. Her siblings may have helped; but the chances are that Mausolus, like those Roman emperors who later designed and built their 'Mausolea' during their own lifetimes (e.g. Augustus and Hadrian), may have conceived his colossal tomb as an integral part of his city. As the founder or *oikist* of 'new' Halicarnassus, Mausolus knew that Greek tradition would allow his commemoration, or even cult, in the centre of the city, close to its market-place. And he was also aware of other traditions, both local and extraneous, which would legitimate both the scale and ostentation of this monument.

Locally, there was a tradition of the family tomb which heroized both husband and wife, and an accumulation of their ancestors. Such tombs were especially prominent in neighbouring Lycia, where again a measure of cultural independence did not deflect prominent individuals from employing Greek sculptors to execute memorials that combined what the Greeks would have called a hero-chapel (*heroon*) with a gallery of ancestors (*syngenikon*). The best-known of the Lycian tombs is what we call the Nereid Monument from Xanthos, now reassembled in the British Museum (*ill. 120*). It is a sign of Lycian marginality in Greek history that we can only guess whom this pseudo-temple celebrates, and simply surmise that he saw himself as a second Achilles (hence the Nereids, mythical marine female friends of Achilles' mother, Thetis), and had his military triumphs extensively trumpeted in the friezes of the monument. One suggestion is that he was a ruler of Xanthos called Arbinas (a Persian-sounding name), formerly tyrant of Tlos (another Lycian city). The reliefs also probably contain some allusions to the exploits and vicissitudes of past generations: a part of the decoration shows a city under siege, and may represent the late sixth-century BC attack on Xanthos by Harpagos the Persian (recounted by Herodotus). The decoration of the frontal pediment is pure dynastic glorification: what scholars sometimes take to be a pair of deities at its centre is more likely to be the couple in whose honour the tomb was raised. Presumed to have been put up around 400–380 BC, this was very likely a tomb with which Mausolus was personally familiar.

The question of whether Mausolus ever visited Persia is open: as a satrap, he may have been occasionally required to go. Had he been to Pasargadae, he may have seen the sixth-century BC tomb of Cyrus (or what then remained of it), who was considered the founder of the Persian empire. This was not a massive monument in absolute terms, but it was undoubtedly once conspicuous in its simple, plain and solid construction. A substantial terraced podium was surmounted by a gabled tomb chamber: the height was sufficient to command the view for miles around. Mausolus might well have regarded this Persian precedent as one from which his own architects could reasonably depart. The stepped part of his own tomb was the roof rather than the podium, and in its dimensions it recalled not so much Persia as Egypt, and in particular the pyramids – the *erga*, the achievements, so wonderingly described by that famous son of old Halicarnassus, Herodotus.

120 The 'Nereid Monument' from Xanthos, Lycia, in Asia Minor; early fourth century BC.

The columns of the Mausoleum, however, are in the Ionic order. And, like the Lycian chiefs, and indeed the Persian kings, for the decoration of his tomb Mausolus called in Greek sculptors. Later sources speak of an assortment of 'great masters' brought over for the commission: the names of Scopas, Bryaxis, Leochares, Timotheos and Praxiteles are mentioned, and there is supposed to have been a sort of competition between several of these sculptors, each taking a different side of the monument. On stylistic grounds this has so far proved impossible to demonstrate, and attributing the various and numerous fragments of the Mausoleum's decoration to named sculptors is likewise a fairly fruitless exercise. But anyone who looks closely at even the more battered remains of the Mausoleum's sculptures (*ill. 122*) is bound to agree that whoever they were, the sculptors called to Halicarnassus were as capable as any on the Greek mainland. And in iconographic terms, they pandered fully to their patron's Hellenizing tendencies.

Uncertainties remain about precisely how the relics recovered from the site (mostly in 1857 by Sir Charles Newton of the British Museum) relate to the building. But the sculptural programme of the Mausoleum may be hypothetically detailed as follows (descending in order from the top of the building):

1. On top of the stepped pyramidal roof: a four-horse chariot. There may have been a rider in this chariot – some suggest Mausolus himself, others propose Helios. The latest nomination is Herakles, whose apotheosis was accomplished in a chariot, and from whom Mausolus (in company with Alexander, and divers other Hellenistic despots) may have claimed his ultimate ancestry. In any case, such quadrigas were to become standard emblems of royal power: the bronze horses now in San Marco at Venice may come from one of the many Hellenistic groups of this sort.

2. Around the base of the chariot group: a frieze depicting Greeks against Centaurs. By the mid-fourth century BC, this theme had become almost an essential token of the Classical. There is no reason why Mausolus should not have embraced its broadest symbolic meaning, and aligned himself with the civilization of the Greeks as challenged by outsiders.

3. At the foot of the sloped roof: patrolling lions. Greece (Delos), Lycia and Persia might all offer precedents for these, whose function (beyond the decorative) may be described as apotropaic.

4. Below the roof: a colonnade of thirty-six Ionic columns. On the inner wall of this colonnade was a second frieze, showing chariot-racing: a reference, perhaps, to the Homeric-style games that would mark the funeral of Mausolus. Some freestanding figures – possibly Hekatomnid ancestors of Mausolus – may have stood between the columns.

5. Immediately below the colonnade: a third frieze. Both the largest and best-preserved, it shows an Amazonomachy. Less cluttered than some of its Classical predecessors (e.g. the Amazonomachy from Bassae), it was made readily comprehensible to a viewer below by lavish indulgence in what Kenneth Clark called 'the heroic diagonal' (*ill. 123*) – sharp postures of combat, strikingly outlined against a simple background of shields and flying cloaks. Like the Centauromachy, this theme was inherently Classicizing, but it may also have had some family pertinence, since we are told that the Hekatomnids claimed to possess, as a sacred relic, the axe of Hippolyte, Queen of the Amazons. Slab number 1008 in the British Museum shows 'Herakles destroying a principal Amazon lady': it may be that some epic was composed for Mausolus, linking his ancestors with this feat. It is worth noting that on coinage issued on the island of Kos, which came under his influence, Mausolus is shown in the guise of Herakles.

6. Finally, there were sculptures in the round, apparently on different levels and on different scales, towards the base of the podium. Cuttings in the cornices of the podium indicate that this is where most of the free-

121 *(opposite above left)* The over lifesize statue identified as Mausolus, from the Mausoleum, though it may represent another Carian dynast.

122 *(opposite above right)* Detail of the Mausoleum frieze; carved c. 360–350 BC.

123 *(opposite below)* A detail of Mausoleum frieze: an example of the use of the 'heroic diagonal' in a scene of Greeks fighting Amazons.

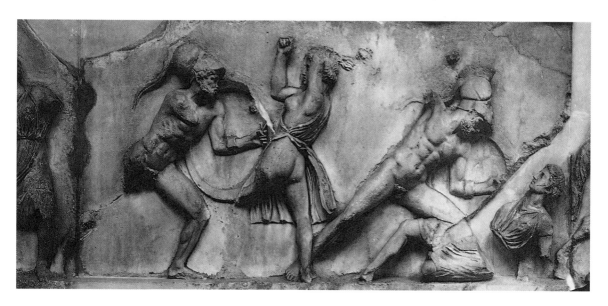

standing statuary must have been, though the fragmentary state of its survival permits only a vague account of it. Imaginative reconstructions of the entire monument have to allow for the fact that the sculptures are on three different scales, from lifesize through to 'colossal' – so some figures have to be elevated either to the colonnade, or the roof (or both). But there is no way of knowing whether the two colossal figures usually identified as 'Mausolus' and 'Artemisia' are actually the royal couple. 'Artemisia', faceless as she is, has been reckoned to strike an 'adoring' pose; 'Mausolus' (*ill. 121*) displays physiognomic features, and a splendid moustache, that relate closely to other images of Persian satraps (as evident, for example, from numismatic portraits of Tissaphernes and Pharnabazus, who ruled in these parts in the late fifth century BC). However, it may be wiser to reserve the remains of one colossal enthroned figure as Mausolus; and as for the rest of the figures, the distance between immediate family and heroic ancestors may never have been easy to ascertain even when the monument was intact.

The Mausoleum was an excessive tomb. Excavations of the royal chamber underneath have revealed traces of an equally excessive cremation. Only some of the tomb treasures (*keimelia*) have survived, but a vast deposit of bones of sacrificed animals was found at the chamber's entrance, adding archaeological substance to the literary sources that record a funeral for Mausolus conducted in Homeric style. The monument itself was included in the Hellenistic compilation we know as the Seven Wonders of the Ancient World, and by the late first century BC the term 'Mausoleum' had become eponymous for any ambitious sepulchre.

Mausolus had his own court bard: one Theodektes, who would design his own tomb, to be situated between Athens and Eleusis, and include portraits of all *his* ancestors, among whose number he claimed Homer. At the funeral of Mausolus it was a Greek rhetorician and historian, Theopompus, who delivered the eulogy. As we have seen, the Mausoleum as a concept is largely non-Greek, and non-Greek in some of its details too. But there is no doubt that Mausolus was consistently, and assiduously, Hellenizing. And what the Mausoleum amounts to is an overt architectural manifestation of what we know as ruler-cult, one of the symptomatic traits of 'the Hellenistic period'. Alexander would develop its potential, but he was not the first.

Alexander and his ancestry

'In the studio Alexander used to talk a great deal about many things without any real knowledge of them, and Apelles would politely advise him to be silent, saying that the boys engaged in grinding the colours were laughing at him.'

Pliny's vignette (from *Natural History* XXXV. 36) anticipates the sentiment of Dr Johnson's famously peevish definition of a 'Patron': 'a wretch who supports with insolence, and is paid with flattery'. Apelles, supposedly the only painter to whom Alexander entrusted his portraiture, may have had to endure all sorts of ill-informed commentary from his patron, and he did not stint on the flattery: a notorious event in ancient art historiography is Apelles painting Alexander as *keraunophoros*, 'wielding a thunderbolt', as if he were Zeus himself. The sculptural counterpart of Apelles in Alexander's entourage, Lysippos, allegedly reprimanded Apelles for going too far. But who dictated the limits of the decorum of royal representation?

In modern history, the workings of royal patronage, or indeed anything like a propaganda campaign, are relatively easy to reconstruct. For Louis XIV, 'the Sun King' who created Versailles and ruled France for most of the seventeenth century, we can assemble a great deal of documentation that charts the careful monitoring of messages which projected the king's power: not only paintings and sculpture, but also plays, poems, ballets and public spectacles. The bureaucrats, advisers and scholars involved in this seventeenth-century monitoring process have left us many of the clues we need to recreate its programmatic intentions, and it is perfectly possible to speak of 'the fabrication of Louis XIV'. As for the contemporary moulding of an image of power, usually entrusted to an advertising agency, or a special government ministry, it rarely defies analysis: 'the hidden persuaders' of today may have deeper insights into human psychology, but their methods are essentially similar to those of the offstage masterminds who so successfully controlled the 'theatre state' of Louis XIV.

What emerges from the programmes devised for Louis XIV is a certain reliance on ancient symbols of power. In fact, his sobriquet 'the Sun King' directly connects him with the emperor Augustus, who made much of a perceived divine alliance with Apollo, and Alexander, who was posthumously figured as Helios in parts of his empire, and in Egypt was worshipped as the son of the sun-god Amun-Ra while he was still alive. Yet for both Augustus and Alexander, we have virtually no documentary evidence of how their respective images were 'fabricated'. Patterns of consistency in the images projected can be observed, and deductions made accordingly; and there is an anthropology of symbols of power which can always provide models (hence the concept of 'theatre state', extrapolated by Clifford Geertz from his studies of nineteenth-century Bali, quoted in the epigraph to this chapter); but one numismatist has denied that 'propaganda', understood as a highly co-ordinated and tightly controlled activity, really existed in Hellenistic courts. What we find instead, he argues, is 'the largely unsystematic attempt at irregular intervals to publicize a ruler's actual achievements or omens, legends, and prophecies concerning him in order to enhance his own personal prestige and to provide added reasons for continued loyalty to future members of the dynasty he hoped to establish.'

This was written prior to the discovery, in 1977, of a barrel-vaulted tomb beneath one of the tumuli near Vergina (probably the Macedonian city of Aegae) – the tomb, as reasonably claimed by its excavator, Manolis Andronikos, of Alexander the Great's father, Philip II. Philip was assassinated in 336 BC, and if indeed this tomb is his, he was buried in handsome royal style. Among the rich circumstances of his deposition were some twenty miniature ivory images, including what appear to be portraits of him and his family. His own portrait (*ill. 124*) may be judged by an unusual complement: the reconstruction of his face, from the remains of a skull found in the tomb, by impartial forensic experts in Manchester, England. If that constitutes a reasonable likeness, can we then assume that the little head plausibly identified as Alexander (*ill. 125*), just twenty years old when he assumed his father's place, gives us an equally approximate image? If so, then it has to be said that the fabrication of Alexander the Great was in hand at the outset of his reign. How far he ever matched the quality of his projected image we shall never know, though both the 'good' and the 'bad' sources relating to Alexander attest a conspicuous abundance of natural charisma. What is of importance to us is the apparently early date of such an image. For when he died precociously in 323 BC, Alexander did not cease to wield power – at least, his name and his image were very much at large for some years. It is consequently very difficult to tell which of the many surviving portraits of Alexander should be counted as posthumous. The Vergina find implies, however, that a basic portrait-type was possibly established almost as a part of Alexander's dynastic grooming, or as preparation for his grand eastwards expansion of the Macedonian empire. And, more generally, it forces us both to reassess the sophistication of art in the service of Hellenistic rulers, and to take account of the myth-making ambitions of Macedonian kings prior to Alexander.

It was an earlier Alexander, Alexander I of Macedon (reigning from around 495 until 450 BC), who seems to have generated something akin to a propaganda programme for himself and his successors. Though it is not entirely clear in its terms and nomenclature (and perhaps was never intended to be), the heroic genealogy of Alexander I invokes a son or kinsman of Herakles, called Temenos, who in turn begets Perdiccas, a founding king of Macedonia. Hence the ensuing dynasty may be known as Temenid, and given a broadly Greek or Dorian affiliation. The mythology accompanying this genealogy ascribes some Persian adventures to Perdiccas, however, and probably reflects the political balancing-act that

124 A miniature ivory head, identified as that of Philip II, from his tomb at Vergina.

125 A miniature ivory head possibly of Alexander, from Philip II's tomb at Vergina.

Alexander I maintained through the Persian wars: on the one hand, offering either help or no resistance to the Persian invaders, and on the other extending his formal friendship or *xenia* with the Greeks by qualifying (perhaps thanks to his Heraklean blood) for the Olympic Games, and allegedly supplying Greek forces with useful information about Persian movements before the battle of Plataea (479 BC). Ruler of a hitherto disparate area, Alexander I promoted the fiscal credibility of Macedonia through a centralized mint, producing coins whose images of hunting and horsemanship may have owed something to Persian royal iconography. A later successor, Archelaus (who ruled from around 413 to 399 BC), would adopt the Persian standard of coin weight, while calling on the image of Herakles for mythical validation on those coins. This was the same Archelaus who would patronize the Athenian playwright Euripides at his court, and who developed a new Macedonian centre at Pella. In the fifth century, then, a basis was laid for what we will recognize as 'ruler-cult': in simplest terms, the divine right of kings. While Herakles was not a very original choice as progenitor of the Temenids, he was by the same token an effective pan-Hellenic hero-god; and if the campaigns of Philip II reveal the first principle of Temenid foreign policy, then that must be judged to have been the domination of Greece by Macedon.

Chaeronea may or may not be regarded as a battle which settled that ambition: Greek states subsequently revolted against Macedonian rule whenever they could. But the tholos-chapel which Philip endowed within the sanctuary at Olympia – close to the Temple of Zeus, and suggestively rivalling the cult statue of Zeus by displaying a semicircle of chryselephantine family portraits – is a significant attestation of propaganda. The 'Philippeion' was a harbinger of what would happen within pan-Hellenic sanctuaries under the rules of royal patronage. At Delphi, for example, three Hellenistic monarchs – Antigonos the One-eyed and his son Demetrios, from Macedon, and later Ptolemy III, of Egypt – had the effrontery to replace Athenian heroes on the Marathon memorial (see Chapter 6) with their own 'heroic' nominees (doubtless in their own respective likenesses). Such were the delicacies of absolute self-promotion witnessed in these old arenas of 'peer polity interaction'.

We do not know what the young Alexander looked like in the Philippeion. The statues were attributed to a sculptor called Leochares. But historical tradition (for what it is worth) tells us that Alexander the Great settled on another sculptor, Lysippos, to execute all his portraits. Only this sculptor, says Plutarch, possessed the finesse (*akribeia*) to render faithfully the king's charisma: his 'melting gaze', 'leonine mane' and 'tilted neck'; others, in their effort to convey those commanding features, tended to lose their subject's heroic manliness.

Here we should admit a problem. Surveying the range of Alexander-images, most of us will soon find ourselves able to recognize the essential Alexander features: a powerful profile, full lips, a gaze which is somehow both far-off and penetrating, and above all, a head of hair that is thick and dishevelled in the most perfect face-framing fashion (*ills 126* and *127*). At the same time, we might feel less easy about accrediting all these portraits to just one sculptor; or, given that they may often be copies done posthumously, believing that they all stem from a single prototype. Perhaps Lysippos did indeed create an *Ur*-Alexander, but the evidence surely points to a rapid diffusion and weakening of that original type, and consequently one may wonder just how profound was Alexander's control over the reproduction of his own image.

Notwithstanding those doubts, a fair summary of the effect of Alexander's portraits can be proposed:

126 A marble head of Alexander, from Alexandria, with the classic features of a thick mane of hair, a moody gaze and full lips.

The warrior irresistible. 'The Alexander Mosaic', seemingly a copy of a painting of the king in the full tumult of battle with his Persian enemy Darius III (at the battle of Issus on the north Syrian border, in 333 BC), is generally taken to present a 'realistic' image of Alexander; that is, with some attention to the detail of military accoutrements and so on. That may be a naive view, but the painting probably incorporates a sculptural type of Alexander on horseback. Here, on his trusty 'ox-headed' horse Bucephalus, he plunges into a hedge of long Persian spears, his eyes flashing for the death of Darius. The Persians, and their king, 'flee like cattle before the lion'. At least one statue-type, perhaps created by Lysippos, shows Alexander as a cavalier; and he may appear on horseback in the paintings at Vergina. His military acumen was demonstrated while he was still young, at Chaeronea; he thought of himself as a second Achilles (from whom his formidable mother Olympias claimed descent), to the point of making a pilgrimage to Troy and paying his respects to his Homeric alterego. All the historical narratives imply that Alexander, like his father, earned the respect of his troops by leading from the front; he was seemingly invincible (*aniketos*).

127 A head of Alexander, from Tarsus, Asia Minor.

The numinous gaze. The sources tell us that Alexander, though wellproportioned, was not a physically large man. When he tried to sit on the throne of the Persian king, his legs swung well short of the ground, and minions hurriedly brought a stool. His friend Hephaisteion was of more impressive stature, and the ladies of the defeated Persian king's harem instinctively threw themselves for mercy at the feet of Hephaisteion, not Alexander. But Alexander had a gaze that none of his contemporaries could match. Directed heavenwards, his eyes brimmed with 'diffuseness' and moisture (*diachysis, hygros*); they generated ecstasy because they contained so much of what the Greeks called *enthousiasmos* – divine inspiration. So in his portraits Alexander is often shown like some lachrymose medieval saint, transfixed and transfigured, only much more muscular. His eyes rested on a divine vision; his ears were attuned to divine instructions. He was divinity on earth (*theia epipnoia*); to his subjects he shone like Apollo.

The sun of righteousness. Plutarch asserts that the parts of the world unvisited by Alexander stayed sunless. Alexander possessed the looks and hairstyle associated with Helios the sun-god; this facilitated his progress in the East, where the cult of Sol Invictus was so entrenched by the third century AD that the Christians would have to compromise with it and celebrate the birth of Christ at the time of the solstice. Lysippos made a famous chariot-group driven by Helios; the Colossus of Rhodes was Helios too; the Macedonian kings used a radiant sun as a regal insignium (Alexander's father had a sun-burst on his golden casket at Vergina); and when Alexander conquered Egypt, the local equation of pharaoh with the blessed sun – his rise saluted by baboons in the desert, his function the seasonal guarantee of Nilotic fertility – naturally encouraged Alexander to accept honours as the offspring of Amun-Ra (the Greek Ammon, often identified with Zeus).

The leonine man. From the leonine mane came the leonine man. This was a type recognized in fourth-century BC handbooks of physiognomy and it comprised more than simply a shock of long hair. 'Wide brows', for instance, went with the stock leonine features. Alexander's name, which literally means 'warding off men', fitted this typology nicely, as did his spiritual kinship with Achilles, whom Homer so often describes as fighting savagely like a lion. But for his portraitists, Alexander's thick mane of hair was the most suggestive index of his lionhood.

Long hair – *to koman* – has in recent years been associated with youthful defiance of authority, the reverse of its ancient meaning. To the biblical Samson it was the source of his prodigal strength. To the Spartans, it was a means of sowing terror among their enemies. No wonder Roman emperors became so sensitive about their baldness. In Alexander's case, his rich coiffure was not only a sign of his royalty, but also his divinity – likening him further to Apollo and Helios – and a measure of wisdom. We may recognize, again, an anticipation of Christian iconography, when either the naturally tawny colour of such hair, or else a sprinkling of gold dust, confers upon Hellenistic rulers a sort of spiritual nimbus or halo.

Not only was Alexander leonine, he was, like the Persian kings, a champion hunter of lions (*ill. 95*). Frescoes in one of the burial chambers at Vergina include scenes of lion-hunting, a motif repeated in mosaics at the other Macedonian royal centre, Pella; and when one of the provincial monarchs under Alexander's tutelage came to order a tomb for himself, he chose to show his protector in the thick of the chase. This is the mislead-

128–9 Macedonians fighting
Persians *(above left)* and
Persians and Macedonians
hunting together *(above
right)*. Details from the
'Alexander Sarcophagus'.

ingly named 'Alexander sarcophagus', now in Istanbul, which probably contained the remains of King Abdalonymus of Sidon. Abdalonymus was a local royal who had been down on his luck until Alexander 'liberated' Sidon from the Persians after the victory at Issus in 333 BC. Abdalonymus seems to have acknowledged his benefactor accordingly on the reliefs of his own coffin. There are scenes of battle (perhaps Issus) between Macedonians and Persians (*ill. 128*); but there are also scenes of Persians and Macedonians hunting together (*ill. 129*), probably in a dedicated game-park (*paradeisos*). Their prey are lion and deer. Hunting was a favourite pastime of the Macedonian elite, and also a well-known symbol of Persian royal power: here Abdalonymus allows the ideological affinity of Persians and Macedonians as much decorative space as their political opposition.

Anyone who reads Plutarch's biography and the other ancient histories of Alexander will realize that, however unreliable they may be in detail, the overall impression they leave us is that Alexander's power – including his ability to command as much loyalty as fear – was largely due to his personal charisma. That is why his portraiture makes such intriguing study. We cannot prove that the odour of Alexander's body, as his biographers say, was a marvellous perfumed essence. Nor can we readily separate Alexander's leonine endowments from his diplomatic shrewdness (as Machiavelli would indicate to his Renaissance readers, the prince who is nothing but leonine will not last very long: there must be an element of the fox in him too). But we are permitted, thanks to the portraits, to sample Alexander's *ethos*. And in all but the most ragged examples, the effect is unarguably impressive. Humans, notoriously, crave strong leadership. What we see in the image of Alexander is its classic physiognomy: it is, in sculptured form, the individual awesomeness that Shakespeare articulates with verbal majesty when describing Mark Antony:

> His legs bestrid the ocean, his rear'd arm
> Crested the world, his voice was propertied
> As all the tuned spheres, and that to friends;
> But when he meant to quail and shake the orb,
> He was as rattling thunder. For his bounty,
> There was no winter in't; an autumn it was
> That grew the more by reaping. His delights
> Were dolphin-like, they show'd his back above
> The element they liv'd in. In his livery
> Walk'd crowns and crownets; realms and islands were
> As plates dropp'd from his pocket.

(Antony and Cleopatra, V.ii)

A host of sub-texts might be added here, but we shall confine ourselves to a trio. In the first place, it is worth noting that the most definitive description of Alexander's appearance comes from writers (such as Plutarch) who only saw his portraits. Given that most of the surviving portraits are undoubtedly posthumous, however much we may suspect that Alexander was genuinely an inspirational figure, we are bound to talk in terms of his 'fabrication'.

Secondly, we should note that Alexander's style of rule was essentially Macedonian. The Temenids developed a method of monarchical rule as thoughtfully as they shaped their military tactics. This admitted a circle of power-sharing colleagues who were deemed 'companions' (*hetairoi*). There are awkward moments in the historiography of Alexander when he demands, after his Persian conquests, that he be paid the symbolic dues of self-abasement (*proskynesis*) by those in his presence. But it seems that he stopped short of entitling himself 'king of kings' (*basileon basileus*); and while he took a Persian wife, he did not consider himself heir to the Persian throne (he may in fact have thought himself rather grander – *basileus Asias*, King of all Asia). A year before his death, he sent an edict to his Greek subjects requiring that he be worshipped as a god. Some historians regard this as a sign that he was failing to modulate his self-image with due sensitivity to local customs; that he was losing his grip, thinking that Egyptian or Persian ruler-cults could be imported to democracy's home. But as we shall see, it was not very long before the citizens of Greek city-states were falling over themselves to worship this or that monarch as a divine protector. Alexander knew what he was doing.

Finally, it is worth noting that numismatists do not agree whether Alexander issued coins bearing his own self-portrait. This seems surprising, but again accords with a Macedonian style of qualified tolerance rather than outright domination. Alexander's coinage is in fact fairly homogeneous: many of his issues carry what the Greeks would broadly recognize as an image of the enthroned Zeus, holding eagle and sceptre; but this image could double as Gilgamesh in Babylon, as Baal in Cilicia and as Melquart in Syria and Phoenicia. The accompanying image of Herakles wearing a lion's scalp was likewise a relatively ecumenical imprint, and in due time easily assimilated to the portrait features of Alexander himself. Otherwise, Alexander allowed his subject-kings and satraps to issue their own images locally. It was not so much Alexander, then, who made numismatic capital out of his image, but his successors. Since this is probably true of his portraiture generally, it is to those successors that we now turn.

Alexander's legacy

Alexander died young, at Babylon, of an illness possibly compounded by heavy drinking. His 'companions' and generals then became his official 'Successors' (*hoi Diadochoi*), for whom his image was patently talismanic. According to their local spheres of influence and military experience, they divided up Alexander's empire between themselves. With varying success, they then attempted to create their own dynasties. It was in the early part of this process that the indebtedness to Alexander's image, the Alexander-*mimesis* of his Successors, appears as an essential element of ruler-cult. Before we examine the programmes of sculpture commissioned by one of these post-Alexander dynasties, the Attalids at Pergamum, it is worth sketching the nature of this ruler-cult as it is manifest in the various parts of the 'Hellenistic' world.

The prize possession was Egypt: rich, easily defended and with a native population already used to saluting Alexander as son of Amun-Ra, or (at the oasis sanctuary of Siwah) Zeus-Ammon. One of the most sensitive pieces of Alexandrian sculpture is the series of reliefs which decorate the chapel added to the temple at Luxor. These show Alexander enjoying the same formal relationship with the Egyptian deities as any pharaoh; and, more importantly, there is no difference in style or symbolism from what had gone before in the long history of this temple. To anyone unable to read the hieroglyphs in the cartouches relating to the reliefs, Alexander could just as easily be Ramesses III. There was no doubt of his divinity in Egypt: Alexander was son of Amun, and openly worshipped as such.

Egypt fell to a close Macedonian colleague of Alexander's, Ptolemy, who would in due time be styled Ptolemy I Soter, 'the Saviour'. Ptolemy not so much lionized Alexander as elephantized him – showing him on coins wearing an elephant's scalp head-dress, sign of his Dionysiac conquest of India. And Ptolemy went further than numismatic homage. When he heard that a massive funeral caravan was setting out from Babylon to transport the body of Alexander back to Macedonia for interment in the royal tumuli at Aegae, Ptolemy intercepted the cortège, and re-directed it. He claimed that Alexander had wanted to be buried at the oasis sacred to Zeus-Ammon at Siwah, and accordingly hijacked the golden sarcophagus containing Alexander. In the event, the place of deposition (and cult) was first Memphis, and ultimately Alexandria, though the tomb has not been found – it is *not* under the Russian embassy, as used to be rumoured and a recent claim of the discovery of a Macedonian-style tomb at Siwah needs further investigation before we can clarify Ptolemy's appropriation of Alexander's magical relics.

Ptolemy declared himself *basileus* in 305/304 BC. He was one of the more successful dynasty-founders. His plump features and those of his successors are a feature of local coins and sculpture until the Roman annexation of Egypt. Alexander's tomb provided a focus, a *sema*, for the worship of each Ptolemy and his wife as 'saviour gods' (*theoi soteres*); at temples along the Nile, the Ptolemies followed Alexander in using traditional pharaonic iconography to express their divinity, or at least the divine sanction of their power. Ptolemy's son, Ptolemy II Philadelphus, also sustained a consistently Hellenizing policy (of which the great library at Alexandria was the cultural cornerstone), and initiated the tradition of carnival processions that involved the portage of giant images of both Greek and Egyptian deities. It is worth noting, however, that although Egyptologists speak of a Ptolemaic hybrid (*gemischtstil*) in sculpture, in fact relatively little cross-fertilization between Greek and traditional Egyptian styles took place. This may reflect a basic aesthetic reluctance to mix styles which had stood apart since the earliest Greek settlement in Egypt (see Chapter 3).

In literature, however, the 'Hellenistic' facets of Ptolemaic patronage are more obvious. Especially memorable is the hymn to Ptolemy II composed by the Greek bucolic poet Theocritus (*Idylls*, XVII). In this unstinting encomium, Ptolemy's father is envisaged aloft in heaven with Zeus, Alexander ('bane of the Persians') and Herakles, from whom the Ptolemies claimed the usual Macedonian descent. He himself is hailed as master of not only Egypt, but a string of satellite territories – including Libya, Pamphylia, Lycia, Caria and the Cyclades – and more: 'All the sea and the land and the roaring rivers admit the lordship of Ptolemy, and about him gather horsemen and shielded warriors in hosts, harnessed in flashing bronze'.

We can recognize the style of this paean to Ptolemy's lordship (*anasso Ptolemaio*). It is positively Homeric in its archaizing portrait of the heroic demi-god (*hemitheos*). Ptolemy is a warrior who has a sense of justice, a man of wealth who is generous, and he is both divinely descended and reverent to the gods. Theocritus ends by urging him to ever greater acquisition of heaven-sent glory (*arete*), but that should not be taken as a shadow of criticism, but simply more craven obsequies from an artist – any artist – compelled to work by *force majeure*.

The Ptolemies fit a general pattern. Another Macedonian general of Alexander's, Seleucus, converted his satrapy of Syria into a dynastic basis for greater ambitions. Those ambitions need not concern us here, but we should note the ideological justification with which Seleucus invested his despotism. He asserted a special relationship with Apollo, claiming that it was that god's oracle at Didyma which had instructed him not to return to Macedonia, but stay in Asia. His coinage from about 300 BC was stamped with the laureate head of Apollo, or the prophetic tripod; and he conspicuously endowed Didyma and nearby Miletus. A fragment of inscribed verse from Erythrai, on the Lydian coast, makes explicit the divine ancestry: 'Praise with hymns at the libations of Apollo the dark hair of his son Seleucus, whom the god of the golden lyre himself begat; praise him and forget not'.

In Macedonia itself, Alexander's own family did not survive local wrangling. Eventually the country became 'Antigonid', after its seizure by the son of Antigonus Monophthalmus ('the One-eyed'). Antigonus Monophthalmus was a senior general on Alexander's staff, and arguably the only Successor who might have reunited Alexander's empire. His son Demetrius inherited his aggressive ambitions, embodied in his sobriquet, Poliorketes – 'besieger of cities' – but he reserved a tender attitude towards Athens, which the Athenians amply repaid in sheer flattery. They regarded Demetrius as a tutelary deity, a brother of Athena and a second Dionysos. In 290 BC a special Athenian chorus, perhaps complete with joyous erect phalloi, welcomed Demetrius to the city in the most fulsome terms: they declared him to be 'pre-eminent in beauty' (*kallei diaphoros*), radiant as the sun (with his friends as stars) and 'the only true god' (*monos theos alethinos*). Other gods (the chorus went) were made of wood or stone, and consequently impassive and unresponsive to prayers: but Demetrius was better than them, since he was a living manifestation of divine power. This hymn (preserved for us by Athenaeus, in his *Deiopnosophistae*, 253b–d) is a signal recantation of certain basic principles of Greek trust in images, not to mention a grovelling document of Athenian impotence. It mocks the reported scepticism that Athenians voiced when Alexander made his request for divine honours in 324 BC ('Why not?' the scornful Demosthenes had allegedly retorted. 'He can be the son of Zeus and Poseidon too, if he wants').

Well: Demetrius Poliorketes did indeed bid for Poseidon's paternity too. Emboldened by his success in a substantial naval engagement with Ptolemy off Salamis, in Cyprus, in 306 BC, he assumed a trident and posed on his coins as Poseidon's own favoured son. And very likely it was

Demetrius who provided the world with one of its most flamboyant statues, the Nike of Samothrace (*ill. 130*). Samothrace, an island in the north Aegean which the Macedonians considered theirs, offered a naturally spectacular site for architectural endowment, and it was in the *exedra* or portico of the elevated sanctuary of the Great Gods that this massive Nike was displayed, shown as if she were alighting on the prow of a ship. The sculpted prow itself was set in a pool of water, whose surface must have been ruffled by sea breezes. This, combined with her flying and extravagantly deep wind-channelled drapery, and the huge outstretched wings, resulted in a Nike to make all others of her type seem static. In the face of such statuary scholars are apt to reach for art-historical anachronisms such as 'Baroque', or impose a 'theatrical' mentality upon its designers; but it can be explained equally well in terms of the competitive patronage fostered by Alexander's legacy. A coin issue of Demetrius Poliorketes features a Nike on a prow; although in this case she blows a long trumpet (as the Nike of Samothrace seems not to have done), it makes sense for Demetrius to have advertised his victory at Salamis with a sculptural landmark to drive home his numismatic message. The Samothracian sanctuary, while remote, maximized the effect of the statue. A similar effort, from the market-place of Cyrene, must have been much less striking. Traces of rival monuments have been noted at Epidauros, Lindos and Thasos: but nothing seems to have challenged the Nike of Samothrace as a monumental concept until, in the mid-third century BC, the son of Demetrius, Antigonus Gonatas, endowed the sanctuary of Delos with a colossal marble basin, supported by Persian-style bovine capitals – and placed in the basin a complete warship, dedicated *ex voto* to Apollo.

What we witness in the wake of Alexander, then, is more than the assertion by individual kings of their divine right to rule. Alexander's own claim of divine paternity was aped brazenly by the Ptolemies, the Seleucids, the Antigonids and others. These claims naturally involved the kings in expense, for piety towards their own divine parentage had to be publicly manifested; and the most obvious means of making a show of piety was to commission new buildings and new statues. Such commissions looked even better when made in the context of old sanctuaries. Unlike certain Roman emperors, the Hellenistic monarchs did not steal from the pan-Hellenic centres. This is one reason why 'Greek sculpture', properly considered, continues to flourish under royal patronage. The idea that some sort of artistic decline set in after Alexander is difficult to support on anything other than purely subjective grounds. It is true that by itself, the style of what we call 'Hellenistic' sculpture is relatively static: a piece such as the Nike of Samothrace may be (and has been) plausibly dated on stylistic grounds to anywhere between the late fourth and the late first centuries BC (in fact one suggestion for the battle it commemorates is Actium, in 31 BC). Yet in terms of complex composition, subject-range, variations in scale and sheer *jeu d'esprit*, there is nothing decadent about Greek sculpture in this period. The ambitions and pretensions of many monarchs ensured that: but pride of place must be given to the Attalids of Pergamum.

Pergamum: the Athens of the East

As part of the preamble to his *History of the Peloponnesian War*, Thucydides makes a very intelligent observation. Departing from an almost archaeological speculation about the power of ancient Mycenae, he notes that the protagonists of the war he is about to describe, Athens and Sparta, would look like very ill-matched opponents, when judged purely on their monumental remains. Of simple Sparta, he says, a future archaeologist would surely never accept that she once controlled large tracts of the Peloponnese; and of Athens, by the same token, one would be deceived by her spectacular buildings into thinking she was much more powerful than actually was the case.

The citadel of Pergamum may be said to be similarly misleading. A visitor to the site today (about 96 km or 60 miles north of modern Izmir) is immediately struck by an Athenian-style grandeur. There is a magnitude and a sophistication to the planning of this eminence which give it the air of the capital of a great territory. But in fact the kingdom of Pergamum was the daintiest of all the relics of Alexander's empire. It incorporated the land once known as Mysia, and contained some valuable natural resources, but pine forests and silver deposits cannot by themselves explain Pergamene development. This was more by accident than design.

When Alexander died, he had amassed substantial reserves for the Macedonian treasury – largely booty seized from the Persians. Not surprisingly, his Successors quarrelled over it. At the battle of Ipsus in 301 BC, Lysimachus, a Macedonian ruling in Thrace, contested its possession with Antigonus, a Macedonian fighting in Asia Minor for his dominions there (and whose family would eventually rule Macedonia itself). Supported by Seleucus, Lysimachus prevailed. Much of the treasury he took to Thrace. But a portion he left in Asia Minor, to be guarded there by a deputy governor, one Philetairos, son of a Macedonian general called Attalos. The place chosen for safekeeping the treasure – 9000 talents, the value of which may be impressionistically conveyed by pointing out that all the gold on the colossal statue of Athena Parthenos amounted to a mere 44 talents – was a natural stronghold in territory assigned to Lysimachus. That stronghold was Pergamum.

Philetairos was a scrupulous curator. His portraits show him as a jowly and self-satisfied banker. He held on to his bullion when Lysimachus died; and he held on to it equally carefully when the erstwhile ally of Lysimachus, Seleucus, was assassinated in 281 BC. Eventually there was dynastic confusion about the status of Pergamum and its precious contents. Since Philetairos had taken precautions to arrange suitable defences, he might claim that Alexander's old treasure was safer with him than with anyone else. Pergamum was nominally under Seleucid supervision, but when Philetairos died in 263 BC, another safe pair of local hands took over: his nephew, Eumenes. In the next two decades, this Eumenes effectively made Pergamum independent within Asia Minor; and though he never actually assumed the title, we know him as 'Eumenes I' – the effective creator of the Attalid dynasty.

That is a summary account of the emergence of Pergamum. The significant point about the treasure is that it was not squandered. First a fortress was built to protect it. Then it was used as the basis for constructing a marvellous city, complete with its own Akropolis (*ill. 131*) – the difference from the Athenian Akropolis was that the Pergamene version provided a residence for rulers as well as gods. Then it was used either to finance military expeditions, or else to buy off enemies who could not be dealt with on the battlefield. The Attalids were first-rate stewards of the 9000 talents. And what is important to us is that they also liked to invest in art. With good reason the historian Theodore Mommsen described the successor to Eumenes, who styled himself Attalos I, as the Lorenzo de' Medici of antiquity.

And a good case can be made for describing Pergamum as 'the Athens of the East'. Athena was chosen as the city's guardian goddess; cults of Athena Nikephoros ('Victory-bringer') and Athena Polias were instituted; a Pergamene version of the Panathenaic festival seems to have been created; and over a library stocked with Classical Athenian texts, copied of course on to parchment or *pergamenum* (a local invention, to rival Egyptian papyrus), a marble copy of the Athena Parthenos presided. Schools of philosophy gathered here, after the Athenian model; and so, too, did the sculptors.

It has been established elsewhere in this book that we really know very little about the sculptors of Classical Athens, but it is true to say that we know even less about the sculptors of Pergamum, despite the likelihood that they were numerous and much in demand. One name, Phyromachus, crops up in divers sources as predominant, probably during the first half of the second century BC; we also have mention of a Pergamene Myron, to whom that memorable statue, the 'Drunken Old Hag' (*ill. 132*) is attributed. Some commentators hold this statue up as an example of 'Hellenistic' interest in ugliness or poverty, and wonder where such a piece could possibly have been displayed. In fact there is, at Pergamum, a perfectly sound potential votive provenance – the Temple of Dionysos – and a perfectly good cult occasion too, the *lagynophoria*, at which respectable citizens could get drunk, directly from enormous jars (*lagynoi*) of wine.

Whether the statue (of which we only have copies) was actually created by a sculptor called Myron is not important. But it is significant to find an echo of the name of a 'celebrated' Classical Athenian sculptor at

132 The 'Drunken Old Hag': a copy of an original by Myron of Pergamum; *c.* 200 BC.

Pergamum, for Attalid patronage was not only philhellene; it was positively Atheno-centric. Like Periklean Athens, Attalid Pergamum felt itself to exemplify civilized life; and like Periklean Athens, Attalid Pergamum was beleaguered by barbarians. For the Attalids, these were not the Persians, but the Gauls. In terms of artistic symbolism, however, those Gauls could be directly descended not only from the Persians, but also such mythical prototypes of barbarism as the Amazons and the Giants.

'Gauls' is deceptive. *Galati* is strictly what we should term them: Celts who around 300 BC began to migrate more or less down the course of the Danube, and through the Balkan peninsula. Eventually they would settle in an area uncomfortably close to Pergamum – an area which became known as Galatia. They are recorded as having attacked the sanctuary of Delphi in 280/279 BC and though their aggression might be harnessed by hiring them as mercenaries, these Gauls troubled various Hellenistic kingdoms through most of the second century BC. It appears that around 240–230 BC Attalos I met them in battle at the River Caicus. The portraits of Attalos I, who ruled from 241 to 197 BC, suggest a would-be Alexander (*ill. 133*), but a lack of Alexander-style documentation means that we do not know how serious an engagement this was. Since the Pergamenes were not averse to buying off their enemies when it was expedient to do so, it may not even have been much of a battle. But it was commemorated as a great victory in the Pergamene Akropolis, specifically in the sanctuary of Athena Nikephoros, where a statue-group comprising three lifesize bronze figures was set up. Two of the figures were of a Gaul and his wife. Having killed his wife (in order to prevent her capture and violation), the Gaul is heroically turning his sword upon himself too. The third figure is the statue

133 A head of Attalos I of Pergamum, depicted in the style of an Alexander.

134 The 'Dying Gaul': a Roman copy of a statue from a group at Pergamum; *c.* 220 BC.

we know as the 'Dying Gaul' (*ill. 134*). The original bronzes probably stood in Pergamum until AD 64, when Nero may have removed them; but good marble copies or adaptations were made locally, perhaps in the mid-first century BC, and transferred to Rome, quite possibly to grace the gardens of some Roman involved in the conquest of Gaul (Julius Caesar makes an attractive potential patron for these recontextualized 'copies'; and some scholars argue that new 'Dying Gauls' were actually commissioned by late Republican Romans).

As we shall see, the political and ideological links between Pergamum and Rome are essential to understanding the continuity of the Classical tradition in sculpture. The broadly Celtic identity of the enemies of both Pergamum and Rome made the transference of statuary commemorating triumph over Gauls almost natural. However, that is a later recontextualization. The original Attalid group was set up with a more specifically Hellenizing motive. This can be appreciated from a roughly contemporary poem written by the Alexandria-based Callimachus, in whose *Hymn to Delos* there are injured references to the marauding Gauls. Callimachus not only styles them as barbarians, but as 'latter-day Titans' (*opsigonoi Titenes*: line 174); he then goes further, and describes them as a 'senseless tribe' (*aphron phyle*). In the Attalid group, we may see Titanic features in the body of the Gaul killing himself (especially his swollen, twisted thorax); and in the Dying Gaul, the indicators of barbaric 'Otherness' are clear. Hence the distinctive Celtic torc, or golden choker; and the moustache, hair and the curved battle-trumpet surrounding the moribund warrior.

Writing a century or two later, Diodorus Siculus (V. 28.1–3) tells us how the Gauls washed their hair in limewater, making it dense and tousled, and consequently looked like satyrs, or even Pan. From Pan comes panic – a good thing if you create it on the battlefield (as has been claimed for one of the Macedonian kings, Antigonus Gonatas), but dangerous to be on the receiving end. The group created for Attalos I retains respect for the enemy: these are images of not only physically formidable opponents, but also of a people with pride – the same refusal to surrender, the same dignity in defeat that Tacitus and other Roman writers would guardedly admire in the Celts. Of course, the achievement of Attalos in defeating such spirited enemies is thereby heightened. But the likeness of the Gauls to chaotic Titans also invites the Pergamene partisan to reflect on the divine alliance between Attalos and the gods: a special relationship which would be fully publicized by the next Attalid, Eumenes II.

The rule of Eumenes II lasted from 197 to 160/159 BC, a period which witnessed extensive remodelling of the citadel at Pergamum. Eumenes was a bibliophile, and built the library; he also added the theatre, which largely survives, and a gymnasium. And it is probably under his sponsorship, some time after 168 or 166 BC, that the Great Altar of Zeus was raised. Now in

Berlin, the friezes that decorated this altar constitute the most ambitious project of Greek sculpture since the Parthenon.

Unlike the Parthenon frieze, however, the sculptural programme of the Great Altar was easily visible. The subject is easily summarized, too: it shows the primordial battle of the Gods against the Giants. Since this was mythically the establishment of supremacy by Zeus and his fellow Olympians over the earth's undisciplined aboriginal inhabitants – of heavenly power over 'the earth-born ones', the *gegeneis* – it might be considered as a perfectly suitable subject to decorate a place where Zeus was worshipped. But the proximity of the library at Pergamum, and the supposed influence of court philosophers, have encouraged scholars to speculate on literary sources and allegorical meanings. One suggestion is that the seventh-century BC texts of Hesiod supplied the instructions for the iconography. Another would have the struggle permeated with metaphors of Stoic ideology: divine immanence exemplified.

The traces of names of the Giants involved may imply that some textual agenda guided the frieze's designer, though (as with the Parthenon) no ancient account of the Great Altar illuminates us. We cannot even propose a name for a master-designer, though sixteen executive sculptors have left their identities on the work. Nor do we have any account of the Gigantomachy that might qualify as canonical. In some versions of the myth, it is Athena's birth which either precipitates or coincides with the struggle: in that case, the Athena-phile Pergamenes may have enjoyed seeing their goddess in action. But it is even more likely that the Pergamenes appreciated the physiognomic affinities shared by these insolent Giants and the Gauls. What the viewer gets from the frieze is an impression of tumult, but a tumult in which the faces of the Olympians are invariably calm, and those of the Giants contorted; a battle in which the superiority of one side over another is absolute. As the Attalids were supreme patrons, and had employed mercenary troops to effect their victories, there was no place here for any depiction of the citizen body of Pergamum itself. The divinely-inspired Attalids could relate directly to the Olympians, who fight using their customary attributes. Hence we see Artemis dancing over the torso of a flattened Giant as mistress of the animals, her pet lion sinking its teeth into the nape of another failing challenger. Their tapering snake bodies anchor the Giants to the earth, defining them as reptilian; frequently we see them being yanked by the hair, raging but essentially impotent. The action, though one-sided, is never dull; the carving is dynamic throughout, and the combat artfully involves the viewer by appearing to spill off the edge of the relief and on to the altar steps (*ill. 135*).

Up the stairs, a quieter inner relief explained the heroical and divine dynastic origins of the Attalids. By now the reader should be expecting a

Heraklean input here: and sure enough Herakles is among the recognizable survivors of this now incomplete minor frieze, which presents an almost continuous narrative of the early history of Pergamum's prehistoric founder, Telephus. The details of the adventures of Telephus – a foundling either fathered or launched on his way by Herakles – can be partially reconstructed from literary sources; perhaps what is most important is the marginal involvement of Telephus in the Trojan War, where he appears alternately as a victim and an ally of the Greeks. Such mythical equivocation would suit the Attalids very well: for their philhellene cultural attitudes had to be increasingly balanced with a foreign policy oriented towards Rome. If the Romans were tracing their own origins from the Trojan side of the Trojan War, then it made sense for the Attalids to align themselves as old Troad neighbours.

Pro-Roman *entente* was furthered by Attalos II (160–138 BC), but still the Athenian connection was maintained. It was Attalos II who endowed Athens with a new stoa along the east side of the Agora (now reconstructed), around 150 BC: a discreet token of eastern influence was signalled by the 'Pergamene' capitals of this stoa, using Asiatic palm-leaf designs. For the kings of Pergamum to make their presence felt at Athens was not new: Attalos I had added himself to the Eponymous Heroes group in the Agora, for example; but it seems that Attalos II was particularly generous towards Pergamum's spiritual model. On the Athenian Akropolis itself, as Pausanias relates, there was a Pergamene donation of statues representing four separate (but symbolically connected) battles: of the Gods against the Giants; of the Athenians against the Amazons; of the Athenians against the Persians at Marathon; and of the Pergamenes against the Gauls in Mysia (see Pausanias I. 25.2). Unfortunately, Pausanias only tells us that 'Attalos' made the donation, without specifying which one; and though he gives some idea of the scale of the figures (about half lifesize), he does not indicate their quantity. On the basis of copies, it has been estimated that each combat group consisted of about fourteen figures, making a total of at least fifty figures altogether. It is presumed that the figures Pausanias saw were bronzes, since one was reportedly blown into the Theatre of Dionysos below by a freak wind; but we cannot be sure that in Pergamum there were not marble replicas.

Attalos II was a brother of Eumenes II, and campaigned against the Gauls during the reign of Eumenes in 168–167 BC. It may be this Attalos who raised the Athenian groups, prior to his actual monarchy: in which case a date of some time after 167 BC seems likely. Whatever the precise date, there is no doubting the ideological links of the quartet of battles. Each one seems to have included utterly prostrate corpses – of Giants, Amazons, Persians and Gauls. Triumphant figures, some on horseback, were also repeated; and figures pathetically kneeling, sheltering themselves

from blows. It is as if each victory was sanctioned by the same universal moral justification. The Giants threatened proto-divine order in an excess of *hubris*: they were put down. The Amazons threatened prehistoric Athens: they were repulsed. The Persians threatened historic Athens: they too were beaten back. Finally, the Gauls threatened Pergamum, Athens of the East: and thanks to Attalos, they suffered the same fate as their predecessors. This 'Lesser Gaul Group' (as it is called, to distinguish it from the earlier monument of Attalos I featuring the Dying Gaul and Gaul killing his wife) was patently programmed by someone who had studied patterns of symbolism in Classical Athenian iconography (the friezes of the temple of Athena Nike, for instance, and the paintings of the Stoa Poikile). The fact that a Pergamene king was able to count on a second-century BC audience's ability to recognize a genealogy of civilization-versus-barbarism images should be a great comfort to those students of Classical art who sometimes worry about seeing anti-Persian symbolism in every Gigantomachy or Amazonomachy.

The conclusion of our account, however, belongs not with Athens, but Rome. Attalos II was succeeded by Attalos III, whom the sources describe as a curmudgeon. Perhaps he was. After five years in power (138–133 BC)

135 Okeanos and marine deities in a battle against the Giants: detail of the Great Altar at Pergamum. The figures spill out from the frieze on to the steps of the altar.

he died childless. In his will, he closed the Attalid dynasty. He bequeathed Pergamum, and all its possessions – including the nucleus of the treasury entrusted to Philetairos a hundred years previously – to Rome. In retrospect, this seems an act moved not so much by spite as by foresight. Pergamum had already joined forces with the Romans campaigning against Macedon, at the battle of Pydna in 168 BC: Attalos III looked at a future which was likely to be Roman, and sheer prescience may have impelled him to anticipate the eclipse of his little kingdom.

One statue may epitomize all this. 'The swansong of Pergamum', as Bernard Andreae calls it: the Laocoon (*ill. 136*). What we see of this group today is a very fine marble copy of what must have been a bronze original. The copy was made of Italian marble, probably in the time of either Augustus or Tiberius (although Nero, with his penchant for the Fall of Troy, is an attractive possible sponsor). It may be that the commission to make the copy came directly as a result of the popularity of Vergil's *Aeneid*: for in Book Two of his epic, Vergil puts a vivid description of Laocoon's fate into the mouth of his hero Aeneas, while recounting the desperate events that caused his emigration. This is the occasion involving the Wooden Horse, which the Greeks have surreptitiously left as a 'gift' for the Trojans. It is Laocoon, a priest, who says that he does not trust the Greeks even when they come with gifts, and casts a lance at the horse's flank. While Laocoon is preparing a sacrifice by the shore, however, his doubts appear to be severely punished: as Aeneas records, 'two giant arching sea-snakes' suddenly reared out of the sea 'with blazing, bloodshot eyes, and tongues which flickered and licked their hissing mouths'; they foamed on to the beach, heading for Laocoon. First they seized his two sons; then they coiled around Laocoon, binding him 'in the giant spirals of their scaly length . . . His hands strove frantically to wrench the knots apart. . . . His shrieks were horrible and filled the sky, like a bull's bellow when an axe has struck awry . . .' (*Aeneid* II. 201–27).

According to the plot of a play (now lost) by Sophocles, Laocoon was punished for an act of sacrilege. In Pergamene terms, his act of defiance has been translated into heroism. And for sound patriotic reasons, as much as in any aesthetic response, the Romans admired this statue. Eventually it would stand in the imperial residence of Titus, and Pliny would describe it as 'a work to be preferred to all that the arts of painting and sculpture have produced' (*Natural History* XXXVI. 37). Since Pliny was writing ostensibly in honour of Titus, we may find his judgment pragmatic. But Laocoon may be considered a hero of Rome's myth-history: despite his punishment, he had at least spoken his mind; and he was right – the Wooden Horse did bring disaster upon Troy.

Those who study the Laocoon cannot deny the group's patent indebtedness to the Great Altar at Pergamum. Though the copyists who made the

136 The Laocoon Group: perhaps a Roman copy of a Pergamene bronze original of *c.* 140 BC.

marble version are named as three Rhodians (Hagesander, Polydorus and Athenodorus), there is little doubt that the style is essentially Pergamene. And, upon reflection, it seems a thoroughly plausible Pergamene commission. Pergamum was not only ideologically connected with Troy (through her mythical founder, Telephus); she enjoyed a similar topographical and geographical location. In the second half of the second century BC, it became increasingly clear that as an independent bastion of treasures and high culture in Asia Minor, Pergamum was unlikely to survive. What better symbol of her pseudo-Trojan fate than a sculptural evocation of Laocoon's death?

10

GRAECIA CAPTA

When Athens sinks by fates unjust,
When wild Barbarians spurn her dust;
Perhaps ev'n Britain's utmost shore
Shall cease to blush with stranger's gore,
See arts her savage sons control
And Athens rising near the pole!

Alexander Pope, from 'Chorus of the Athenians',
in *Minor Poems* (London 1954), 151–2

Himmler paid a brief visit to Athens in May 1941, chiefly – it seems – to see
the Acropolis.

Mark Mazower, *Inside Hitler's Greece* (New Haven 1993), 219

The rights and wrongs of plunder

To plunder was an ancient right of war. The seizure and display of booty
is a less conspicuous aspect of modern warfare, though Napoleon
indulged, and in World War II it was Nazi policy to build up secret collections of looted art (Russian soldiers invading Berlin in 1945 were happy to
reciprocate openly). And so we are likely to forget plunder's martial logic.
To annex works of art is to express superiority: by taking your enemy's
cherished objects of self-esteem and self-definition, you symbolically
incorporate and assimilate him. We have already seen how the Greeks
themselves operated this logic: the city-state treasuries at Olympia and
Delphi were designed to expose fruits of victory, and on the Athenian
Akropolis the display of spoils (*aristeia*) taken from the Persians was conspicuous. When the Carthaginians attacked the Greek colonial city of
Akragas (Agrigento) in 406 BC, they, too, are recorded as having carried off
'all kinds of works of art' (*kataskeuasmata*). And as for Alexander, he is
reckoned, during his Persian campaigns of 333–331 BC, to have accumu-
lated 180,000 talents of booty. This is estimated (depending how much is
counted as gold) to equate to between £1.7 and 22 billion or $2.5 and 33
billion.

The plundering of Greek statuary by the Romans is sometimes described as a part of the Roman conquest of Greece during the second century BC. This is too tidy a summary. It is true that Rome pursued a policy of political and military expansion in the eastern Mediterranean – in the course of which the kingdom of Pergamum (to some Roman surprise) surrendered itself to Rome's possession. But Romans helped themselves to Greek art in three different military situations. To begin with, they were intervening as allies in the struggles between the various Hellenistic kingdoms, and the Greek cities, or leagues of Greek cities, attempting to assert independence. This developed into Rome's annexation of Macedonia in 146 BC, including the province they would designate separately in 27 BC as Achaea. But once Roman rule had been more or less established in those areas broadly denoted as *Graecia*, a third context for plunder was created, when Greece hosted certain key campaigns of the Roman civil wars during the first century BC. This is not to mention the subsequent depredations of certain powerful individuals, notoriously Verres, who went beyond legality in seizing works of art in Cilicia and Sicily, and of certain emperors, notoriously Nero, who pillaged with impunity.

Greek sanctuaries, since they were already places where booty of old had been displayed, invited the plunderer's hand. Plutarch (*Life of Sulla*, XII. 3) tells us that Sulla stole from Epidauros, Olympia and Delphi. When the priests at Delphi reported that Apollo's lyre had been heard in the sanctuary, angrily lamenting the robbery, Sulla flippantly retorted that this was a sign of the god's contentment, not anger: he would accordingly carry off more. Gnaeus Octavius, an associate of Aemilius Paullus in the decisive campaigns against the Macedonian king, Perseus, in 171–168 BC, sacked the Macedonian sanctuary at Samothrace; Verres, among his multiple raids of private property, was accused of stealing from the Heraion on Samos; and Nero is said to have removed five hundred bronzes statues from Delphi, as well as the figure of Odysseus from an ensemble of nine Achaean heroes at Olympia. As noted earlier (Chapter 6), if the Riace Bronzes are indeed from the Marathon memorial at Delphi, then they too must be counted among these Roman lootings of Greek sanctuaries.

The case of Verres illustrates what scruples conditioned the appropriation of Greek art, whether from sanctuaries or elsewhere. He was prosecuted in 70 BC by Cicero, whose prolix indictment meticulously chronicles Verres' worst abuse of his powers, which was precisely the seizure of art treasures. So we learn that when Verres descended on Aspendos in Pamphylia, not a single statue escaped his greedy trawl. In addition to the Samian Heraion, Chios, Erythrai and Halicarnassus were also plundered. As for his governorship in Sicily, it left many cities and private individuals short of their cherished possessions. The great danger of inviting Verres to dinner was that his henchmen would be around the next day to carry off the silver dinner service. But many provincial governors were doubtless similarly light-fingered. What Cicero charges against Verres is not so much his theft of art (though that was excessive), but two secondary crimes: firstly, that he acted against Roman interests by including Rome's allies, such as Antiochus of Syria, among his victims; and secondly, that instead of making proper inventories of his collection, and passing a proportion to the public chest, he kept everything for his own purposes. This evidently was a key element of culpability in this case: Cicero's prosecution was carried.

No legal proceedings, however, were brought against Sulla. Sulla relied on booty to pay his troops. His use for bronze statues was pecuniary in the most direct sense: he would have the statues melted down and struck into coins. Other generals cashed their plunder less destructively. It could be turned into great political capital, when transported home and exhibited in triumph; especially if its consignment to state coffers relieved Romans of their own tax burden. There was no law obliging a general to hand over booty to the state, but a moral obligation can be measured in Roman political oratory; and the morale boost provided by widespread tax cuts, the concession of holidays and the staging of triumphal processions and associated entertainments encouraged all politically sensitive commanders not to reserve their booty entirely for themselves, but distribute it around the city. Livy tells us (XXV. 39.1–3) that the first Roman general to display looted Greek art-works as 'embellishments of the city' (*ornamenta urbis*) was Marcellus, after his sack of Syracuse in 211 BC; and, in Livy's eyes, that was a decidedly mixed blessing.

Booty boosted the war effort, and when used as urban ornament it promoted Rome's Mediterranean status (Livy will later note that the physical appearance of the city of Rome was the butt of jokes among Macedonian aristocrats: XL. 5.8). Yet the distribution also promoted an appetite for collecting Greek works of art which some Romans (Livy among them) considered unhealthy. In a sense, the two phenomena were necessarily connected: if generals brought back works of art as booty, the state treasurers would want to turn at least some of that art into cash by selling it off to supply wealthy collectors. But Romans who believed in the old Republican ideals of plain talking and hard work harboured a strong sense of inverted snobbery about Greek art. The Elder Cato (234–149 BC) represents this Hellenophobia best: he would have applauded Sulla's consideration of Greek bronzes as so many pieces of junk metal waiting to be turned into something useful. And Livy, nostalgic for the imagined purities of the early Republic, feels obliged to take the line of resistance towards the import of Greek culture. Despite the fact that in Livy's own time, Greek statues were being deployed for apparently valid civic functions (such as on the temple of Apollo Medicus sponsored by Caius Sosius, for whose decoration entire Classical Greek pedimental groups were brought over, probably from Eretria), Livy remained austere. The import of Greek art was corrupting inasmuch as it stimulated the taste for *privata luxuria*, and politically antipathetic, since it encouraged private individuals in the Roman Republic to surround themselves with the palatial baubles usually associated with Hellenistic monarchs. But Livy was too late in his censure: the battle, on that front, was already lost.

'Captive Greece made captive her uncultured conqueror'

'Graecia capta ferum victorem cepit et artis intulit agresti Latio': Livy's contemporary, Horace, indicates that poets may show better judgment than historians. This summary (from his *Epistles*, II. 1.156–7) of how Greece culturally colonized Rome, 'and brought the arts to rustic Latium', is made with an eye on literary culture, and it is not an entirely original sentiment: referring to the art of eloquence generally, Cicero had said 'we were conquered by conquered Greece' (*vincebamur a victa Graecia*: see *Brutus* 73. 254). But both Cicero and Horace would have conceded that eloquence and literature were not alone as Greek cultural victories. Roman generals themselves were conquered: despite a Republican moral tradition which considered nudity the basis of many evils, these old soldiers liked the image of Greek athletic prowess, and allowed or instructed Greek sculptors to give them the bodies of stalwart athletes, even though their portrait-faces told a different story (*ill. 137*).

In one sense the Roman attitude here was like a renunciation of ambitions: art is something they will leave to the Greeks. Vergil phrases this attitude as if it were an accepted law of ethnic disposition. When Aeneas is shown the course of future Roman greatness by his father Anchises, the paternal wisdom includes a warning not to try anything in sculpture. 'Others shall beat more delicately the breathing bronze, coax living faces out of marble' (*vivos ducent de marmore voltus: Aeneid* VI. 847–48): Romans should concentrate on what they do best, which is the business of conquering and governing the world. Once established, this resignation from endeavour by the Romans freed a new status for Greek art. Cicero, when bringing his case against Verres, disingenuously affects not to know very much about Greek productions. But his letters to friends reveal a lively interest in the collecting and connoisseurship of what would soon be known as *nobilia opera* – 'the great works' – of the Greeks, which educated Romans felt they had inherited from the old cultural centre of the Mediterranean, and which uneducated Romans took to be the prizes of imperial expansion. So it was that the rich collected statues because statues

137 The 'Pseudo-athlete': a Roman portrait from Delos; c. 100 BC.

signified riches; while the more cultivated man (*homo doctus*) would express his intellectualism by displaying figures of the Muses, busts of philosophers and so on; or commissioning programmes of statuary illustrating myths or literature of which he was especially fond. Although some worthies collected Greek sculpture through their enthusiasm for Hellenic culture generally (like the emperor Hadrian), the acquisition of statues, or sponsorship of copies, cannot be described as a fetish or craze among the Romans. It was a process of absorption which, from the late first century BC onwards, was virtually taken for granted. The manipulation of Greek imagery in Roman contexts was probably far more subtle than we shall ever appreciate: all we can do here is register the extent of Roman patronage. By the third century AD, the city, with its environs, is estimated to have had a statue-population of half a million.

Many of these statues will have been what are usually described as 'copies' of Greek originals. The tell-tale signs are obvious enough, especially when it is a case of a copy in marble of an original in bronze: extra supports have to be brought in for the marble versions, and some of these – most commonly, the palm tree growing into the side of an athlete's thigh – look downright ridiculous. But caution is required when speaking of copies. Though there is some evidence of plaster casts of Greek statuary being taken in the Roman period, the fact remains that accurate 'pointing-off' techniques for copying were not developed in antiquity. So while Roman sources speak of the 'canonical' figure of the spear-carrier (Doryphoros) made by the Classical Athenian sculptor Polykleitos as an ideal model for all sculptors to follow (words like *lex*, *magister* and *exemplum* are used of the Doryphoros), no amount of measuring from the twenty-five surviving Roman 'copies' of this statue-type will restore to us the precise dimensions of the original.

So a great deal 'copying' was done with some creative licence, and Roman connoisseurs, if they could not get hold of (say) an Archaic Greek *kore* for their garden, could always have a statue made to look like one. But while more and more stories are generated about the 'great masters' of the fifth and fourth centuries BC, we hear very little about the many Greek sculptors actually working to Roman orders. One exception is a highly versatile sculptor from Magna Graecia called Pasiteles, whose devotion to the old ethic of faithfulness to nature nearly cost him his life: down in the docks of Rome, where jungle beasts were being unloaded for the circus, he was moulding an image of a lion at close quarters when a panther got loose from a cage and mauled him (as Pliny relates: *Natural History* XXXVI. 40). But already with Pasiteles (active at the end of the first century BC) there is the feeling that nothing new can be done in sculpture. Pasiteles himself is said to have assembled a five-volume tome detailing *The World's Great Masterpieces*: what else was there to do save pay homage to *nobilia opera*? And Pliny, rather condescendingly, can only praise Pasiteles as 'the most conscientious of artists' (*diligentissimus artificis*). Pasiteles was clever and adept: but he could never match the achievements of his fellow-countrymen of earlier centuries.

Such was the Roman respect for great works that some even came to appear on coins, such as Myron's much-applauded bronze heifer, which ultimately stood in Vespasian's Temple of Peace. No wonder that certain statues were perceived as public property. When the emperor Tiberius, in the early first century AD, decided to expropriate from public view the original bronze figure of an athlete scraping himself, the Apoxyomenos of Lysippos (*ill. 138*), to keep in his own quarters, there was a protest vehement enough to force the statue's return. But of course there was no limit to what wealthy Romans could commission in private. To Tiberius we may probably attribute one of the most imaginative private displays of Greek sculpture known to us: the mini-theme park of statuary in the grotto at Sperlonga, on the coast south of Rome. Here marble groups depicting select adventures of Odysseus, some of them extremely complex, were placed in a huge marine grotto where dinner could be taken, and conversation turned, no doubt, on the many philosophical and literary topics arising from the Odyssean scenes.

The statues at Sperlonga were saved for us by a collapse of rock. In Rome, the statues once placed in temples, colonnades, *fora*, baths and gardens were mostly doomed when Constantine transferred his capital to Byzantium in AD 330. Bronzes suffered their usual fate in furnaces; and medieval Romans found that marbles, too, had some use. The processing of statues into building lime is recorded at Rome as late as 1443. Then came the Italian Renaissance, and with it a resurrection of Roman connoisseurship of Greek statues.

138 The Apoxyomenos ('Scraper') by Lysippos: a Roman copy of a late fourth-century BC bronze original.

A brief history of modern collecting

Not all Classical statuary suffered in the Middle Ages. On a parapet on the front of the basilica of St Mark's cathedral in Venice stood a set of bronze horses which was almost certainly taken from Constantinople in 1204, during the Fourth Crusade. They are recorded in Venice in 1364, and may well be work of the fifth or fourth century BC, though no exact Greek provenance can be fixed for them. And as Umberto Eco showed in his 1959 monograph *Art and Beauty in the Middle Ages*, medieval asceticism coexisted with a degree of medieval aestheticism. But reverence for the achievements of Classical sculpture is not really evident until the early sixteenth century, when we have our first notice of excavations dedicated to finding antique statuary. In Vasari's *Life of Giovanni da Udine*, we are told

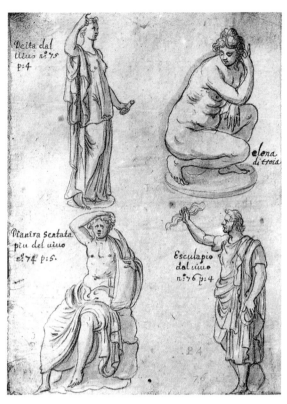

how young Giovanni (1494–1564) went digging in the ruins of the palace of Titus, 'to find statues' (*per trovar figure*); and it was from the palace of Titus that the Laocoon group was recovered in 1506, allegedly in the presence of Michelangelo. Contemporary scholars would have known of Pliny's high esteem for the Laocoon, and the matching of Roman esteem with an excavated object encouraged immediate fresh celebrity for the Laocoon.

It was put in a niche in the Vatican's dedicated Belvedere ('lovely to see') statue court, and artists paid homage to it as artists were increasingly bound to do: by sketching in front of 'great works' (*ill. 139*). Although certain popes worried about nudity, and periodically insisted on the application of fig leaves over male genitalia, some of the first pieces of antique sculpture collected in Renaissance Rome were female nudes, including the Aphrodite of the Lovely Buttocks (*Kallipygos*) and the Crouching Aphrodite, sketched by one artist as 'Helen of Troy' (*ill. 140*). The Farnese family, including Pope Paul III (1468–1549), and his grandson Cardinal Alessandro Farnese (1520–89), were particularly assiduous collectors:

139 The Laocoon, as sketched in the Belvedere gardens of the Vatican. Engraving of 1539.

140 Sketches of statues once in the collection of Charles I of England, including one labelled 'Helen of Troy' but in fact based on the Crouching Aphrodite (*see ill. 116*) from the ruins of the Baths of Caracalla, which lay on their own property, they salvaged some spectacularly large pieces of Hellenistic–Roman production, notably a colossal marble Herakles and a group showing the sons of Antiope tying Dirce to a rampant bull.

Francis I of France communicated some of this new enthusiasm north of Italy, but the Vatican maintained control over collecting sculpture, though very little that was not Roman or Hellenistic had yet come to light. It is all the more astonishing, then, that when Winckelmann entered the employ of Cardinal Albani (1692–1779), he was able to construct an entire history of ancient art based on the Vatican holdings. Explorations of Hadrian's villa at Tivoli had swelled the collection, but it was still limited in its range. Winckelmann's work, however, awakened strong interest in aristocrats in France, Britain and Germany: the idea of the 'Grand Tour' was developing, and sculptures made excellent souvenirs of such tours. Since Greece was apparently thought dangerous and bandit-ridden by most grand tourists, Italy, and Rome in particular, remained the main market for Classical antiquities in the eighteenth century. A good example of what was then considered a very fine collection is represented by the Townley Marbles, now displayed separately in the British Museum as a curiosity in the history of taste.

The prestige status of Classical statuary can be measured by a list of what Napoleon Bonaparte and his revolutionary French forces confiscated in Italy during 1796. From Venice they gathered the horses of St Mark;

141 Napoleon and his court inspecting the Laocoon, brought from Rome to Paris, in the Louvre at night.

from the Vatican, all the celebrated pieces, including the Laocoon, the Apollo Belvedere, and the so-called 'Belvedere Torso' (*ill. 141*). These were laboriously transported back to Paris overland, lest the English navy pounce on them: and when they were triumphantly deposited in the Louvre in 1798, a banner proclaimed:

> 'Monuments of Ancient Sculpture. Greece gave them up;
> Rome lost them;
> Their fate has twice changed:
> It will not change again!'

That was a rash boast: in 1816, after Waterloo, the neoclassical sculptor Canova escorted nearly all the looted material back to Italy.

A change in taste was imminent; compounded, ironically, by Napoleon's occupation of Italy. Two British artists, James Stuart and Nicholas Revett, had ventured to Greece and Asia Minor in the mid-eighteenth century, and in 1762 they published the first volume of their handsome account of *Athenian Antiquities*. Apart from meticulously detailing what was to be seen at Athens and elsewhere, they demonstrated that the difficulties of travelling in Turkish-occupied Greece might be regarded as more óf an adventure than a series of inconveniences; and the footloose British aristocrat, since Bonaparte had taken Italy, needed a new destination to complete his education. So Greece became available. And one of those who desired the 'Grecian gusto' described by Stuart and Revett was Thomas Bruce, the Seventh Earl of Elgin, who occupied a rather gloomy ancestral home at Broomhall in Fifeshire. He thought he could combine a diplomatic posting to Constantinople with an expedition to Athens, to collect some sketches and plaster casts of architectural mouldings that might ennoble his stately home.

The rest of the Elgin saga is so well documented by others that it requires no repetition here. Much of the invective directed at Elgin came from Romantics who liked their ruins to be in a perpetual (but fixed) state of picturesque decay: whereas he himself became an unquestioning apostle of the Enlightenment, who believed in the didactic utility of stripping the Parthenon of its decoration, and placing it in a guarded collection, before it decayed beyond repair *in situ*. Of course, there was an element of nationalistic competition here, and Elgin would have removed very little had Nelson not prevailed over the French at the battle of the Nile in 1801; and there must be a measure of retrospective disingenuousness when Elgin wrote, in 1831, that he had taken the Parthenon marbles 'wholly for the purpose of securing to Great Britain, and through it to Europe in general, the most effectual possible knowledge, and means of improving, by the excellence of Grecian art in sculpture and architecture.' But there can be no doubting that the subsequent display of the Parthenon sculptures in the British Museum caused a minor revolution in taste for Greek sculpture. There was some initial hostility, on the grounds that the figures were damaged and incomplete: but resistance soon crumbled. The statues were purchased for the nation; the cult of Pheidias began; the associations of the Parthenon with Periklean Athens were vigorously exaggerated; and in the British Museum itself, continued external polemic over the rights of possession of these sculptures only added to their cherished status. Students of fine art were sent to set up their easels and learn how to draw in front of the sculptures (in 1879, over 15,000 sketching permits were issued), and though no artistic revival has ever come about in Britain as a result, the creation in 1933 of an extra-spacious Olympian refuge for the Parthenon sculptures, at Lord Duveen's expense, and with two Classical archaeologists (J.D. Beazley and Bernard Ashmole) advising, has maintained a hallowed place in London for Elgin's trophies.

Today, collectors must rely on the circulation of formerly collected pieces, or the fruits of illicit looting, to furnish their needs. The main peril of twentieth-century collectors is being duped by a forgery; but that is a natural effect of strong demand and limited supply in a lucrative market. The twentieth century has seen further switches in taste: modernists either rejected the authority of Classical models entirely, or else chose to admire the simplicities of Archaic Greek work. And the pervasive relativism of the late twentieth century has generally reduced the force of Western admiration for the achievements of Greek sculpture. In the Museum of Fine Arts at Boston, and the Metropolitan Museum of New York, for instance, Greek collections no longer occupy their central positions of old: the masks and totems of what is (still patronizingly) termed 'primitive' art are reckoned to be as germane, if not more so, to our collective self-comprehension.

'We do not want either Greek or Roman Models if we are but just & true to our own Imaginations', cried William Blake in 1804. Blake suffered from a religious mania that made him convinced that Greek sculptors had filched their masterpieces from Hebraic originals: the Laocoon group he believed to be a copy of a representation of Jehovah and his sons Satan and Adam in Solomon's Temple. Such delusion cannot be argued with. The aesthetic authority of Greek sculpture has been resented by other artists for better reasons, and doubtless tastes will vacillate this way and that in years to come. Anyone visiting the British Museum nowadays, however, will usually find one or two art students sketching in front of the Parthenon sculptures. Modernism rejected the authority of Classical models; but in the Postmodern world, the charm of the Classical has been saluted as one of a medley of charms from the past; and the fact that Classical statuary is so often fragmentary adds – in Postmodernist eyes – to its particular appeal.

EPILOGUE

One underlying assumption of this book has so far gone unstated. Since it is the ultimate justification for all that has been written here, this premise should at last be admitted. Greek sculpture is worth studying because Greek sculpture is great sculpture.

What does that mean? It is a value-judgment, obviously, and one which some might regard as the stubborn arrogance of an author who believes in the canonical status of 'the Classics'. But the word 'great' is used here with more than the straight sense of generic approbation. In the first place, Greek sculpture is, by common consensus, technically 'great'. Examining original bronzes – such as the Delphi charioteer (*ill. 52*), or the Riace pair (*ill. 91*) – anyone with expertise in the metal-casting process readily admits that these are great, in the sense that such figures represent in their execution the highest degree of difficulty. Likewise, modern marble-workers remain amazed at the carving and finish of pieces as chronologically disparate as the Moscophoros (*ill. 60*) and the Laocoon (*ill. 136*).

There is, however, a further sense in which Greek sculpture is 'great'. This is because of its subject matter. So many of the themes of Greek sculptors were determined – according to their patrons' agenda – to be expressive of heroism, excellence and piety. The result is that Greek sculpture is never abstract, rarely trivial and generally ennobling. Even when the sculpted bodies of heroes and deities were marked with geometric patterns (following the prevalent Greek artistic style in the eighth century BC), a tangible, non-abstract ideal was still the aim. As Apollo was 'great' in his divinity, so his sculptural representation must equate to a definition of greatness. And since that definition was made in anthropomorphic or human-shaped terms, it became an inspiration to all mortal viewers.

In modern parlance it is still possible (though mannered) to exclaim, 'How divine!' in front of a work of art. In ancient Greek usage, to declare a sculpture 'godly' (*entheos*) was not a simply aesthetic response, but an article of faith. And this is how Greek sculpture was invested with its ennobling qualities. The viewers of divine or heroized forms believed that their sculptors had done more than provide souvenirs of greatness. A spirit, an animated power, had been caught in the stone, clay or bronze. This spirit – be it of a deity, a Homeric warrior, a deceased priestess or a prematurely lost infant – reserved a message for all who gazed on its sculpted form. Thus Greek sculptures served a genuinely vicarious function. They were accessible; they communicated – and what they communicated was mostly encouragement and consolation to their viewers.

So it is neither elitist nor eccentric to assert that Greek sculpture is great. In the conspectus of global art history, there is general agreement about the particular contribution of the Greeks: they pioneered, or even 'discovered' naturalism in art. This is the significance of the phrase, 'the Greek Revolution'. To those who are culturally unfamiliar with it, the sight of a collection of Greek sculpture can be a shock, and that must also have been the case in antiquity. Some non-Greeks – Jews and Christians especially – abhorred its idolatrous significance; others – certainly the Etruscans and perhaps, too, the Buddhist peoples of Gandhara, in northwest India – altered their own traditions of image-making as a result of it; and of course, one or two Greeks – notably Plato – remained suspicious of the illusionistic obsessions endemic among the sculptors of their day. Tracing the ripples created around the world by 'the Greek Revolution' is a study in itself. But what have we done in this present exploration to illuminate the dynamics of this global achievement?

Most handbooks of Greek art trace the chronological development of style. This is easy enough to do, following the broad rule that Greek art is progressively more naturalistic over a timespan of about 800 to 100 BC. Working from the piecemeal notice of names in ancient literature, and a small number of signed works, a history of Greek sculpture may be created which is effectively a chronicle of the activities of ever more skilful and ambitious craftsmen, whose drive for greater illusionistic effect is then imputed to a highly competitive environment. In such chronicles, great sculpture is explained as the handiwork of great masters.

Our study has been more or less chronological, and has not denied the element of competition among individual sculptors. It is recklessly dogmatic to describe them as the 'secret heroes' of Greek civilization. Some of them clearly traded on self-advertisement, and it can probably be said of certain known sculptors – Pheidias, Praxiteles, Lysippos – that camouflage was not their strong suit. At the same time, it has to be acknowledged that only a very few Greek sculptors were celebrated in their own times. More were retrospectively lionized by Roman collectors of sculpture, and yet more have been invented for (and by) modern connoisseurs. Thus 'the Greek Revolution' has been set into the artificial framework of a supposed aesthetic of artistic 'progress', and peopled with protagonists who make the running. In reality, this framework is a very flimsy structure, whose weakness was fully demonstrated when the Riace Bronzes were found. Matching names to pieces involves more guesswork than good sense.

Biographical information is a common craving, and it is in human nature to collect and catalogue rare objects according to their actual or imagined authorship. We love to have systems for ordering things, and names make marvellous systems, especially when they can be organized into fathers and sons, pupils and followers, workshops and schools. But the message of this book is that a better understanding of both the themes and the stylistic accomplishments of Greek sculpture can be reached if we abandon our craving for names, and transfer our attention away from those who made Greek sculpture, in the direction instead of those who asked for it and paid for it.

Of course there are problems with this approach also. One undeniable truth is that some pieces of Greek sculpture, familiar to us for many years, continue, despite their apparent familiarity, to provoke much varied speculation as to their meaning. The Parthenon frieze is one such: here, one of several possible interpretations has been argued for, but it cannot be definitive. Most of the commissions for Greek sculpture were sacred, and few documents survive that relate to the commission itself. It is not surprising, perhaps, that faced with some major obstacles to an understanding of what ancient works of art mean, scholars prefer to concentrate on questions of attribution. Here we have provided examples of how to overcome difficulties of interpretation; and a threefold summary of methods may serve as both a conclusion and a manifesto for future efforts.

Firstly, it should be clear that no understanding of Greek sculpture can be gained without drawing on philological sources. By 'philological' are meant those literary and historical records which get us as close as possible to the ambience in which the sculptors originally operated. Possibly too much faith has been entrusted here to Pausanias, writing in the second century AD, but he was travelling with a lively eye for surviving traditions; and knowledge of those traditions, however distant, is a massive help in itself. It is a great pity that Herodotus, writing in the mid-fifth century BC, was not as interested in Greek ritual as he was in Egyptian. Unfortunately (for our purposes) he could doubtless assume that his Greek audience needed no instruction about their own cultural peculiarities. But the philological materials yielded by the literate societies of Athens and elsewhere from the sixth century BC onwards remain essential points of reference for students of Greek sculpture. (It has to be admitted that our nineteenth-century predecessors, with their more rigorous Classical educations, were often more sensitive to this fact than we are.)

Secondly, we need theory. It need not be some all-explanatory model for the production and display of Greek sculpture, but a component of analysis used as and when appropriate. A century ago, J.G. Frazer, Jane Harrison and others were using the relative evidence from anthropological research to fathom the meanings of Greek art. As we have seen, certain models derived from direct studies of other cultures, such as the notion of the Balinese 'theatre state', can usefully be applied to illuminate ancient

Greek conditions. Likewise, the interdisciplinary approaches favoured by archaeologists, particularly prehistoric archaeologists, should be brought to bear on the Greek evidence. Systematic methods for deciphering the iconography of ritual, for example, are all the more important if Greek writers remain silent on such matters.

Lastly, and most importantly: students of Greek sculpture must be archaeologists. Once statues are ensconced in museums, and labelled with their dates and styles and supposed authorship, it is too easily forgotten that they usually had to be disinterred to get where they are now. Too often, in the chequered history of Classical archaeology, the prime concern of excavators has been to dig up *objets d'art*, caring little about precise provenance and stratification. Most surviving Greek sculptures come from sanctuaries: but how those sanctuaries functioned remains unclear to us, and the fault must partly lie with the way in which excavations were once conducted. Studying the modes of worship – for instance, the reverence of family ancestors, and cult heroes – are now more important to archaeologists, and our understanding of ritual objects can only improve as a result.

One reason why new explorations of Greek sculpture need to be produced is because archaeology steadily yields new evidence. It is instructive to consider that when the father of Classical art history, J.J. Winckelmann, compiled his first account of Greek art in 1764, he not only had no knowledge of the Athenian Akropolis, but many key sites – Olympia, Delphi, Samos, Pergamum – had yet to be excavated. Distinguished scholars in the first half of this century had little knowledge of the Athenian Agora; and only in the last thirty years have such crucial materials for the history of Greek sculpture as the Riace Bronzes, and the finds from Vergina, become available, and such discoveries continue. The re-excavation and renewed analysis of certain sites first explored in the last century, such as the Mausoleum, is also genuinely adding to our knowledge and understanding.

Our aim here has been to restore to Greek sculpture a measure of the imaginative sympathy it required of its ancient viewers. Modern viewers cannot hope to engage so comprehensively with it as their ancient predecessors. But this should not deter us from making the effort to recover at least some of the original and powerful enchantment of this art.

SOURCES AND FURTHER READING

This list is predominantly of works in English, and certainly not comprehensive. Those seeking more detailed accounts of the dating and attribution of Greek sculpture should consult A.F. Stewart, *Greek Sculpture* (New Haven 1990), and the following handbooks: J. Boardman, *Greek Sculpture: the Archaic Period* (London 1978); J. Boardman, *Greek Sculpture: the Classical Period* (London 1985); J. Boardman, *Greek Sculpture: the Late Classical Period* (London 1995); and R.R.R. Smith, *Hellenistic Sculpture* (London 1991). For a sound annotated anthology of translated sources, consult J.J. Pollit, *The Art of Ancient Greece* (Cambridge 1990).

1 Introduction (pp. 7–15)

The opening tale comes from *Constantinople in the Early Eighth Century: the* Parastaseis Syntomi Chronikai, A. Cameron and J. Herrin (eds), Leiden 1984, 88–91. The quote from St Jerome is from his rendering of Eusebius' *Chronici Canones*, 314.24. For Eusebius and the *Vita Constantius*, see *A Select Library of Nicene and Post-Nicene Fathers*, Vol. 1, P. Schaff and H. Wace (eds): section 3.54 of the *Vita* is particularly relevant. I have drawn on Cyril Mango, 'Antique Statuary and the Byzantine Beholder', in *Dumbarton Oaks Papers* 17 (1963), 55–75 (reprinted, with the same pagination, in C. Mango, *Byzantium and its Image: History and Culture of the Byzantine Empire and Heritage*, London 1984); also useful is T.C.G. Thornton, 'The Destruction of Idols – Sinful or Meritorious?', in *Journal of Theological Studies* 37 (1986), 121–4; and C. Mango et al., 'The Palace of Lausus at Constantinople and its Collection of Ancient Statues', in *Journal of the History of Collections* 4 (1992), 89–98. The letter ascribed to St Augustine is in the Loeb edition of *Select Letters*, no. 16.

G. Mendel's three-volume publication of statuary in the Istanbul Museum (*Catalogue des Sculptures*, Constantinople 1912–14) is comprehensive, though only illustrated by line-drawings.

The epigrams of Christodorus were collected in the Palatine Anthology, and are translated in Vol. I of W.R. Paton's Loeb edition of *The Greek Anthology*. For an exegesis, see R. Stupperich, 'Das Statuenprogramm in den Zeuxippos-Thermen: überlegungen zur Beschreibung durch Christodorus von Koptos', in *Istanbuler Mitteilungen* 32 (1982), 210–35.

For Jacob of Saroug (or Serug), see P. Martin, 'Discours de Jacques de Saroug sur la chute des idoles', in *Zeitschrift der Deutschen Morgenländischen Gesellschaft* 29 (1875), 107–47 (Syriac text with French translation).

Those foreign to the tenets of Postmodernism should start with D. Harvey, *The Condition of Postmodernity* (Oxford 1990). The quotation regarding the Christian basis of Constantinople is taken from R. MacMullen, *Constantine* (London 1970), 154. Berenson's eloquent views on the Arch of Constantine may be found in his monograph, *The Arch of Constantine, or the Decline of Form* (London 1954).

2 'The Greek Revolution' (pp. 17–53)

Goethe's denomination of the *Urpferd* is often quoted, but rarely sourced or explained. (The original German runs: 'Es sieht so übermächtig und geisterartig aus, als wenn es gegen die Natur gebildet wäre, und doch, jener Beobachtung gemäss, hat der Künstler eigentlich ein Urpferd geschaffen'.) His use of the term belongs to an essay written *c.* 1823, and the phrase cited here comes from Vol. 36 (*Zur Morphologie*, ed. W. Wasielewksi) of *Goethes Werke* (Berlin-Leipzig, n.d.), 286. For the original text of the passage quoted from Eckermann, see J.P. Eckermann, *Gespräche mit Goethe* (Basel 1945), Vol. I, 278. The phrase of Ernst Buschor is the opening line of his *Pferde des Phidias* (Munich 1948).

'The Greek Miracle': W. Deonna, *Du miracle grec au miracle chrètien* (Basle 1946–6; cf. *L'Antiquité classique* 6 (1937), 181–230). The New York exhibition, *The Greek Miracle*, was published in a catalogue of the same title edited by D. Buitron-Oliver (New York 1993).

'Discovery of nature': E. Loewy, *The Rendering of Nature in Early Greek Art* (London 1907). The quote on Kritian Boy comes from H. Payne and G. Mackworth-Young, *Archaic Marble Sculpture from the Acropolis* (London 1936), 45. Surprisingly little has been written about Winckelmann's idealization of Classical sculpture: but perceptive remarks will be found in F. Haskell, *History and its Images* (New Haven 1993), 217ff., and a longer account of Winckelmann's proclivities in A. Potts, *Flesh and the Ideal* (New Haven 1994).

Egyptian comparisons: I have quoted from W. Davis, *The Canonical Tradition in Ancient Egyptian Art* (Cambridge 1989), 220; see also H. Schäfer, *Principles of Egyptian Art* (Oxford 1974); and (for a severely mathematical analysis), G. Robins, *Proportion and Style in Ancient Egyptian Art* (London 1994).

Euandria and related contests: see three articles by N.B. Crowther: 'Male Beauty Contests in Greece: the Euandria and the Euexia', in *L'Antiquité classique* 54 (1985), 285–91; 'The Euandria Competition at the Panathenaia Reconsidered', in *Ancient World* 15 (1987), 59–64; and 'Euexia, Eutaxia, Philoponia: Three

Contests of the Greek Gymnasium', in *Zeitschrift für Papyrologie und Epigraphie* 85 (1991), 301–4. Also: J. Neils, 'The Panathenaia and Kleisthenic Ideology', in W. Coulson et al. (eds), *The Archaeology of Athens and Attica under the Democracy* (Oxford 1994), 151–60.

On Polykleitos: A.F. Stewart, 'The Canon of Polykleitos: a question of evidence', in *Journal of Hellenic Studies* 98 (1978), 122–31; and E. Panofsky, *Meaning in the Visual Arts* (Harmondsworth 1970), Ch. 2. The measuring relief in Oxford is discussed in E. Fernie, 'The Greek Metrological Relief in Oxford', in *Antiquaries Journal* 61 (1981), 255–63.

Anthropomorphism: see N.J. Spivey, 'Bionic Statues', in A. Powell (ed.), *The Greek World* (London 1995); B. Alroth, 'Changing Modes in the Representation of Cult Images', in R. Hägg (ed.), *The Iconography of Cult in the Archaic and Classical Periods* (Athens-Liège 1992), 9–46; and A. Schnapp, 'Are images animated: the psychology of statues in Ancient Greece', in C. Renfrew and E. Zubrow (eds), *The Ancient Mind* (Cambridge 1994), 40–4.

Dio Chrysostom's *Olympic Discourse* (generally reckoned to be his best oratory) is available in an excellent edition of Dio by D.A. Russell (Cambridge 1992).

For Ovid's Pygmalion, see J. Elsner, 'Visual Mimesis and the Myth of the Real: Ovid's Pygmalion as Viewer', in *Ramus* 20 (1991), 154–68.

Walter Benjamin's essay 'The Work of Art in the Age of Mechanical Reproduction' is in the collection of his writings entitled *Illuminations* (London 1970).

3 Daedalus and the Wings of Techne (pp. 54–77)

On Herder and his relativism, see generally I. Berlin, *The Crooked Timber of Humanity* (London 1990), 74ff. The quote here comes from Herder's *Auch eine Philosophie der Geschichte* (ed. M. Rouché [1774]), 144–6. See also A. Potts, 'Herder's *Plastik*', in J. Onians (ed.), *Sight and Insight* (London 1994), 341–51.

The best account of the mythologization of Daedalus is F. Frontisi-Ducroix, *Dédale: mythologie de l'artisan en Grèce ancienne* (Paris 1975). A much more complex study is S.P. Morris, *Daidalos and the Origins of Greek Art* (Princeton 1992). I have quoted from the review of this by S. Sherratt in *Antiquity* 67 (1993), 915–16.

On the disparagement of *banausic* activity, see R. Mondolfo, 'The Greek attitude to manual labour', in *Past and Present* 6 (1954), 1–5.

Sculpture in wood: the mostly literary evidence is surveyed best in R. Meiggs, *Trees and Timber in the Ancient Mediterranean World* (Oxford 1982), 300–24. See also A.A. Donohue, *Xoana and the origins of Greek sculpture* (Atlanta 1988).

Sculpture in stone: S. Adam, *The Technique of Greek Sculpture* (London 1966); the various papers in the Getty Symposium, *Marble: Art Historical and Scientific Perspectives on Ancient Sculpture* (Malibu 1990); M. Korres, *From Pentelicon to the Parthenon* (Athens 1995); and for a practising stonemason's account, P. Rockwell, *The Art of Stoneworking* (Cambridge 1993). Generally, N. Penny, *The Materials of Sculpture* (London 1993) is instructive.

The latest, and clearest account of bronze-working is D. Haynes, *The Technique of Greek Bronze Statuary* (Mainz 1992). C.C. Mattusch, *Greek Bronze Statuary from the beginnings through the fifth century* BC (Ithaca 1988) is also trustworthy. Further technical information can be gleaned from the misleadingly-entitled colloquim *Small Bronze Sculpture from the Ancient World* (Getty Museum, 1990: large bronzes are also discussed). On the influence of armoury, see J.F. Kenfield, 'The Sculptural Significance of Early Greek Armour', in *Opuscula Romana* 9 (1973), 149–56.

For Oriental bronzes recovered from Samos, see U. Jantzen, *Ägyptische und orientalische Bronzen auf dem Heraion von Samos* (Bonn 1972).

Olympia bronzes: A. Furtwängler, *Olympia IV: Die Bronzen und die übrigen Kleinfunde* (Berlin 1890); and W-D. Heilmeyer, *Frühe Olympische Bronzefiguren (Olympische Forschungen XII)* (Berlin 1979).

On polychromy: G. Richter, 'Polychromy in Greek Sculpture', in *American Journal of Archaeology* 48 (1944), 321–33; J. Gage, *Colour and Culture* (London 1993), 11ff.; and V. Manzelli, *La policromia nella statuaria greca arcaica* (Rome 1994).

4 Sacred Decoration (pp. 78–104)

On the archaeological problems generally, see C. Renfrew, *The Archaeology of Cult: the Sanctuary of Phylakopi* (London 1985), 1–26. For a useful summary of the Greek material, see M. Robertson's contribution to P.E. Easterling and J.V. Muir (eds), *Greek Religion and Society* (Cambridge 1985).

The quote concerning the Pre-Socratics comes from F.M. Cornford, in the *Cambridge Ancient History* Vol. IV (Cambridge 1930), 522. Related discussion in G.E.R. Lloyd, *Demystifying Mentalities* (Cambridge 1990).

The structure of the survey of votive occasions here largely follows the old but still valuable study by W.H.D. Rouse, *Greek Votive Offerings* (Cambridge 1902). See also F.S. van Straten, 'Gifts for the Gods', in H.S. Versnel (ed.), *Faith, Hope and Worship* (Leiden 1984), 65–151, and (for the source of the *kourotrophos* quote), T. Hadzisteliou Price, *Kourotrophos* (Leiden 1978).

The estimate of 20,000 *kouroi* comes from Anthony Snodgrass: see P. Garnsey, K. Hopkins and C. Whittaker (eds), *Trade in the Ancient Economy* (London 1983), 21. The *kouroi* as symbols of interaction: C. Renfrew, in C. Renfrew and J.F. Cherry (eds), *Peer Polity Interaction and Socio-Political Change* (Cambridge 1986), 11–12. On the development of Olympia: A. Mallwitz, 'Cult and Competition Locations at Olympia', in W. Raschke (ed.), *The Archaeology of the Olympics* (Wisconsin 1988), 79–109; and C. Morgan, *Athletes and Oracles* (Cambridge 1990).

5 Heroes Apparent (pp. 105–122)

G. Nagy, *The Best of the Achaeans* (Baltimore 1979) is an excellent philological delineation of the hero in Greek literature; for a summary of debate about the archaeology of hero-cults, see J. Whitley, 'Early states and hero-cults: a reappraisal', in *Journal of Hellenic*

Studies 108 (1988), 173–82. Relevant to both this chapter and the preceding one are certain essays in C. Dougherty and L. Kurke (eds), *Cultural Poetics in Archaic Greece* (Cambridge 1993): in particular, L. Kurke, 'The Economy of *kudos*', 131–63.

On the meaning of the *kouroi*: A.F. Stewart, 'When is a Kouros Not an Apollo? The Tenea "Apollo" Revisited', in M. del Chiaro (ed.), *Corinthiaca* (Missouri 1986), 54–70; and A.M. d'Onofrio, '*Korai e kouroi* funerari attici', in *Annali dell'Instituto Orientale di Napoli* 4 (1982), 135–70.

The Tyrannicide literature is large, and best dealt with by M.W. Taylor, *The Tyrant Slayers: The Heroic Image in Fifth Century B.C. Athenian Art and Politics* (New York 1981), though for the historical background it is still worth consulting F. Jacoby, *Atthis* (Oxford 1949), 152–68. For 'the Harmodius blow' see B.B. Shefton, 'Some Iconographic Remarks on the Tyrannicides', in *American Journal of Archaeology* 64 (1960), 173–9. The inscription from Chios was published by E. Pernice, in *Österreichische Jahreshefte* 13 (1910), 106.

Recent work on Attic grave-reliefs (by Christopher Clairmont) is perhaps too unwieldy: readers should return to K.F. Johansen, *The Attic Grave Reliefs of the Classical Period* (Copenhagen 1951). For earlier *stelai*, see G.M.A. Richter, *Archaic Gravestones of Attica* (London 1961). For discussion of the handshake motif, see E.G. Pemberton, 'The *Dexiosis* on Attic Gravestones', in *Mediterranean Archaeology* 2 (1988), 45–50. The context of ancestor worship is best discussed by S. Humphreys: 'Family Tombs and Tomb Cult in Ancient Athens: Tradition or Traditionalism?', in *Journal of Hellenic Studies* 100 (1980), 96–126. For the interpretation of the Dexileos relief as part of a *heroon*, see S. Ensoli, 'L'Heróon di Dexileos nel Ceramico di Atene', in *Atti della Accademia Nazionale dei Lincei* 29 (1987). The archaeology of the Kerameikos is described in U. Knigge, *The Athenian Kerameikos* (Athens 1988); on beliefs and funerary monuments generally, see R. Garland, *The Greek Way of Death* (London 1985), and D. Kurtz and J. Boardman, *Greek Burial Customs* (London 1971).

6 From Marathon to the Parthenon (pp. 123–151)

J.S. Mill on Marathon: see F.M. Turner, *The Greek Heritage in Victorian Britain* (New Haven 1981), 188. The battle itself: N. Hammond, 'The Campaign and Battle of Marathon', in *Journal of Hellenic Studies* 88 (1968), 13–57 (= *Studies in Greek History*, Oxford 1973, 170–250). (For an opposite view, i.e. disbelieving Herodotus, see A.W. Gomme, 'Herodotus and Marathon', in *Phoenix* 6 (1952), 75–83.)

On the burial: W.K. Pritchett, *The Greek State at War*, IV (California 1985), 126–9. The archaeology of the tumulus is described and put in context by James Whitley, in 'The Monuments that Stood before Marathon: Tomb Cult and Hero Cult in Archaic Attica', in *American Journal of Archaeology* 98 (1994), 213–30.

For the development of 'the Marathon Paradigm', see N. Loraux, *The Invention of Athens* (Harvard 1986), esp. 155–71 (though Loraux, like her Athenian orators, forgets the role of the Plataeans at Marathon); also R. Thomas, *Oral Tradition and Written Record in Classical Athens* (Cambridge 1989), 224–5.

The Athenian Treasury at Delphi: here I largely follow W. Gauer, 'Das Athenaschatzhaus und die marathonis-chen Akrothinia in Delphi', in F. Krinzinger et al. (eds), *Festschrift Bernhard Neutsch* (Innsbruck 1980), 127–36.

The Stoa Poikile: T. Hölscher, *Griechische Historienbilder des 5. und 4. Jahrhunderts v. Chr.* (Würzburg 1973), 50–84. On Echetlaeus: M. Jameson, 'The Hero Echetlaeus', in *Transactions of the American Philological Association* 82 (1951), 49–61. For the suggestion that Pausanias got Oenoe in Argos confused with Oenoe near Marathon, see E.D. Francis and M. Vickers, 'The Oenoe Painting in the Stoa Poikile and Herodotus' Account of Marathon', in *Annual of the British School at Athens* 80 (1985), 99–113.

Athena Promachos: for epigraphic records, see *Inscriptiones Graecae* I.3, Fasc. I (ed. D.M. Lewis, Berlin–New York 1981), no. 435.

The Marathon Trophy: E. Vanderpool, 'A Monument to Marathon', in *Hesperia* 35 (1966), 93–106.

Several scholars have proposed a provenance of the Riace Bronzes from the Marathon monument at Delphi, including Werner Fuchs and John Barron: here I follow the argument of Antonio Giuliano, summarized in 'I grandi bronzi di Riace, Fidia e la sua officina', in *Due Bronzi da Riace* (Supplementary volume of *Bollettino d'Arte*, Rome 1985), 297–306).

The case for viewing the Parthenon overall as a commemoration of the Persian wars is best summarized in D. Castriota, *Myth, Ethos, and Actuality* (Wisconsin 1992). Questions of chronology and symbolism are further explored in E.D. Francis, *Image and Idea in Fifth-Century Greece* (London 1990). A new account of Athenian –Persian relations is forthcoming from Meg Miller. Otherwise, see A.R. Burn, *Persia and the Greeks* (second edition, with postscript by D.M. Lewis, London 1984). The strongest version of the argument that the Parthenon frieze attempts parity with the Apadana at Persepolis is given by M.C. Root, in 'The Parthenon Frieze and the Apadana Reliefs at Persepolis: Reassessing a Programmatic Relationship', in *American Journal of Archaeology* 89 (1985), 103–20. I have quoted from A.W. Lawrence, 'The Acropolis and Persepolis', in *Journal of Hellenic Studies* 71 (1951), 111–19; see also J. Boardman, *The Diffusion of Classical Art in Antiquity* (London 1994), 28ff. Arguing that the Parthenon frieze defies thorough interpretation: R. Osborne, 'The Viewing and Obscuring of the Parthenon Frieze', in *Journal of Hellenic Studies* 107 (1987), 98–105: against this, see P. Veyne, 'Conduct without belief and works of art without viewers', in *Diogenes* 143 (1988), 1–22.

Interpreting the frieze: see I. Jenkins, *The Parthenon Frieze* (London 1994). The case for a Panathenaic reading is best made by E. Simon, in *Festivals of Attica* (Wisconsin 1983), 55–72. J. Boardman's proposal is detailed in 'The Parthenon Frieze – Another View', in U. Höckmann and A. Krug (eds), *Festschrift für Frank Brommer* (Mainz 1977), 39–49. For the Erechtheus case, see J.B. Connelly, 'Parthenon and Parthenoi: a Mythological Interpretation of the Parthenon Frieze', in the *American Journal of Archaeology* for January 1996.

Supporting the Vitruvian aetiology of Caryatids, I follow M. Vickers, 'Persepolis, Vitruvius and the Erechtheum Caryatids: the iconography of Medism and servitude', in *Revue Archéologique* 1985, 3–28. On the Nike temple friezes, see E. Harrison, 'The South Frieze of the Nike Temple and the Marathon Painting in the Painted Stoa', in *American Journal of Archaeology* 76 (1972), 353–78; and on the sacrificial scenes of the parapet, M. Jameson, 'The Ritual of the Athena Nike Parapet', in R. Osborne and S. Hornblower (eds), *Ritual, Finance, Politics* (Oxford 1994), 307–24.

7 In Search of Pheidias (pp. 152–171)

On Alma-Tadema: V.G. Swanson, *Sir Lawrence Alma-Tadema* (London 1977). The quote from Ruskin comes from *Aratra Pentelici* (using the London 1907 edition), 196. For ideas of genius generally, see P. Murray (ed.), *Genius: the History of an Idea* (Oxford 1989), esp. Ch 1; and E. Kris and O. Kurz, *Legend, Myth, and Magic in the Image of the Artist* (New Haven 1979). A. Burford, *Craftsmen in Greek and Roman Society* (London 1972) is a useful corrective; I have drawn also upon her essay 'The Builders of the Parthenon', in *Parthenos and Parthenon* (*Greece and Rome* Supplement, ed. G. T. W. Hooker, Oxford 1963), 23–34. The details of the Erechtheum accounts come from G.P. Stevens et al., *The Erechtheum* (Harvard 1927), 387ff.; for a discussion of the artisans recorded here, see R.H. Randall, 'The Erechtheum Workmen', in *American Journal of Archaeology* 57 (1953), 199–210.

The literature on the 'Pheidias-Process' is large, beginning with the great K.O. Müller's *De Phidiae vita et operibus* (Göttingen 1827), and best summarized in P. Stadter, *A Commentary on Plutarch's* Perikles (North Carolina 1989), 284–97. The case for following Philochorus' account of events is forcefully put by G. Donnay, 'La date du procès de Pheidias', in *L'Antiquité classique* 37 (1968), 19–36. Of recent Pheidian literature, a dense and enlightening handbook is recom-

mended: C. Höcker and L. Schnieder, *Phidias* (Hamburg 1993). To point out that Pheidias may have had little to do with carving the Parthenon marbles is not entirely original: see N. Himmelmann, 'Phidias und die Parthenon-Skulpturen', in *Bonner Festgabe J. Straub* (Bonn 1977), 67–90. Michelangelo's managerial skills are thoroughly documented in W.E. Wallace, *Michelangelo at San Lorenzo: the Genius as Entrepreneur* (Cambridge 1994). The quote from Percy Gardner comes from P. Gardner, *New Chapters in Greek Art* (Oxford 1926), 69.

On the Parthenos: G.P. Stevens, 'How the Parthenos was made', in *Hesperia* 26 (1957), 350–61. N. Leipen, *Athena Parthenos: a reconstruction* (Toronto 1971), presents the Toronto mock-up. C.J. Herington's monograph, *Athena Parthenos and Athena Polias* (Manchester 1955) is still valuable, and B.S. Ridgway's survey of 'Images of Athena on the Akropolis', in J. Neils et al., *Goddess and Polis* (Princeton 1992), 119–42, gathers new ideas about the *peplos* (or rather *peploi*) woven in Athena's honour. B. Fehr has argued that the iconography of the Parthenos reflects many elements of the Delian Apollo, emblematic of Athens' control of Delian League funds: for these theories, see his three articles under the title 'Zum religionspolitischen Funktion der Athena Parthenos im Rahmen des delisch-attischen Seebundes', in *Hephaistos* Nos. 1–3 (1979–81: 71–91, 113–25 and 55–93).

On the Olympian Workshop of Pheidias, see A. Mallwitz and W. Schiering, *Die Werkstatt des Pheidias in Olympia* (Berlin 1964), and W. Schiering, *Werkstattfunde* (Berlin 1991). For a general, though slightly inaccurate, account of the statue and its vicissitudes, see M.J. Price, 'The Statue of Zeus at Olympia', in P. Clayton and M. Price (eds), *The Seven Wonders of the Ancient World* (London 1988), 59–77.

8 Revealing Aphrodite (pp. 173–186)

Generally: L.R. Farnell, *The Cults of the Greek States*, Vol. II (Oxford 1896), 618ff.; G. Grigson, *The Goddess of Love* (London 1976); P. Friedrich, *The Meaning of Aphrodite* (Chicago 1978). For the associated cult of Adonis, and

the perfumed elements of Aphrodite's worship, see M. Detienne, *The Gardens of Adonis* (Princeton 1994).

Temple prostitution at Corinth – Strabo VIII.6.20.

Knidos: interim excavation report by Iris Love in *American Journal of Archaeology* Vol. 74 (1970), 149ff., and Vol. 76 (1972), 61ff. and 393ff. C. Blinkenberg, *Knidia* (Copenhagen 1933), collects the statuary; see also J. Closuit, *L'Aphrodite de Cnide* (Paris 1978), and C.M. Havelock, *The Aphrodite of Knidos and her Successors* (Michigan 1995). On the Roman 'copies' or Hellenistic 'editions' of the Knidian statue: M. Pfrommer, 'Zur Venus Colonna: Eine späthellenistische Redaktion der Knidischen Aphrodite', in *DAI Istanbuler Mitteilungen* 35 (1985), 173–80. Foucault's discussion of Lucian's dialogue comes in the third volume of his History of Sexuality, *The Care of the Self* (Harmondsworth 1990), 211ff.

On the Venus from Melos: A. Paquier, *La Vénus de Milo et les Aphrodites du Louvre* (Paris 1985). Further Aphrodite-types are documented in D.M. Brinkerhoff, *Hellenistic Statues of Aphrodite* (New York 1978).

Kallipygeia: see G. Saflund's monograph *Aphrodite Kallipygos* (Uppsala 1963).

9 The Patronage of Kings (pp. 187–217)

The Mausoleum was subject to a series of Danish excavations until 1977, clarifying much of its construction and decoration: see K. Jeppesen's summary in 'Tot operum opus. Ergebenisse der dänischen Forschungen zum Maussolleion von Halikarnass seit 1966', in *Jahrbuch des Deutschen Archäologischen Instituts* 107 (1992), 59–102, and the various articles in J. Isager (ed.), *Hekatomnid Caria and the Ionian Renaissance* (Odense 1994). I have leaned heavily on S. Hornblower's *Mausolus* (Oxford 1982): Hornblower's new edited volume of the Cambridge Ancient History (Vol. VI: *The Fourth Century* BC, Cambridge 1994), is also valuable, especially for political and historical background.

On the Nereid Monument, see W.A.P. Childs and P. Demargne, *Fouilles de Xanthos VIII* (*Le monu-*

ment des Néréides, le décor sculpté: Paris 1989). The Tomb of Cyrus is well published in D. Stronach, *Pasargadae* (Oxford 1978), 24–43.

The quotation on the nature of Hellenistic numismatic propaganda is taken from R.A. Hadley, 'Royal Propaganda of Seleucus I and Lysimachus', in *Journal of Hellenic Studies* 94 (1974), 51. A handy account of coins and kings is given by N. Davis and C.M. Kraay, *The Hellenistic Kingdoms: Portrait coins and history* (London 1973). That Tomb II of the Vergina excavations is the burial of Philip II is not universally accepted (see e.g. E.N. Borza, *In the Shadow of Olympus: The Emergence of Macedon*, Princeton 1990); but the conviction of the excavator, Manolis Andronikos, is infectious. See M. Andronikos, *Vergina: the Royal Tombs* (Athens 1987). Terming the Macedonian dynasty of Alexander I as 'Temenid' is likewise not universal (the title 'Argead' is often preferred): for the Temenid bias, see N. Hammond and J. Griffith, *A History of Macedonia* Vol. II (Oxford 1979).

A large literature on the image of Alexander now exists. The latest contributions are A.F. Stewart, *Faces of Power* (California 1993), and J.O. Carlsen (ed.), *Alexander the Great: Myth and Reality* (Rome 1993).

Nike of Samothrace: see P.W. Lehmann and K. Lehmann, *Samothracian Reflections* (Princeton 1973), 181ff.; and A.F. Stewart in P. Holliday (ed.), *Narrative and Event in Ancient Art* (Cambridge 1994), 137–53.

Alexander's Successors: for an illuminating commentary on Ptolemaic propaganda (and the deployment of giant robotic statues), see E.E. Rice, *The Grand Procession of Ptolemy Philadelphus* (Oxford 1983).

Pergamum: the standard account of the history is E.V. Hansen's *The Attalids of Pergamum* (Ithaca 1971). On the Great Altar: E. Schmidt, *The Great Altar of Pergamon* (Leipzig 1962). Its dating to post-166 BC is based on pottery evidence: see P.J. Callaghan, 'On the date of the Great Altar of Zeus at Pergamum', *Bulletin of the Institute of Classical Studies* 28 (1981), 115–21. Important documentation about the 'Lesser Attalid Group' is collected in B. Palma, 'Il piccolo donario pergameno', in *Xenia* I (1981), 45–84.

In attributing the Laocoon originally to Pergamum, I follow Bernard Andreae: see his *Laokoon and die Kunst von Pergamon* (Frankfurt 1991). For the Pergamene effect on Augustan Rome, see P. Hardie, *Virgil's Aeneid: Cosmos and Imperium* (Oxford 1986), especially 125–43.

10 Graecia Capta (pp. 218–227)

S.E. Alcock, *Graecia Capta* (Cambridge 1993) fully documents the archaeology of the Horatian epitome quoted here. On booty and plunder: D.B. Thompson, 'The Persian Spoils in Athens', in S. Weinburg (ed.), *The Aegean and the Near East: Studies Presented to Hetty Goldman* (New York 1956), 281–91; M. Vickers and D. Gill, *Artful Crafts* (Oxford 1994), 55–70; and (specifically Roman), I. Schatzmann, 'The Roman general's authority over booty', in *Historia* 21 (1872), 177–205. See also C.C. Vermeule, *Greek Sculpture and Roman Taste* (Michigan 1977); J.J. Pollitt, 'The Impact of Greek Art on Rome', in *Transactions of the American Philological Association* 108 (1978), 155–74; and E.S. Gruen, *Culture and National Identity in Rome* (London 1993).

Two good case studies: A.F. Stewart, 'To entertain an emperor: Sperlonga, Laokoon and Tiberius at the dinner table', in *Journal of Roman Studies* 117 (1977), 76–90; and P.G. Warden and D.G. Romano, 'The Course of Glory: Greek Art in a Roman Context at the Villa of the Papyri at Herculaneum', in *Art History* 17.2 (1994), 228–54.

On copying: B.S. Ridgway, *Roman Copies of Greek Statues* (Princeton 1984); M. Marvin, 'Copying in Roman Sculpture: The Replica Series', in E. D'Ambra (ed.), *Roman Art in Context* (Englewood Cliffs 1993), 161–88. Statues in gardens, and so on: E. Moorman, *La pittura parietale romana come fonte di consocenza per la scultura antica* (Maastricht 1988).

The best survey of Renaissance and post-Renaissance collecting is F. Haskell and N. Penny, *Taste and the Antique* (London 1981). B.F. Cook, *The Townley Marbles* (London 1985) documents an exemplary eighteenth-century collection. For the disposition of the Parthenon marbles in the British Museum, see I. Jenkins, *Archaeologists and Aesthetes* (London 1992). The muddled ideology of British phil-hellenes is made evident in I. Jenkins, '"Athens Rising Near the Pole": London, Athens and the Idea of Freedom', in C. Fox (ed.), *London – World City* (London 1992), 143–53.

ILLUSTRATION CREDITS

Frontispiece: Olympia Museum. Map: Tracy Wellman. 1 Musée du Louvre; © RMN. 2 Capitoline Museums, Rome; photo Michael Duigan. 4 British Museum, London. 5 National Museum, Athens, no.18135; photo DAI Athens. 6 Vatican Museums, Rome, no.344. 7 From E. Curtius and F. Adler *Olympia*, III, pl. 1 (1894). 8 From Piranesi, *Statue Antiche* (1791). 9 Akropolis Museum, Athens. 10 British Museum, London. 11 After G. Robins *Proportion and Style in Ancient Egyptian Art*, fig. 1.4 by Ann S. Fowler, London (1994); redrawn by Tracy Wellman. 12–13 Olympia Museum; photo Hirmer. 14 Olympia Museum. 15 Vatican Museums, Rome. 16 Staatliche Museen zu Berlin, no. F4221. 17 From: *Polyklet: der Bildhauer des griechischen klassik*, Frankfurt (1990). 18 Accademia, Venice. 19 Ashmolean Museum, Oxford. 20 By kind permission of the Allard Pierson Museum, Amsterdam. 21 Piraeus Museum; photo Hirmer. 22 British Museum, London. 23–4 Birmingham City Museum and Art Gallery. 25 By kind permission of the Managing Committee of the British School at Athens and L.H. Sackett and Prof. J.A. MacGillivray. 26 Photo Joan Stubbings. 27 Musée du Louvre, Paris; photo Hirmer. 28 Archaeological Museum, Palermo. 29 Photo DAI Athens. 30–1 British Museum, London. 33–4 Paestum Museum. 35 Drawing by Amanda Claridge. 36 From H. Schrader (ed.) *Die archaischen Marmorbildwerke der Akropolis*, pl.30, Frankfurt (1939). 37 From *Journal of Hellenic Studies, Archaeological Reports*, 1964–5, fig. 15. 38 Staatliche Museen zu Berlin, no.31098. 39 Staatliche Museen zu Berlin, no. 2294. 40 Agora Museum, Athens, no.5741. 41 Cerveteri Museum; photo DAI Rome. 42 Museo Nazionale, Reggio di Calabria. 43–4 Museum of Classical Archaeology, Cambridge. 45 From H. Thiersch, *Artemis Ephesia*, pl.53.2, Berlin (1935). 46 Fitzwilliam Museum, Cambridge. 47 Medelshavsmuseet (Museum of Mediterranean and Near Eastern Antiquities), Stockholm. 48 National Museum, Athens, no.126. 49 By C.R. Cockerell, from *The Temples of Jupiter Panhellenicus at Aegina, and of Apollo Epicurius at Bassae near Phigaleia in Arcadia*, London (1860). 50 Delphi Museum; photo Emile Seraf. 51 Olympia Museum; photo Hirmer. 52 Delphi Museum. 53 By kind permission of Fondazione G. Whitaker, Motya; photo G. Leone. 54 National Museum, Athens, no.3344. 55 Akropolis Museum, Athens, no.1329. 56 National Museum, Athens, no.3526. 57 National Museum, Athens, no.4472. 58 Akropolis Museum, Athens, no.1332. 59 Akropolis Museum, Athens, no.682; photo Hirmer. 60 Akropolis Museum, Athens, no.624. 61 Ashmolean Museum, Oxford, G8. 62 National Museum, Athens, no.15161. 63 From *Investigations at Assos*, Boston (1921), 145. 64 Corfu Museum; photo DAI Athens. 65–6 Akropolis Museum, Athens. 67 Akropolis Museum, Athens; photo Hirmer. 68 After C. Renfrew and J. Cherry (eds) *Peer Polity Interaction and Socio-Political Change*, fig. 1.10, Cambridge (1986); redrawn by Tracy Wellman. 69–71 British Museum, London. 72 From V. Laloux and P. Monceaux *Restauration d'Olympie*, Paris (1889). 73–4 By C.R. Cockerell, from *The Temples of Jupiter Panhellenicus at Aegina, and of Apollo Epicurius at Bassae near Phigaleia in Arcadia*, London (1860). 75 Munich Glyptothek. 76–7 Delphi Museum; photo Hirmer. 78 National Museum, Athens. 79 Cleveland Museum of Arts, 53.125. 80 Musée du Louvre, Paris, MA 2792. 81 Archaeological Museum, Naples, 6009/6010. 82 National Museum, Athens, no.56. 83 National Museum, Athens, no.1959. 84 Baracco Museum, Rome. 85 Kerameikos Museum, Athens; photo DAI Athens. 86 National Museum, Athens, no.869; photo Michael Duigan. 87 Ashmolean Museum, Oxford (Michaelis 203). 88 Staatliche Museen zu Berlin; photo Michael Duigan. 89 Delphi Museum. 90 Akropolis Museum, Athens. 91–2 Museo Nazionale, Reggio di Calabria. 93 British Museum, London. 94 Photo Alison Frantz. 96 From A.M Dieulafoy *L'Art Antique de la Perse*, III, pl.8, Paris (1885). 97 Photo Hirmer. 98–102 British Museum, London. 103 Photo Michael Duigan. 104 British Museum, London. 105 Birmingham City Museum and Art Gallery. 106 Royal Ontario Museum, Toronto. 107 National Museum, Athens, no.129; photo Michael Duigan. 108 National Museum, Athens, no.128; photo Michael Duigan. 109 Reconstruction by Siân Frances; by kind permission of the artist. 110 Vatican Museums, Rome. 111 Photo ACL Brussels. 112 British Museum, London. 113 Reconstruction by Siân Frances; by kind permission of the artist. 114 Drawing by Jacques Carrey. 115 Musée du Louvre, Paris; photo Hirmer. 116 Musée du Louvre, Paris, MA 2240; © RMN. 117 Vatican Museums, Rome. 118 From B. Rottier, *Descriptions des Monuments de Rhodes*, 1830. 119 Musée du Louvre, Paris. 120–1 British Museum, London. 122 Mausoleum Museum, Bodrum. 123 British Museum, London. 124–5 M. Andronikos. 126 British Museum, London. 127 Ny Carlsberg Glyptotek, Copenhagen. 128–9 From F. Winter, *Alexander-Sarkophag*, pls 8 and 10, Strasbourg (1912). 130 Musée du Louvre, Paris; © RMN. 131 From R. Bohn, *Pergamon* II, pl.41, Berlin (1885). 132 Staatliche Antikensammlungen, Munich. 133 Staatliche Museen zu Berlin. 134 Capitoline Museums, Rome. 135 Staatliche Museen zu Berlin. 136 Vatican Museums, Rome. 137 National Museum, Athens, no.1828. 138 Vatican Museums, Rome; photo DAI Rome. 139 British Museum, London. 140 Windsor Castle, The Royal Collection © 1996 Her Majesty The Queen. 141 Musée du Louvre, Paris.

INDEX

Numbers in *italic* refer to illustrations